PRESIDENTS, BUREAUCRATS, AND FOREIGN POLICY

The Politics of Organizational Reform

PRESIDENTS

BUREAUCRATS

AND FOREIGN

POLICY

The Politics

of Organizational Reform

I . M . D E S T L E R

PRINCETON UNIVERSITY PRESS

PRINCETON, NEW JERSEY

1972

TO MY FATHER

Scholar, Author, and Example
to his Son

"The real organization of government at higher echelons is not what you find in textbooks or organization charts. It is how confidence flows down from the President."

Dean Rusk, January 1969

"The nightmare of the modern state is the hugeness of the bureaucracy, and the problem is how to get coherence and design in it."

Henry Kissinger, August 1970

Contents

Preface

THIS book is about the problem of organizing our government for foreign policy. It is intended for government officials, scholars, students taking courses on American foreign policy, and general readers concerned about why our government sometimes behaves so "irrationally" and what we *might* be able to do about it. The book assumes that we want this government to exercise some degree of influence over people and events outside our borders. It assumes further that we wish to have this influence exercised by coordinated government actions which support conscious, central United States policy purposes. It seeks to illuminate the potentials and limitations of particular organizational devices and strategies as means to these ends.

The book makes no assumption about what our policy purposes should be. While the author is personally critical of a number of things the United States government has done in foreign affairs over the past two decades, whatever lessons this book holds are equally useful for those of differing persuasion. Some may question the appropriateness of such a book at a time when the substance of American foreign policy occasions such deep and bitter debate. Yet such a debate is little more than empty posturing unless our government and its leaders have the means to turn aspirations into actions. In rightly holding our top officials accountable for what the government does, we tend to forget the often substantial gap between what our Presidents seek and what the bureaucrats officially working for them actually do. How this gap might be reduced is the problem around which most of this book is written. And perhaps it is useful to point out here what I trust the reader would infer from the tone throughout: that the term "bureaucrat" as used here means simply "government official," with no negative connotation intended.

ix

I have sought to stay in that difficult middle ground between the world of scholarship and the world of practice. There is more generalization here about the way the government operates and the problems of organizational change than would be found in the typical official report or reform proposal, or indeed in most previous books on foreign affairs organization. Readers more interested in specific practical problems or cases may wish to skip Chapters Two and Three, moving directly from the Introduction to the treatment of the Presidency and the past three administrations in Chapters Four and Five. But if some bureaucrats may feel there is excessive "conceptualizing" or "theorizing," some academics may feel that serious general analytic problems are not always given adequate attention. The specialist in organizational behavior, for example, may be troubled by the space I devote to analyzing foreign policy "staffs," even though I am unable to provide a rigorous definition which fully distinguishes them from other units in the foreign affairs bureaucracy. Part of my response would be that no absolute distinction is possible. Yet certain types of staffs have been repeatedly employed by high officials to help them control that bureaucracy, so an effort to clarify what these staffs do and what they might accomplish seems essential.

This book was made possible by an International Affairs Fellowship from the Council on Foreign Relations, which enabled me to devote a full year to research and writing. Thus I am particularly indebted to Lester R. Brown—who recommended me to the Council—and to John Temple Swing, whose energetic support and encouragement went well beyond his obligations as director of the Council program. Particularly valuable was the opportunity to present papers for critical comment in the Spring of 1970 to the Council's Discussion Group on Foreign Affairs Organization for the Seventies, chaired by McGeorge Bundy with Edward Hamilton as

Vice-Chairman. I am also indebted to Henry Owen for the opportunity to spend my Council Fellowship year as a Guest Scholar at The Brookings Institution.

I doubt that I would ever have undertaken a study on this subject had not Executive Director Frederick Bohen invited me in early 1967 to join the staff of the President's Task Force on Government Organization chaired by Ben W. Heineman. It was one of those occasions—perhaps not so rare as staff members like to think—when the "principals" knew considerably more about the government they were seeking to change than those of us hired to analyze it for them. If this book shows any feel at all for the foreign affairs government as it looks at the Cabinet or near-Cabinet level, it is due considerably to the brief but intensive education I gained from sitting in on Task Force discussions.

More people contributed directly or indirectly to my thinking as my research progressed than it is possible to mention here. My greatest debt is to Richard Ullman, who has not only offered detailed substantive comment on two complete drafts but valued advice and assistance throughout. The original draft was also read in its entirety by Marver Bernstein, Morton Halperin, and Andrew Scott, and the book reflects many of their insights and suggestions. It was reviewed to my benefit by my father, Chester M. Destler, who took time off from two books he was working on. And my wife Harriett provided invaluable help throughout the writing, not only in keeping faith when it looked as if this book might never be, but in reading page after draft page with a stubborn insistence that it be clearly written and that it make sense.

Many others offered helpful comments and suggestions on specific chapters and preliminary papers. I particularly profited from the detailed criticism provided by Leslie Gelb, Robert H. Johnson, Arnold Kanter, Herbert Kaufman, John Leddy, Henry Owen, and Allen

Schick, as well as a number of government officials whose names must regrettably not be mentioned here. I am also grateful to typist Maybelle Clark, who twice turned some shabby and stapled-together pages into a shiny clean manuscript in less time than I ought to have given her.

I doubt that I have fully met all of the criticisms made by those who took the time to review my work. But their suggestions have, I believe, improved it at many points. It goes without saying that whatever imperfections remain are my own responsibility.

Arlington, Virginia
June 1971

Portions of this book have appeared previously in somewhat different form: in articles in the *Foreign Service Journal* and *Foreign Policy*, and in a paper delivered to the 1971 American Political Science Association Convention. Their cooperation in arranging transfer of copyright to the Princeton University Press is gratefully acknowledged.

CHAPTER ONE

Introduction

IN MARCH 1971, Senator Stuart Symington made a speech denouncing "the concentration of foreign policy decisionmaking power in the White House" which had deprived Secretary of State William P. Rogers of his rightful authority. What got the headlines was the Senator's ad-libbed remark that Rogers was "laughed at" on the cocktail circuit as "Secretary of State in title only."[a] But what he was really attacking was "the unique and unprecedentedly authoritative role of Presidential Adviser Henry Kissinger," who had become, said Symington, "clearly the most powerful man in the Nixon Administration next to the President himself."[1]

Much of the press reaction inevitably centered around the personalities of Kissinger and Rogers, and their relative influence as individuals in power-conscious Washington. President Nixon's response to a news conference question two days later treated the issue mainly in these terms. He sought to bolster Rogers' prestige by characterizing "Senator Symington's attack upon the Secretary" as a "cheap shot," and insisting "very simply that the Secretary of State is always the chief foreign policy adviser and the chief foreign policy spokesman of the administration."[2] But at issue was something more fundamental: how the executive branch of the United States government should be organized for the central management and coordination of foreign policy. Though never really saying so publicly, Nixon had chosen—apparently quite consciously—to build an or-

Bibliographical notes begin on page 297.

[a] To refute this claim, the Republican National Committee staff polled two Washington society columnists and four "prominent Washington hostesses," and "reported their 'unanimous' testimony that 'they had never heard the Secretary of State laughed at.'" (John Osborne in *The New Republic*, March 27, 1971, p. 13.)

ganizational system which would give his Assistant for National Security Affairs the central responsibility for foreign affairs short of the President. Symington was arguing that the Secretary of State was the official who should play this role.

In protesting the weakening of the Secretary, the Senator was in good company. Of eleven major studies or proposals on foreign affairs organization which had addressed the subject since World War II, seven had urged that overall foreign policy coordination be built mainly around the Secretary and his department.[b] Only two backed alternative solutions. And the best of the studies—that conducted by Senator Henry Jackson's national security subcommittee—had explicitly warned against efforts to base foreign policy coordination on a "super-staff" in the White House.[3]

President Nixon also had ample precedent when he proclaimed the primacy of his Secretary in form while weakening it in practice. The Kennedy Administration had described the Secretary's role as "agent of coordination in all our major policies toward other nations," but its major organizational innovation was the creation of a White House foreign policy staff which actually did much of the coordinating. In 1966, Lyndon Johnson created a network of general interdepartmental committees to support the Secretary in exercising his "authority and responsibility" for "the overall direction, coordination, and supervision of interdepartmental activities of the United States government overseas." But there was little evidence that either he or his Secretary of State Dean Rusk took the committees seriously. Rich-

---

[b] They varied in their emphases. The 1949 Hoover Commission report, for example, argued that State's efforts should be supplemented by the creation of Cabinet-level interdepartmental committees with their memberships and mandates determined by the President. By contrast, the 1967 Heineman Task Force report and the 1968 AFSA report both endorsed a far-reaching and unambiguous leadership role for the Secretary.

ard Nixon went both of his predecessors one better. Immediately after his inauguration he established a policy-making system providing unprecedented White House staff authority, all the while reaffirming "the position of the Secretary of State as his principal foreign policy adviser."[4]

The President built this system because he had a goal —Presidential control over foreign policy. The State Department had not achieved this for other Presidents, and Nixon apparently concluded that a White House-centered system had better prospects for success. The system was not designed mainly to shut out Congress, though it did tend to have that effect. What Nixon primarily sought to control, rather, was "his" part of the government, the executive branch. As Kissinger put it somewhat later, "The nightmare of the modern state is the hugeness of the bureaucracy, and the problem is how to get coherence and design in it."[5]

It is a bureaucracy which could neutralize an explicit order by President Kennedy-that our obsolete and provocative Jupiter missiles be removed from Turkey, simply by not implementing the order. It is a bureaucracy which could at the same time pursue delicate negotiations with North Vietnam and unleash bombing attacks on Hanoi which destroyed any chance of the negotiations succeeding. It is a bureaucracy which could locate a blockade around Cuba in October 1962 not where the President wanted it in order to minimize the danger of a rash Soviet response, but where the Navy found it most consistent with standard blockade procedures and the military problems as the Navy saw them. It is a bureaucracy which can provide unbalanced or incomplete information, continue outmoded policies through its own inertial momentum, and treat the needs of particular offices and bureaus as if they were sacred national interests.[6]

It is also a bureaucracy which contains considerable

3

talent and unrivalled expertise, coupled with the means for giving Presidential decisions real effect; thus it is indispensable. It is filled with men generally loyal to the President, and to a certain degree responsive to him. But because they tend to be responsive even more to the demands of their own particular jobs and organizations, they see things very differently from the way he does. To get "coherence and design" from this bureaucracy is an enormously difficult task. Yet to seek it is essential to our conducting an effective foreign policy at all.

This book is about this problem—how the government should be organized for *purposive* and *coherent* foreign policy. By "policy" we mean here not what we aspire to accomplish but what the government actually does. To have policy that is "purposive" means, then, to have what we do relate to what we aim to do; drawing on Webster, it is policy "having or tending to fulfill a conscious purpose or design." By wishing it to be "coherent" we mean we want the various things we do to be consistent with one another and with our broader purposes. Moreover, we do not mean consistency in the sense of being in line with certain general principles, or appearing to be. We mean instead consistency in effect. Thus a "coherent" foreign policy could well include defending one country against "aggression" and not another.[c]

The aim of coherent and purposive foreign policy has been shared by most analysts, pundits, and high-level practitioners in post-war America. Twenty-five years ago Walter Lippmann complained that "our foreign rela-

---

[c] Of course, we don't just want foreign policy to be purposive and coherent. We also wish it to be "effective," and most of all "good." It is assumed that purposiveness and coherence will, on balance, contribute to effectiveness. It is hoped that the resulting policy will be "good." But while organizational devices can help men achieve good policies—are indeed indispensable to that purpose—the fact that organization is essentially a means implies that it can be employed for "poor"/"bad" policies as well.

tions are not under control, that decisions of the greatest moment are being made in bits and pieces without the exercise of any sufficient overall judgment."[7] Since then men of such divergent policy viewpoints as Senator Jackson and George Kennan have stressed the need for our government to "speak with one voice," and have sought to show how it might be organized to do so.[8] And most international relations scholars assume that states do or should act "rationally," as purposive units.[9] Whether speaking of the "science" of "statecraft" or the "art" of diplomacy, they have tended to assume the existence of a central intelligence and guiding force.

Yet the goal does raise certain problems both of definition and of desirability. Precision is impossible, for example, in distinguishing "foreign" from other types of national policy. International issues are becoming more and more intertwined with a range of domestic policy interests, from the textile industry fighting Asian imports to young men resisting the draft for a foreign war. But this book assumes the broadest reasonable definition. "Foreign policy," as used here, means activities by government officials which influence (and whose purpose, in large part, is to influence) either events abroad or relationships between Americans and citizens of other countries, especially relations between the U. S. government and other governments. Specifically included is a wide range of defense issues, since our armed forces are intended mainly for providing security against actual or potential threats from other countries, influencing events beyond our borders, or strengthening our international bargaining position generally. Thus our use of the term "foreign policy" encompasses what others call "national security policy." It also includes international economic policy, specifically aid, trade, monetary, and commercial policy.

Another important question relates to whether we really want our foreign policy to be entirely coherent.

5

In stressing the need for the government to pursue calculated, purposive policies aiming to affect the world or parts of it in certain intended ways, this study tends to understate the degree to which governmental institutions perform useful functions simply by acting as a focal point for the resolution of the various foreign policy-related interests in our society. It is hard to make a case in theory that all of our government's overseas actions should be entirely consistent, and it is certain in fact that they will not be. There is clearly room for different programs pursuing values important to particular segments of our society, such as development assistance, cultural exchange, or the Peace Corps. It is also perfectly reasonable and legitimate for unions and industries directly affected by particular imports to undertake campaigns to restrict them, however much those favoring a liberal trade policy may regret their doing so.

When one reaches the political-military sphere, however, the case for "pluralism" becomes weaker, and the need for central control more urgent. Neither our armed forces, nor their network of overseas bases, nor our various intelligence activities can reasonably be considered ends in themselves. To the degree that they become so, they pose threats not only to international but to internal security. They must instead be the instruments of foreign policy purposes. It is also in the political-military area where we face the danger of irrevocability—in a matter of days, through failure to control our military actions in another Cuban missile crisis; or over a period of years, if an uncontrolled arms race eventually creates a condition where one nation feels it has to "strike first."

Yet there can be no clear separation between the political-military (or national security) policy area and other U. S. government foreign affairs-related activities. The Marshall Plan was more than an economic program. The problem of U. S. troops in Europe is at once a military, diplomatic, and balance of payments issue of the first rank. For this reason, this study will continue to speak about bringing coherence to foreign policy as a whole. But as the careful reader will notice, the emphasis throughout is on the political-military side, with the main examples drawn from this sphere and the analysis and proposals directed mainly toward it.

Once these general problems are clarified, a study about organizing for coherent foreign policy must cope with other types of questions. At one level, these are the "practical" ones raised repeatedly by both analysts and practitioners. Can the foreign affairs government be effectively run from the White House staff? By the State Department? What devices are available to help assure that important issues are brought before top decision-makers in the most thorough and balanced way, and that decisions are in fact carried out? To what extent can broad advance planning make our actual policy more "rational?" Will coordinating committees really coordinate? And perhaps most important of all, once it is decided that a certain official or institution should play a central policy role, how does one go about increasing the chances that he (or it) will actually play it?

But a review of how others have sought to answer these questions forces us to face broader issues. For in seeking to use organizational changes to promote purposive and coherent policy, experts and practitioners alike have often produced both strikingly inadequate recommendations and notably ineffective remedies. The first Hoover Commission, for example, urged in 1949 that the State Department should serve as "the focal point for coordination of foreign affairs activities throughout the Government," but neglected to even discuss how its bureaucratic rivals were to be made receptive to such coordination. Thirteen years later the Herter Committee on Foreign Affairs Personnel placed its hopes for State Department management and interagency coordination on the creation of a new, "Number Three" job, Executive Under Secretary of State. Never once did it raise the obvious question of how the incumbent could develop sufficient influence over those whom he was to "manage." Yet this recommendation was endorsed in 1968 by a major foreign affairs professional organization, and in 1969 by an important independent study.[10]

Both the Hoover and Herter reports failed to resolve (or even to treat) the central problem of how their chosen coordinators could develop sufficient leverage within the bureaucracy to be effective. It may not be just coincidence that the Herter proposal was not adopted, and that the Hoover recommendation did not work. Nor, given this track record, is it surprising that Presidents have increasingly disregarded expert counsel to build foreign policy coordination around State, and sought instead to construct an alternative mechanism in the White House. Yet practitioners often do just as badly. The Eisenhower Administration's elaborate policy planning machinery was apparently more effective in burying key issues than in highlighting them. The 1969 State Department sought to emulate the White House and Defense by creating a staff to support the Secretary on critical current policy issues, yet undermined its prospects for effectiveness by the way it organized the staff in relation to other departmental units. Even the Nixon-Kissinger system, the product of considerably more sophisticated analysis of the ways of bureaucracies, has developed a number of quite serious weaknesses which threaten the achievement of the President's goals.

An effort to analyze why reforms so often fail makes us face a more "theoretical" question: How in general can we make organizational changes affect what the government actually does, in the way we intend to affect it? And to seek an answer to this question is to raise still another: What sorts of motivations and influences

8

do affect how government officials behave in the day-to-day bureaucratic world? Or to change that question slightly: How is policy in fact made?

A serious study of foreign affairs organization, then, must involve an effort to relate organization to the "real world" of policy-making. This book seeks to do so in three ways. The first is relatively theoretical—a search for what general things scholars have to say about the foreign affairs governmental process. The second is more practical—a look at what has happened in the foreign affairs government since 1960, with special attention to the White House and the State Department. The third is an effort to assess the utility of specific organizational devices, such as central staffs and coordinating committee systems, and in particular to discover the circumstances which contribute to their effectiveness. All three assume the goal of purposive and coherent foreign policy. All seek to throw light on how, and how much, it can be achieved.

The remainder of this chapter seeks to provide a brief introduction to the foreign affairs government and its organizational problems. Chapter Two looks at the most prominent post-war organizational approaches, seeking to uncover their central thrusts and their apparent underlying assumptions. A resulting dissatisfaction with their treatment of the major problems sets the stage for Chapter Three, which delves into academic studies of bureaucratic politics for illuminating concepts about how foreign policy is actually made. This creates a general framework for Chapter Four, which puts forward a tentative foreign affairs organizational strategy.

Chapter Five looks at the approaches of our last three Presidents, with one important theme being the increased role of the White House staff. Chapter Six investigates why the State Department has been unable to play the coordinating role, and assesses a range of proposed or attempted departmental reforms. Chapter

Seven looks briefly at the utility of particular organizational devices as means of strengthening central management. Chapter Eight treats the problems and potential of central substantive foreign policy staffs, and relates White House and Defense experience to the problem of staffing the Secretary of State. Finally, Chapter Nine seeks to draw on preceding analyses to propose a comprehensive strategy aimed at using organization as a tool to promote the making of purposive and coherent foreign policy.

Since this study seeks to develop a realistic view of how organization can influence foreign policy, the author must stand ready to be judged on the practicality of his specific proposals. Yet they may be the least important part of the book. No single organizational scheme, whatever its built-in flexibility, can fully accommodate the differing personalities and priorities of different Presidents and Administrations. But if this study proves at all useful, the questions raised and the experience analyzed should clarify the choices that are available. Thus the ultimate aim of this study is not to "solve" the problem. It is to provide a framework and a line of analysis useful to those who must grapple with parts of it either as analysts or as practitioners.

The Foreign Affairs Government

At the official center of the foreign affairs government is the Department of State. Its Secretary is the senior member of the Cabinet, and his Department has since 1789 been responsible for the basic conduct of our foreign relations. Its Foreign Service officers (FSO's), numbering about 3,000, represent our country overseas, conduct negotiations with other governments, and analyze and report on events in particular countries. Above all they are charged with carrying out American foreign policy and contributing—through their analysis, information, and advice—to the decisions and actions of top leaders. Half of these FSO's are in Washington, where they and others of State's approximately 6,800 employees deal with envoys of 117 different countries represented there. The other half are overseas, the senior layer of a State Department presence totalling about 6,200 Americans in 124 diplomatic missions.[11]

By itself the Department is large enough and dispersed enough to constitute a formidable management problem. But State is only part of the foreign affairs government today, and by no means the predominant part. For example, its overseas staffs represent just 29 per cent of the approximately 21,500 officials in our diplomatic missions, and only 16.6 per cent if one subtracts those State officials who are there to provide administrative services to other U. S. agencies. By contrast, 28.7 per cent of the Americans attached to these missions are Defense Department (DoD) officials, 21.3 per cent represent the Agency for International Development (AID), and 5.6 per cent work for the United States Information Agency (USIA). Others represent such predominantly domestic departments as Treasury, Agriculture, Commerce, Labor, Justice, and Transportation. These numbers may or may not include Central Intelligence Agency (CIA) officials,[d] about whom no government statistics are supplied.[12]

The size of the foreign affairs bureacracy is also reflected in dollars spent. With the massive exception of defense, money is not as central to foreign policy as it is to domestic. But the Nixon Administration's proposed FY 1972 budget still listed, under the category of "inter-

---

[d] Various published analyses of the CIA give estimates, of which Stewart Alsop's are reasonably representative. "The whole 'intelligence community,' " he writes, "spends on the order of $3 billion a year, and employs about 160,000 people. Of this, the CIA's share is around a half-billion, and less than 16,000 people (other than agents and other foreigners). The code-breaking National Security Agency spends the most money—on the order of $1 billion—and employs, incredibly, over 100,000 people." (*The Center*, Harper and Row, 1968, p. 240.)

11

national affairs and finance," outlays totalling over $4 billion, including $2.3 billion for foreign economic assistance, $962 million for the Food for Peace program, $438 million for general State Department activities, $197 million for USIA, $290 million for the Export-Import Bank, and $73 million for the Peace Corps. This was, of course, entirely outside of the $76.0 billion for "national defense," which included $1.0 billion for military aid. Americans in 1971 tend to have less expansive notions than they once had about what these expenditures can achieve. But since most of our international activities reflect a long-range trend of increased interdependence among nations, an abandonment of very many of them for very long is most unlikely.[13]

Even if we could start from scratch in organizing this government for foreign policy, the geographic, substantive, and programmatic range of our activities poses unavoidable dilemmas. First there is the classic problem of dividing the work. Should the principal organizational subdivisions be by country and region? By substantive problem? By specific operating program? If we decided to put all of the foreign affairs government into one large agency organized on a regional basis, how would we then assure that the aid programs in various countries conformed to general standards on terms of loans and quality of programs, or could draw on personnel with economic development expertise? Alternatively, if we group all of the functions in a central aid organization, how do we make our aid program in Brazil consistent with our general policy there, rather than just a reflection of what the aid agency wants? Thus, however we establish our main organizational subdivisions, we face the need for cross-cutting mechanisms to meet the needs for coordination neglected by the basic organizational subdivisions.

These dilemmas are reflected in our actual foreign affairs organization. The State Department is organized primarily on a geographic basis, with functional and administrative units handling those activities not assignable to regional bureaus. Other agencies—like Defense, CIA, AID, USIA, and the Arms Control and Disarmament Agency (ACDA)—have been established to administer particular programs (aid and information), work on specific policy problems (arms control), or provide important policy support functions and instruments (military force, intelligence gathering, and covert action). And the domestic departments involved in foreign affairs have primarily functional *raisons d'être*.

But for those seeking to bring coherence and central purpose to this government, the overriding organizational problem is one of coordination. For the major foreign affairs issues simply aren't divisible into components which can be handled more or less on their own terms. Not only, for example, is the problem of our troop deployment in Europe critical to our defense posture (Defense), our balance of payments (Treasury), and our relations with several important countries including the Soviet Union (State). It is also very difficult for an action to be taken by an agency concerned with one of these elements without it having an impact on another. Foreign affairs bureaucrats, of course, like to treat issues as *military* or *diplomatic* or *aid* or *agricultural* matters; if a problem can be easily classified and assigned, everyone's job is easier. But it is difficult to do so on very many questions, and impossible on the most important. Whether the problem be our response to an India threatened by famine or by China, our bases in Japan or the textiles Japan ships here, the future shape of "the Alliance" or the "Alianza," it almost inevitably involves at least two agencies, and usually more.

Yet in any large system which organizes thousands of people to perform parts of a complex body of work, most individuals will tend to think and act in terms of quite narrow perspectives shaped by their particular sets of responsibilities. Means must somehow be found to bring their particular actions into accord with larger purposes.

One useful type of coordination is lateral coordination. We avoid the left hand not knowing what the right is doing by the three "C's"—committees, clearances, and compromises. Committees must assure that various departments' expertise, interests, and program responsibilities are brought to bear on the issue; clearances are required to show interdepartmental agreement on outgoing cables or policy documents of broad importance; compromises are needed to reach such agreement. The development of a network of interagency relationships for lateral coordination has been one of the most important organizational developments of the post-war era. Richard Neustadt noted in 1963 that ". . . in the pre-Korea years . . . a Secretary of Defense could forbid contacts between Pentagon and State at any level lower than his own, and within limits could enforce his ban. That happened only 14 years ago. In bureaucrtic terms it is as remote as the stone age."[14]

But lateral coordination has brought problems of its own—slowness in resolving issues, the extreme difficulty of getting anything significant "cleared" at all, or interagency deals which postpone the most difficult problems or settle them on "least common denominator" grounds. So coordination among relative equals isn't enough. We need coordination from above as well.

Such coordination is, of course, a major goal of the Nixon-Kissinger system which has caused Symington, and no doubt Rogers, so much anguish. It was the purpose also of the first post-war effort to harmonize policies on critical issues, the establishment of the National Security Council.[e] And it is the subject of most of this

[e] The NSC was created by Congress in the National Security Act of 1947, which also established the office of Secretary of Defense. It

book. Before beginning our own analysis of the problems of achieving such coordination, however, it is first necessary to see how others have sought to do the job. That is the purpose of Chapter Two.

---

is chaired by the President, and the other statutory members at present are the Vice President, the Secretary of State, the Secretary of Defense, and the Director of the Office of Emergency Preparedness. Its original official purpose was to relate military and weapons policies more closely to foreign policy. Its actual role has varied widely, reflecting Presidents' differing organizational preferences and operating styles.

CHAPTER TWO

How Not to Reorganize the Government

BUREAUCRATS and academics alike have tired of the subject of foreign affairs organization. Both question the relevance of past studies to present problems. Both wonder whether organizational forms affect policy-making in anything like the intended ways. Both have doubts about the utility of "another study" to turn over ground already so amply plowed.

Such skepticism has ample justification. Few problems have been probed as often since World War II as that of organizing our government for coherent and purposive foreign policy. At least thirteen major studies or proposals have appeared, most with some degree of official sponsorship.[1] Five Presidential Administrations have sought to handle the problem in at least five different ways. There also have been many narrower reviews, focused on personnel administration or particular problems like foreign aid. And accompanying them all has been a chorus of published commentary by officials, scholars, and assorted prominent citizens.

Not only have many looked into the problem, they also have come out of their reviews saying similar things. Studies of foreign affairs organization have fed substantially on other studies, tending to raise the same issues and repeat (or reject) the same proposals. Incoming Administrations have responded mainly to the foreign affairs experiences of their predecessors, whether emulation or avoidance was their aim. And in general, neither the recommenders nor the practitioners have sought very many insights from either the experience of the domestic government or the work of scholars in possibly relevant fields.

Any new look at foreign affairs organization must cope

16

with this legacy, and establish a need to go beyond it. Such is the purpose of the present chapter. It seeks to analyze the post-war reform tradition not by summarizing and criticizing each individual proposal or report, but by a broader analysis of some of their common themes. Such an approach has its dangers. No two of the post-war studies are identical in either content or quality, and there have been significant differences in practical efforts as well. A review which treats most of this legacy in a broader framework risks not being completely fair or thorough about any specific part of it. Yet the recurrence of similar answers to the question of how to organize the government for coherent foreign policy underscores the need for a broader assessment than a study-by-study analysis could offer.

The great majority of post-war "solutions" to the foreign affairs organizational problem can be grouped under eleven general categories. These are:

1) The Separation of "Policy" from "Operations"
2) The Joining of "Authority" and "Responsibility"
3) The Creation of a New Central Official
4) The Strengthening of Career Services
5) The Elimination of "Over-Staffing"
6) Coordination from the White House
7) Coordination by the State Department
8) Bringing Other Government Foreign Affairs Activities into the State Department
9) Foreign Affairs Programming
10) The Establishment of General Interagency Coordinating Committees
11) The Use of Central Policy Staffs

Since they have different advocates, some of these "solutions" are inconsistent with others. There is also overlap among them, with many studies and reforms combining two or more.

17

This chapter will concentrate on the first five of these solutions,[a] treating them as a reasonably representative sample of what the post-war tradition has to offer. Most of the major studies have recommended one or more of them, and each of the five has backers who see it as *the* major solution to the problem of coherent foreign policy-making. A look at their virtues and limitations, then, should serve as a useful introduction to the post-war literature, and as the basis for a broader critique.

1. *The Separation of "Policy" from "Operations"*[b]

One of the most frequent approaches to organizing for coherent foreign policy is to separate responsibility for "policy planning," or "policy formulation" from responsibility for "operations." The usual aim is for the former to control the latter. There have been two major applications of this distinction. The first involves the separation of the State Department from operating programs. The second has been an effort to control day-to-day activities of all agencies through a central policy formulation process.

[a] The others are discussed elsewhere: White House coordination in Chapter Five, "solutions" 8, 9, and 10 in Chapter Seven, and the uses of staffs in Chapter Eight. The limitations of the State Department as the lead agency for foreign policy are treated in Chapter Six, the possibilities for correcting them in Chapter Nine.

[b] This use of the word "policy" obviously differs from our Chapter One definition of the term as "what the government actually does." It is closer to Morton Halperin's definition of policy as "an authoritative statement describing a general situation desired by the U.S. or prescribing general criteria for action." (See his forthcoming study of bureaucratic politics, discussed in Chapter Three.) To avoid confusion, this book will use such phrases as "policy formulation," "policy objectives," and "policy guidelines" when the latter sense is intended, or will simply enclose the word "policy" in quotation marks.

Also, the "policy-operations" and "planning-operations" distinctions discussed interchangeably here are not strictly speaking the same. But often "planning" in this context seems to mean "policy formulation," as in the Eisenhower Administration example. Both dichotomies are distinct from, but bear a family resemblance to, the State Department's internal "substance-administration" dichotomy referred to in Chapter Six.

The Hoover Commission in 1949 urged that State Department responsibility be concentrated on "formulating [for the President] proposed policies in conjunction with other departments and agencies." State "should not be given responsibility for the operation of specific programs," but rather be "the focal point for coordination of foreign affairs activities throughout the government." Other studies of the time criticized this recommendation, but it was clearly attractive to the career Foreign Service. It has also been favored by top officials. No Secretary of State since World War II appears to have considered program operations to be an important part of his—or his Department's—job.[2]

It is not clear that all proponents of this division of labor saw policy formulation as a way to control operations. Dulles and others in State apparently considered "operations" (defined as ongoing programs), as an encumbrance to be shunted aside, insufficiently important for their attention. The Hoover Commission seems to have been interested mainly in a tidy division of labor between State and other agencies. But the NSC staff system under Eisenhower separated policy formulation and operations in a way that clearly saw the former as a management tool to shape the latter. The system built by his first Special Assistant for National Security Affairs, Robert Cutler, had as its main working organs two interdepartmental committees. These were the Planning Board, charged with preparing issues for National Security Council consideration by drafting papers outlining general policy guidelines; and the Operations Coordinating Board (OCB), created to oversee implementation of decisions taken on these issues. And in this case the "operations" which the planning process aimed to control were not just "programs," but all day-to-day foreign affairs government activities.

The Kennedy and Johnson Administrations, in the words of Special Assistant for National Security Affairs

McGeorge Bundy, "deliberately rubbed out the distinction between planning and operation."[3] But it was given new life under the Nixon system, which has sought to make broad policy studies the basis for general Presidential decisions intended to control specific bureaucratic actions.[c]

The case for separating "policy" from "operations" has some undeniable logic. Unless relatively broad decisions taken at high levels (often called policy) can shape specific actions at the far reaches of the foreign affairs government (often termed operations), the job of carrying out a coherent foreign policy becomes far more difficult, since top officials cannot know and decide every detail. It is hard to dispute the aim espoused by Lannon Walker of "integrated planning and decentralized operations,"[4] and the idea implicit in this phrase that the former should shape the latter.

Yet if carried very far the distinction sounds much like the politics-administration dichotomy which has haunted the field of public administration. For to work it must assume two things: that the processes, policymaking and operations, are separate or separable, and that the first can control the second (or at least point it in clear general directions). Similarly, Woodrow Wilson's 1887 article urging the founding of a "science of administration" assumed that administration could be simply the efficient execution of policy and program decisions previously taken, though he saw policy-making

[c] In form at least, the Nixon Administration also restored the distinction in another way, by making the NSC "the principal forum for consideration of national security *policy* issues requiring Presidential decision," but assigning responsibility to the Secretary of State, "*in accordance with approved policy*, for the *execution* of foreign policy." (Jackson Subcommittee, "NSC: New Structure," February 6, 1969, italics added.) Thus State Department officials found themselves on the operational side of the dichotomy for a change, but with a similar lack of the leverage needed to play the central coordinating role.

as conducted in the broad political arena rather than centered in executive branch institutions.[5] In fact, broad policy decisions seldom provide effective guidance for specific operational situations. Often guidelines are too general to have clear applicability to particular cases, or several different "policies" will offer conflicting cues. For example, an overseas aid official may at once be expected to enforce Washington's project criteria yet encourage the recipient government to play a stronger planning role. Or he may be directed to stimulate grass-roots participation, yet stay out of sensitive host-country matters like a struggle between advocates of centralized power and champions of local autonomy. If an effort is made to avoid excessive generality or conflicting cues through much more detailed policy guidance, it takes away the flexibility that those on the firing lines need in coping with special situations only vaguely understood in highest Washington. Also, circumstances change, and unforseen crises arise which render previous policy declarations obsolete.

For these and other reasons, a large number of operational decisions are made by harassed bureaucrats who treat each issue as it comes and resolve it mainly on its own terms. General policy guidance is only marginally relevant—either they get specific, *ad hoc* signals from their superiors, or they cope as best they can. Even the Hoover Commission's foreign affairs task force recognized that the policy-operations distinction largely upheld in its recommendations was "defective and illusory,"[d] because "the operation alone of any given pro-

---

[d] The Hoover Commission sought to reconcile this apparent contradiction by indicating that other agencies did have a "policy" role, even if State had no proper direct role in "operations." But the lack of any explanation of how State's "policy" efforts would achieve leverage over theirs made unviable State's proposed role of "leadership in defining and developing United States foreign policies," "recommending the choice and timing of the use of various instruments to carry out policies as formulated," etc. ("Foreign Affairs," p. 29.)

gram involves policy decisions," some of the highest importance.[6] In fact, specific operational decisions can influence our broader policy course to a marked degree. What was apparently a lower-level "operational" decision to support the Laotian "Secret Army" in its efforts to retake the *Plaine des Jarres* in 1969 not only constituted a significant immediate change in our policy toward that part of the world, but came back to haunt the President and constrict his range of choice when the Communists counterattacked earlier in 1970. Similarly, a Presidential statement that we are for a peaceful settlement of the Vietnam conflict has its influence, but more important is how we react to specific third-party peace feelers which cannot be anticipated in a planning process, or what Ambassador Bunker says to President Thieu day by day.

This may help explain why the State Department has failed to serve effectively as the "focal point of coordination" for foreign policy, despite its general fidelity to the Hoover prescription. It may also illustrate the charge, "even by certain insiders," that the Eisenhower Administration's major policy papers were "so general that they were meaningless . . . virtually useless as guides to planning and action."[7] Perhaps the best commentary on the broader question, however, came from Senator Hugh Scott after the U.S. Senate passed the Stennis amendment, which had sought to cripple federal desegregation efforts in the South by undermining their legal basis. "Mercifully," said Scott, "this is mere policy and therefore not binding."[8]

2. *The Joining of "Authority" and "Responsibility"*

The second frequently proposed "solution" to the problem of organizing for coherent foreign policy places hopes in giving major officials "authority" commensurate with their "responsibility."

The late fifties brought a lively organizational debate.

It was spurred by Sputnik, dissatisfaction with the formal Eisenhower NSC machinery, and the upcoming Presidential election. It featured critical articles by men such as George Kennan, Henry Kissinger, and Hans Morgenthau. The most sustained and enduring contribution to the debate, however, was the series of hearings and reports begun in 1959 by Senator Henry Jackson's subcommittee of the Senate Committee on Government Operations.

The subcommittee's work was characterized by considerable practical wisdom, and a resistance to sweeping solutions that solved nothing. And for the most part, its pragmatic approach was both encouraged and reflected by its first witness, Robert Lovett, the Secretary of Defense and Under Secretary of State under Truman whom Kennedy later sought in vain for a major Cabinet post. Lovett defined the foreign affairs management problem as "executive department overlap and the clash of group interests," and described "the device of inviting argument between conflicting interests" within the government as "the 'foul-up factor' in our equation of performance." His prescription was more traditional. "This huge organization would be hard enough to run if authority were given where responsibility is placed. Yet, that frequently is not the case," he said. "The authority of the individual executive must be restored."[9/e]

This diagnosis and prescription were quoted with strong favor in Jackson Subcommittee reports. Moreover, giving authority to general executives had long been standard public administration doctrine. The

e In fairness to Lovett, one should also cite his qualifying remarks: "I am not suggesting that a major cure in policymaking delay is in sight or that any real progress will come from something as appealing as 'simplifying' or 'streamlining.' It is wholly unrealistic to talk of making government simple. We can aspire to make it manageable and effective, but its characteristics make simplicity of machinery impossible." But it was the assertion, not the qualification, which was widely quoted.

23

Hoover Commission found that "the President and his department heads do not have authority commensurate with the responsibility they must assume," and made various recommendations for remedying the situation. More recently, the Blue Ribbon Panel on Defense Department reorganization asserted in its July 1970 report that "The lines of authority and responsibility within the Department must be made clear and unmistakable."[10]

But this is easier to say than to do. For the fundamental problem is that the government is far too large, and its activities far too intermeshed, to allow it to be run by clear lines of authority reflecting any one way of subdividing responsibilities. One recent organizational proposal suggests placing State Department line authority in its regional bureaus and eliminating or consolidating the present functional bureaus such as Politico-Military Affairs, Economic Affairs, and Intelligence and Research.[11] Yet could such a State Department deal effectively with non-regional issues like arms control, international trade, or emerging scientific and technological problems if power were centered in units which handled issues overwhelmingly in country or regional terms? More generally, who in the broader government should have "authority" on the issue of possible U.S. troop withdrawals from Europe? The Secretary of State and his European Affairs Bureau? His Politico-Military Affairs Bureau? The Secretary of Defense? The Secretary of the Treasury, given his role as protector of the balance of payments? The Director of the Arms Control and Disarmament Agency, given the relation of troop withdrawals to the military balance? For each of them, "responsibility" on this issue far outruns "authority" to deal with it.[f]

---

f Nor is it clear that it would be desirable to provide absolutely clear lines of "authority commensurate with responsibility," even were

Thus it may be true that, as Stanley Hoffmann writes citing James McCamy, "the present organization violates all the basic rules of bureaucratic organization: duties are not clearly assigned, the diffusion of authority slackens responsibility, the same job is done by different people," etc.[12] But the fault may lie at least partly not in the organization, but in the "rules" themselves.

None of this means that strengthening individual executives is not desirable, or that gains cannot often be made by focusing primary action responsibility in one part of the government while accepting the involvement of others. Later in this book we will argue strongly for steps to strengthen key officials. But the image of proper government which the notion of "authority commensurate with responsibility" tends to convey—of a powerful Cabinet official, the master of his domain, answerable only to the President—is a gross distortion of the complex world in which this Cabinet member must work. As strong a man as Secretary of Defense Robert McNamara, with a clearer general "line" authority than is conceivable for a Secretary of State, needed to cultivate his influence not only with two Presidents, but with his Congressional committees, the Secretary of State, the Special Assistant for National Security Affairs, the Joint Chiefs, the press, and not least of all his own staff. Thus he was in an important sense "answerable" to all of them. "Authority" he may have had, but maintaining it and making it effective was a constant effort.

---

this possible. The danger is that top officials would be "captured" by their line subordinates, since they would have to depend overwhelmingly on these subordinates for information and advice relating to the subordinates' areas of responsibilities. Carried to its logical extreme, joining authority and responsibility leads us to the self-defeating "line solution" to foreign affairs organizational problems discussed critically in Chapter Eight.

3. *The Creation of a New Central Official*

A third approach to coherent foreign policy suggests that we can achieve it if we create a central official whose job is to bring it about.

One prominent proposal, put by Nelson Rockefeller to the Jackson Subcommittee in 1960 and endorsed by men ranging from President Eisenhower and Secretary Dulles to their vigorous critic, Hans Morgenthau, called for the creation of a "First Secretary of the Government." "Deriving his authority from the President and acting in his behalf," and positioned outside of the direct chain of command, this official would have a broad mandate to integrate "the international political, diplomatic, economic and social, military, informational, cultural, and psychological aspects of foreign affairs." He would be "Executive Chairman" of the National Security Council, provided his own staff, empowered to use and reorganize national security planning machinery, and able at the discretion of the President to represent us internationally "at the prime ministerial level."[13] The aim of the reform, of course, was to overcome the pattern of compromised decision-making by putting one official above the fractious departments who could (unlike the President) devote full time to foreign affairs.

A second proposal, made in a 1960 Brookings Institution study prepared for the Senate Foreign Relations Committee, similarly involved creation of a super-official, this time a "Secretary of Foreign Affairs." This official, however, was to be a new level of line authority comparable to the Secretary of Defense, and would similarly direct three component departments—State, a Department for Foreign Economic Operations (aid), and a Department of Information and Cultural Affairs.[14]

Still another proposal was Herbert Hoover's suggestion in 1955 of an appointed Vice President for foreign affairs.

While these sought to build coherence around a new official above the Cabinet level, the Herter Committee sought a solution by going beneath it. It proposed in 1962 the creation of a new, "Number Three" official in State, an Executive Under Secretary, who would undertake to assure 1) the adequacy of our foreign affairs personnel and machinery; 2) the support of policies by action programs with adequate resources; 3) the "effective union" of policy-making, program development, budgeting, and administration; and 4) the coordination of interagency relationships and personnel arrangements. The post would "normally be filled by a career public official or by a person with pertinent experience in the public service." This proposal was endorsed by the American Foreign Service Association in 1968, and by an important independent study the following year.[15]

Criticism of the proposals to create a "super-Cabinet official" were quick in coming. Many decried the danger of "layering," of adding another echelon between the "working level" in the foreign affairs bureaucracy and the top policy-makers. The Jackson staff felt that the President could not "give a First Secretary the consistent backing and support he would require to maintain his primacy over other Cabinet members," without running "the risk that the First Secretary would become an independent force, politically capable of rivaling the President himself." It further suggested that such an official would unduly insulate the President from "the clash of argument and counter-argument between advocates of different policy courses."[16] President Kennedy apparently found these arguments persuasive.

The Herter Committee proposal has received less attention. But it is vulnerable to similar criticisms. Like the First Secretary, the Executive Under Secretary was supposed to do the coordination work his boss needed done but didn't have time for himself. He would have the same dependence on Secretarial support that the

27

First Secretary would have on Presidential. More than that, the Executive Under Secretary would need Presidential support also, since his job was to coordinate across agency lines. The proposal seems to assume they would provide this general support, but devote their personal attention mainly to other things. It is questionable whether either the Secretary or the President would wish to hand such potential power to a career official without becoming closely involved in his activities, which would mean more time spent on "management," not less. But even if they did, the man would probably prove ineffective, for his leverage would ultimately rest on whether he could get the backing of his superiors on major policy issues. Otherwise he would quickly be reduced to the status of an "administrator," a damaging label in State. And it is unlikely he would get this backing, for the President and Secretary would want such issues resolved from their own perspectives, not from those of a man with a quite different orientation.

The Nixon Administration has developed a type of super-official, the Assistant to the President for National Security Affairs. Yet Kissinger's influence seems not to have suffered, but rather benefited, from his lack of a statutory base, an impressive official title, a superdepartment to run, or any other encumbrances which might compete with his loyalty to the President. In fact, as discussed in Chapter Five, the testimony of close observers suggests that Kissinger has given by far his top attention to his role as personal Presidential adviser, to the neglect of supporting his staff and the institutional NSC system in their exercise of comprehensive foreign policy management and oversight.

4. The Strengthening of Career Services

A fourth general approach seeks to build coherence by training and deploying a career group of top quality

28

men committed to the wise conduct of foreign policy, and by protecting them from partisan pressures so that they can do the job boldly and securely.

This solution to foreign affairs management problems has a long history. It is rooted in the revolt against the "spoils system" around the turn of the century, and owes much to the examples of the British foreign and civil services. The idea, basically, is that with proper recruitment and training, a good career official can be expected to act in the national interest. When necessary, it follows, he can be given considerable latitude in doing so.

Most studies have recognized the danger of a career service becoming too narrow or ingrown, whether because of undue restriction on lateral entry, spending too much time abroad (Wriston), or carrying out too narrow a set of functions (Herter). But these problems have been seen not as intrinsic to the nature of a career service, but as flaws to be overcome by appropriate reforms. As Mosher has noted, the reports "apparently assumed as a *given* the desirability of a personnel system based on the closed career principle."[17] Their differences were over other issues, including Wristonization (incorporation of State civil service officials into the Foreign Service); the relative values of the generalist and the specialist; the extent of lateral entry (admission to the officer corps above the bottom ranks); and whether there should be one or several personnel systems for State, AID, and USIA.[g]

On only one issue is there even a suggestion of conflict between the interests of career officials and those of a President. This is the question of independent statu-

[g] The Herter Committee recommendation of an Executive Under Secretary of State job "normally filled by a career public official" assumes a basic compatibility between careerist and Presidential perspectives. And nowhere in Arthur G. Jones' lucid 1962 summary of personnel studies and actions (*Evolution of Personnel Systems*) is the problem of possible incompatibility even raised.

tory existence and authority for the Director General and Board of the Foreign Service. FSO's have strongly supported such autonomy; the Hoover Commission and the Budget Bureau felt that both should be creatures of the President and the Secretary of State.[h]

Yet this obscure bureaucratic conflict highlights a broader issue. As Don Price has written, it is proper "to worry not only about how to protect the career officials from the politicians, but vice versa." Writing mainly of the domestic government, Herbert Kaufman has shown how efforts to build up the "neutral competence" that career merit systems ostensibly foster have weakened "executive leadership" by spawning "self-directing" groups within the bureaucracy. These groups have "cultivated their own sources of support among professional groups concerned with their subject matter . . . among their clienteles, and among appropriate Congressional committees and subcommittees."[18]

The Foreign Service, lacking a domestic constituency and notoriously weak in relations with Capitol Hill, might potentially be more responsive to Presidential leadership. But Presidents like Roosevelt, Kennedy, and Nixon found the Department's men more impediment than ally, loyal first to their own Service and their own values and priorities, tending to believe, in Schlesinger's words, that "the foreign policy of the United States was their institutional, if not their personal property, to be solicitously protected against interference from the White House and other misguided amateurs."[19]

---

[h] Recently the latter view has prevailed. The Foreign Service Act of 1946 provided for "an independent Director General of the Foreign Service charged with enforcing the regulations and procedures laid down by a statutorily independent Board of the Foreign Service." (AFSA, *Modern Diplomacy*, p. 9.) In 1949, the Director General was stripped of independent statutory authority; in 1965 the Board of the Foreign Service was abolished by a Presidential reorganization plan, and simultaneously recreated by executive order as an advisory body to the Secretary, to whom its statutory authority was transferred.

It is not surprising, then, that the dominant foreign affairs personnel emphases of recent administrations have been *not* on strengthening the career services, but rather on controlling and restricting them through appointees who owe allegiance primarily to the top political officials and are attuned to their ways of thinking. These appointees, whether McNamara's "whiz kids" or the exceptional men Bundy and Kissinger recruited for the White House, are not "political" in the old spoilsman sense, and often have only a remote relationship to partisan politics. They can, however, be committed to present leaders and policies in a way that career officials often feel they can't. They have become a major instrument of Presidential foreign affairs management. If State has escaped any large influx of such outsiders, it may be more than coincidence that its much-cited foreign policy initiative and leadership role has tended to slip away to the places where such outsiders have gone, whether the White House or the McNamara-Clifford Pentagon. Rather than preserving its role as the President's prime agent, State is seen as a bureaucracy with its own narrow values and interests by a White House whose main challenge is to control it.

5. *The Elimination of "Overstaffing"*

The fifth approach to coherence involves reducing the government to manageable size.

Senator Jackson's "Final Statement" summarizing his Subcommittee's initial inquiry concluded that "serious overstaffing in the national security departments and agencies" made for "sluggishness in decision and action."

Unnecessary people make for unnecessary layering, unnecessary clearances and concurrences, and unnecessary intrusions on the time of officials working on problems of real importance.

31

Many offices have reached and passed the point where the quantity of staff reduces the quality of the product.[20]

Three years later Jackson's staff quoted with appropriate horror Secretary Rusk's testimony before the Subcommittee in 1963:

> . . . when I read a telegram coming in in the morning, it poses a very specific question, and . . . I know myself what the answer must be. But that telegram goes on its appointed course into the Bureau, and through the office and down to the desk. If it doesn't go down there, somebody feels that he is being deprived of his participation in a matter of his responsibility.

> Then it goes . . . back up through the Department to me a week or 10 days later, and if it isn't the answer that I know had to be the answer, then I change it. . . But usually it is the answer that everybody would know has to be the answer.[21]

The Subcommittee recommended "a determined effort in State to consolidate overlapping functions, reduce layering, trim unnecessary staff, kill committees, and make clear assignments of responsibility." But it saw the size of the Department as one problem among many, and recognized that those who manage foreign affairs must in any case be prepared to cope with the existence of large organizations. Others, however, have joined with George Kennan in seeing "bigness as a dangerous evil in itself," and doubting "that adequate remedial measures can be found short of a basic change in the spirit of administration and a drastic reduction in the scale of the operation." Ambassador Galbraith wrote Kennedy from India in 1961, "Nothing in my view is so important as to get the [State] Department back to manageable size." John Franklin Campbell argued in 1970, "Size is the first problem to attack and bureaucratic surgery is the answer."[22]

The basic problem, critics agreed, was that more officials meant more people to be consulted on particular issues. This in turn meant not only delay but a tendency to compromise issues in ways not conducive to good foreign policy, simply because compromise was necessary to obtain the concurrences needed to act at all. A further difficulty was that larger bureaucracies meant longer lines of communication between top officials and lower-level operators. This increased the likelihood that the former would be insensitive to the problems on the firing line, and the latter would have but a partial or distorted view of what their bosses wanted.[i] All this led one Foreign Service officer to propose "a modest corollary to Parkinson's Law: The chances of catastrophe grow as organizations grow in number and in size, and as internal communications become more time-consuming and less intelligible."[23]

These critiques of a bloated State Department—incidentally the smallest of the 12 federal departments in budget and the second smallest in number of American employees—are consistent with broader assaults on large government bureaucracies in general. Peter Drucker's latest book achieved marked popularity in the early Nixon Administration by attacking a government that "is big rather than strong . . . fat and flabby rather than powerful . . . costs a great deal but does not achieve much."[24] And it is clear that size *is* a problem. Any effort to carry out tasks in a purposive and coherent way becomes enormously more complicated when the number of men who must work together on them is beyond

[i] Thomas L. Hughes characterizes the problem as follows: "The possibilities for broadly based and persistent policy are almost directly disproportionate to the size, complexity, interruptibility, and intertwining bureaucratic underbrush of a government's foreign policy apparatus." ("Relativity in Foreign Policy," *Foreign Affairs*, June 1967, p. 672.)

what an individual or an intimate group can deal with directly; this is, of course, the basic problem of large-scale organization. Furthermore, reductions in the size of the foreign affairs government would undoubtedly be helpful if undertaken in the right places. No one who has worked in it or observed it will argue that there is not substantial fat to be trimmed (though often not in his section).

Yet one cannot help remembering an earlier debate on size, the hot controversy in early twentieth century America about the large business corporation. Men like Theodore Roosevelt and Herbert Croly argued that it was inevitable and that emphasis should be placed on regulating it for the public good. But Woodrow Wilson and Louis Brandeis thought the trend could be reversed and the world of smaller production units and greater competition restored. And, reports Hofstader, the latter view was "more congenial to the country at large" and "to most of the reformers."[25]

Yet the corporation prevailed—because it was better adapted to the demands of the twentieth century. Similarly, one is tempted to conclude that the growth of the bureaucracy is necessitated (at least in part) by changes in the world with which it deals. No doubt some staff cutbacks are in order, to reflect our reduced sense of our ability—or our need—to remake the world in our image. But however much we reduce our overseas involvements, we will still be dealing with over 100 countries, trading with most and probably aiding many, and we will need to maintain both that military force and that intelligence capability which we judge will maximize our security. This is a large and complicated job; we have little choice but to build a large organization to do it.

Moreover, the advocates of drastic surgery can provide only intuitive answers to the question of how big a reduction in size would be necessary to change the *nature* of the system by which foreign policy is made. Morgenthau has said that elimination of half of State's employees "could by itself not fail to improve the operation of the Department." William Attwood considers the figure high, suggesting that "a fourth could be spared to good advantage."[26] But whether it is a cut of 50 or 25 per cent that is advocated, it is hard to find an accompanying argument why reductions even of this magnitude would eliminate "duplication," "concurrences," "government by committee," or general "inflexibility." There is only the assumption that since bigger is worse, smaller must be better and one should lop off a large chunk to start.

In fact, the U.S. government *has* been reducing its foreign affairs personnel. Both the Johnson and Nixon Administrations have carried out special overseas personnel reduction programs, and official estimates report cuts of over 15 per cent for each.[27/j] What effect is this having on foreign affairs policy-making and management?

It is probably too early to tell. But there are reasons to expect, unfortunately, that the impact may not be favorable. One immediate problem is that the first effect of cutting overseas positions is to flood Washington with bodies, so that for the first time there are more Foreign Service officers stationed at home than abroad. But overseas reductions can be followed by Washington cutbacks,

---

j The Johnson Administration inaugurated the "BALPA" (for "balance of payments") operation in 1967 to reduce U.S. diplomatic mission staffs by ten per cent from a base of 23,000 Americans. The Nixon Administration followed this with "OPRED" ("overseas personnel reduction") in 1969-70, aiming to cut 10 per cent from a larger base (200,000 Americans) which also included some military staffs. The Secretary of State's 1969-70 report gives the result of BALPA as an 18 per cent cut, with OPRED achieving a reduction of "more than 15 per cent." (pp. 319-20.)

Such reports must be taken with some skepticism, since the juggling of personnel categories can make the cutting of many positions a paper exercise.

and often are. The more general problem is the effect of the excruciating personnel reduction process on the quality of men retained and programs undertaken. There is, first of all, the problem of seniority rights. One of the fruits of past career service reforms is that men with longer tenure have greater rights to job security. This provides a certain fairness to individuals, protecting most those who have committed the largest part of their lives to government service. Nor is their experience without value to the government. Unfortunately, those who cling hardest to their jobs are those with both seniority and lack of alternatives elsewhere, often men "over the hill" or among the less capable to begin with. By contrast, AID's 1969 reduction-in-force (RIF) eliminated a number of newly hired "management interns," recent university graduates chosen for their high career leadership potential.[k]

Not only do personnel reductions tend to safeguard the most senior rather than the most able, they tend to eliminate those individuals and positions whose functions are hardest to pin down or justify in terms of a concrete job that everyone can understand. Often these people are among the most creative, or occupy general staff positions needed to relate the more specialized jobs to each other and to our broader objectives.

Finally, reductions do not happen instantaneously. They are a painful process, full of inevitable hassles on how the rules are to be interpreted, who should be included and who excepted, how much lead time is required to close out projects and give notice to those being dismissed or brought home, whether agencies are resorting to any of the numerous devices available to render paper cuts meaningless, etc. Both to prevent end

[k] AID also created merriment all over Washington in 1969 by "RIFing" secretaries, one of the town's truly valued and scarce (relative to demand) resources. It was recruiting them with newspaper ads by 1970.

runs and minimize damage to existing operations, they usually involve suspension of new project starts and new recruitment for several months. This also is a major blow to creativity, reducing agency programs to holding operations, making routine hirings an exercise in bureaucratic legerdemain, demoralizing those very officials who are interested in promoting new activities and approaches rather than simply serving time moving the papers for current operations.

To all these reasons against considering size as *the* central foreign affairs organizational problem must be added one more—that in a number of situations the best apparent way to deal with size is to create more size. Faced with a massive Pentagon, Secretaries of Defense have felt the need to build up their OSD staff. Faced with a vast and far-flung government, Presidents have done likewise.

The Five Approaches—Some Broader Problems

Each of these five approaches has some persuasive logic behind it; none lacks attractiveness to those seeking coherence for the foreign affairs government. A policy-operations distinction may seek to separate the inseparable, but surely top leadership needs an ability to make broad choices which can guide lower officials in their daily actions. Elimination of overstaffing may be overrated as a panacea, but certainly some cuts are in order if they can cut the right people. Likewise we need more competent and effective career personnel, and strengthened authority for top officials. We may not need a First Secretary of the Government, but the problems which Rockefeller diagnosed as the reasons for his recommendation were real problems. They still are.

Yet all approaches prove to have very severe limitations, even when discussed as briefly as here. Some are logically impossible to come very close to, like the joining of authority and responsibility. But the more serious question is the relevance of all these approaches to the foreign policy process as it is actually carried on. There are some highly unreal assumptions: that "policy" can control "operations," that the utility of a career service will not be compromised by a strong loyalty to itself that Presidents will find troubling. There is a general failure to discuss proposed solutions in the context of the actual foreign affairs government, to explore whether a new central official can develop the leverage necessary for effectiveness, or to consider the practical results of staff reductions given the pervasiveness of interagency competition and tenure constraints.

In other words, there is a general failure to really cope with the internal politics of policy-making, including the informal bureaucratic practices that tend to persist despite reforms based on how organizations "ought" to operate. Such practices are of course alluded to from time to time. But most often they are characterized as problems to be overcome by the reorganization proposed, rather than as "facts of governmental life."

On the other hand, these approaches are generally consistent with that traditional way of thinking that sees formal organizational structure as the central determining factor in governmental behavior. All five solutions seem to imply that the policy-making system can be fundamentally reshaped by decisive formal action supported by administrative energy, whether it be a strengthening of career services, a restoration of the authority of the executive, or a breaking of the policy process into neat components like "policy-making" and "operations." There is a flavor of a malleable policy process which can be bent effectively to man's will if only he can determine what that will is.

It would, of course, be very convenient if the problem of organizing the government for foreign policy-making could be reduced to one of designing a rational system where each official or unit played a pre-assigned role in a pre-ordained way. As Roger Hilsman has noted, we like to think of policy-making as

> ... a tidy sequence of specialized actions in a logical division of labor—the groundwork laid by staff, approval by high departmental officers, consideration, judgment, and modification by the National Security Council, approval by the President, and appraisal and implementing legislation by the Congress. We tend to think that this procedure is, or at least ought to be, a dignified, even majestic progression, with each of the participants having well-defined roles and powers and performing a standardized function in the consideration of each issue that arises.[28]

But "the reality," adds Hilsman, "is quite different," and our analysis bears him out. Thus we find career services intended to serve only the national interest developing their own parochial interests. Thus we discover that the addition of a new central official would create a welter of internal political problems for those above him and those below, even if the job he is supposed to do clearly needs doing. Thus, in an Eisenhower Administration where men worked tirelessly to build a logically structured foreign policy planning and implementation system, the Secretary of State was "able to carry out foreign policy only by removing his sphere of operations from the formidable coordination procedures established to maintain tidiness," and "departments and agencies often work[ed] actively and successfully to keep critical policy issues outside the NSC system."[29] For in all these cases we are dealing not with "policy machinery" that can be restructured if we have the proper technical expertise, but with relationships among flesh-and-blood individuals and organizational groups who have their own particular interests and ambitions, and who must deal with problems not as they would appear "in the large" to an ideal, rational top-level executive,

39

but as they arise piece-by-piece at various levels of the bureaucracy.

Whether the study group members, scholars, and practitioners who are cited in the preceding pages really believed that this ongoing bureaucratic process was as malleable as their proposals imply is impossible to determine. One can, in fact, rather doubt it. The men and groups quoted here were mostly persons with substantial governmental experience, with surely a deeper sense of the problems than they put to paper. Often, in fact, reports acknowledge the problem of making formal changes effective with introductory or concluding statements to the effect that "of course organization isn't the whole story," a sort of tipping of the hat which substitutes for going further into that "whole story," or perhaps suggests that they believe it impolitic to do so. An analysis of the sort made here may fully reflect the actual organizational thinking of the men quoted. But it also may not. For it draws only on what they wrote or said for the public record.

Moreover, this tendency to avoid the problems of politics is hardly universal. After all, there are strong critics of these approaches who are part of the same general tradition, and a few—like the Jackson Subcommittee—have made very sophisticated analyses indeed. But as a general rule such sophistication is limited to criticizing present conditions or the proposals of others, and does not extend to advancing one's own. For among those who propose changes there is a remarkable lack of explicitness in dealing with the central question of how organizational reform is to affect governmental practice.

How can one explain this failure? Certainly the notion that formal structural or procedural changes will not automatically produce their desired results is somewhat this side of a revelation. There was a time before World War II when authorities on administration treated organization as a "technical problem," and proposed restructuring on the assumption that roles assigned and authorities provided would be effectively implemented.[1] This reflected a broader conception of administration as something separate and distinct from politics, with its aim simply the most efficient implementation of "policies" already determined by executive branch political leadership and the Congress. The Hoover Commission's pronouncements reflected this traditional approach. But wise practitioners always swallowed these ideas with a grain of salt, if at all. And in the past 25 years, scholar after scholar has demolished the assumptions upon which this approach rested. It is now widely recognized that organizations operate through webs of relationships far more complex than formal charts depict; that executive branch officials are not just "neutral" implementers of "policies" handed down by their superiors but play ongoing, day-to-day roles in shaping these policies; and that the typical way the government settles on particular courses of action is not through a group of high officials applying a rational design to specific problems, but by a "pluralistic" process of political competition and compromise involving "players" both inside and outside the government.[30]

Why then aren't foreign affairs organizational proposals clearly designed to influence the "real policy-making world" which these insights help illuminate? Partly, perhaps, because those who developed these insights concentrated mainly on the domestic government and private organizations. By the late fifties and early sixties, men like Samuel Huntington and Roger Hilsman were concluding that strategic and foreign policy decisions were also "the result of controversy, negotiation, and bargaining among officials and groups with

[1] Dwight Waldo writes: "Probably the most pervasive and important model in American administrative study in the Twentieth Century is the *machine model*." (*Perspectives in Administration*, University of Alabama, 1956, pp. 30-31.)

41

different interests and perspectives," and that "policy-making is politics," even in foreign affairs. Yet the dominant approach among international relations scholars was to treat a particular nation's foreign policy as if it were (or ought to be) the product of one central, national guiding intelligence. As Graham Allison has noted, most foreign policy analysts tended to explain and predict the behavior of a particular national government on the (usually implicit) assumption that it acts as a "rational, unitary decision-maker." Recognition that things might be otherwise was inhibited by the fact that most concerned citizens have considered it immoral to "play politics with national security," or to suggest that our foreign policy is inevitably shaped by a process in which vested interests bureaucratic or otherwise play an important role. Even the politically sophisticated Jackson Subcommittee found it wise to use words other than "politics" and "power" when discussing the actual processes of foreign policy-making.[31]

There are strong traditions, then, which discourage aspiring reorganizers from making too explicit an analysis of the nature of the foreign affairs government they seek to reform. Yet the frequent gap between the patterns of formal organization and how business actually gets transacted in government has long been too obvious to ignore. To conclude, however, that this gap must have forced a rejection of these traditions is to underestimate either the persistence of old thoughtways or the ingenuity of man. For there have developed at least three ways of treating the relationship between organization and practice without dealing generally with the practice. All of them, furthermore, have the marked advantage of allowing men to talk about organization in much the same way they did when the formal tradition was paramount. The first is to treat organization as just part of the foreign affairs governmental story, but an important part worthy of investigation on its own terms.

A second is to recognize political phenomena, but as problems which organization should overcome. A third is just the opposite: to see politics as the "reality," but organizational jargon as a convenient means of disguising it.

Organization as Partial but Indeterminate Influence

Men who study organization tend now to preface their studies with introductions stressing the importance of other factors in influencing governmental behavior. But once they have made such disclaimers, they often go on to write about organization in the old ways. An excellent example is the comprehensive Brookings study by Burton M. Sapin. In a two-and-one-half page section on "The Role of Organization," Sapin responds to those "inclined to be skeptical about the role of organizational arrangements" with the suggestion that "the allocation of powers and responsibilities to certain agencies and the specifying of particular relationships among them by statute and executive order" does "establish a basic framework," though "by no means do these provide the complete picture of who is actually doing what." "Statutory prescriptions, executive orders, and organization charts and manuals . . . are not a complete guide to the nature of the work being done," but they "represent a necessary point of departure," and "may even provide a model, an organizational ideal toward which to aim."[32]

Thus a recognition that organization is not the "complete picture" becomes not a reason to paint a broader picture, but a prelude to writing about organization for its own sake, though one who has observed the process and participated in it as much as Sapin frequently relates organization *ad hoc* to other factors.[m] He does his work

[m] Sapin does devote a chapter to "Some Fundamental Characteristics of the System," which includes some perceptive discussion of a number of broader issues concerning the nature of the system to which organization must relate. But the book is devoted mainly to a dis-

43

with uncommon industry, putting other students of foreign affairs organization in his permanent debt. But no general answer is given to the question of how organizational forms affect practice, except perhaps "partly," or "it depends." Formal organization becomes a partial but indeterminate influence. And the sterile debate goes on, in the government and to a lesser degree in academic circles, about whether it is "organization" or "people" that count the most, or whether, as Senator Jackson has written, "good policy demands both good men and good machinery." For it is difficult to exaggerate the pervasiveness of thinking about "organization" and "people" (or other factors) as separate and somehow independent categories, whether expressed as in the Haviland Report—"Organization is only one element in successful administration"—or as in Chester Cooper's introduction to the IDA study—"In the last analysis the force of personality tends to override procedures." Of course both are right. But neither advances us very far either in developing a general view of government incorporating all of these factors, or in relating organizational devices to the overall governmental process in a realistic manner.[33]

Organization as a Means of Transcending Politics

Another widespread tendency is to combine serious diagnosis of the problems of pluralistic policy-making with more or less magical solutions which seek to transcend these tendencies by building up central authority.

---

cussion of organizational units and problems, and Sapin tends to resist generalizing about broader issues and relationships except for indicating their complexity. On the critical question of how organizational reform affects practice, Sapin is "quite skeptical about the efficacy of grand designs or sweeping proposals," and he clearly recognizes that organizational changes alone are not enough to achieve many of the goals that reorganizers seek. Yet he spurns broader generalization about what makes organizational changes effective because of "the lack of relevant doctrine firmly grounded in empirical investigation." (*Making of Foreign Policy*, pp. 11-14.)

Particular emphasis is given to the conflict among agency interests and the need to override the tendency toward making policy through compromises among these interests. One example was Lovett's remedy for the "foul-up factor": restoring the authority of the individual executive; another was the "First Secretary" proposal.[n] Concerning the latter, Rockefeller recognized that "toes will get stepped on, many vested interests within the government will feel imperiled," but this was necessary to have a structure "geared to support the President in developing and executing integrated policy."[34]

The Hoover Commission was less sophisticated. It recognized, for example, "serious frictions" between the State and Army Departments in our policies and operations vis-à-vis the post-war occupied areas, but it saw these not as the product of the division of responsibility (State was responsible for "formulation of policy," the army for "execution and administration of policy") nor as the sort of dispute which was inherent in bureaucratic life. Rather, it was the result of "uncertainty and delay in the preparation and enunciation of policy," presumably by State, "and the consequent tendency of the administrative agency, through its daily decisions, to make its own policy." Also faulted was "the attempt to handle occupied-areas problems below the secretarial level, without clear definition of responsibility and without clear channels for the transmission of policy guidance from the State Department to the theatre commanders." All of these flaws could be corrected, it implied, by improved administration, and the "frictions" thereby elim-

---

[n] Similarly, Hans Morgenthau recognized that the actual foreign policy-making process in the Eisenhower Administration was "legislative," involving considerable lateral bargaining and compromise. But he did so on the way to arguing that it should be "executive," reflecting one central decision-maker and one guiding intelligence, the President. ("Can We Entrust Defense to a Committee?" *New York Times Magazine*, June 7, 1959; reprinted in Jackson Subcommittee, *Organizing*, Vol. II, p. 280.)

inated. No deeper conflict of agency interests was considered, no concept of such "frictions" as an inevitable element in governmental life.[35] Reformers throughout our history have tended to view politics invidiously, as a problem to be overcome rather than as a fundamental form of human activity. To them "politics" has implied undermining the public good for personal or partisan advantage. When the stakes were what men thought them to be in the fifties and early sixties—the very survival of our way of life— we could hardly afford to permit "political infighting" to settle critical policy questions. Confronted with a choice between an invidious and messy process of political decision-making and the prospect, however unreal, of "rationalizing" it through changes in formal structure and process, organizational reformers are strongly tempted to opt for the latter. Thus the way men want things to be—the way it seems they urgently need to be—has discouraged careful attention to the way things are and the more realistic possibilities for reform.*

Working on Two Levels—Administrative Jargon as a "Cover Language" Masking "Political" Motivations

Perhaps the most effective government organization report was that of the President's Committee on Administrative Management, chaired by Louis Brownlow more than three decades ago, which led to creation of

---

* Huntington sees the demand that intra-governmental bargaining be suppressed by strengthened executive controls as "the latest phase in a prolonged confrontation or dialogue between American intellectuals and reformers and American political institutions." (*Common Defense*, p. 173.) Yet often it seems to be not ivory-tower critics but men with considerable bureaucratic experience who cry out for radical, politics-transcending reforms. Kennan and Rockefeller are two of the more striking examples. Perhaps it is the contrast between their sense of how things ought to be and the great difficulties they have experienced trying to get things done in bureaucratic Washington that makes sweeping formal remedies so attractive to them.

the Executive Office of the President. It dealt not specifically with foreign affairs, but across the whole sphere of Presidential activity. As Richard Neustadt has written, "its proposals for the most part were put into practice with promptness and fidelity. And practice, for the most part, has been kind to the proposals, has sustained —indeed has vindicated—key ideas behind them. What a rare experience for an advisory report."

But, Neustadt continues, this was hardly accidental:

> As Brownlow cheerfully acknowledged, his group was in effect a White House "chosen instrument." The Committee urged what Roosevelt wanted. They wrote, he edited. In the election year of 1936 he gave them a "non-political" assignment, "administrative management." After his election they couched their response in appropriate terms, PODS-CORB terms, Gulick-and-Urwick terms (shades of Taylorism), with "administration" set apart from "policy" and "politics." Roosevelt thought it politic that they should do so. But he took care that their proposals met his purposes which were emphatically, essentially political. He wanted to enhance his own capacity to rule.[36]

Partly because "administrative" proposals are more respectable and less controversial than "political" ones, partly because of the persistence of the formal tradition, partly because of the advantages to participants of describing proposals which will increase their own power in "neutral," organizational language, the practice has developed of putting forward organizational changes for political reasons but talking about them in terms of "good management." Bureaucrats are quick to recognize that, in Hilsman's words, "organizational struggles are struggles for personal power and position," and they assess organizational changes in these terms whether their aim is to acquire power or evade it. But organization reports or proposals seldom own up to this type of motivation. Among other things, the difficulty they face in winning support for their proposals "leads reformers as well as other politicians to reach for consensus-building goals, for labels for reorganization objectives that all must applaud," writes Harvey Mansfield. "Professional reformers are well advised," he adds, "to profess neutrality as to substantive goals and insist on the time-honored distinction between administration and policy.[37]

This masking of underlying political aims may be conscious or unconscious, and it does not necessarily mean abandoning all belief that the changes involved are the best in an "objective," "non-political" sense. For example, President Nixon has explained his foreign affairs organizational changes in terms of re-establishing the National Security Council "as the principal forum for Presidential consideration of foreign policy issues."[38] Quite possibly he meant it. But a better statement of the system's utility to him would surely be that it strengthens the power of his personal agent, the Assistant for National Security Affairs. Yet one would not expect to find it justified in these terms.

Thus the practice of using organizational jargon to "cover" shifts in bureaucratic power has real practical uses, and can therefore be expected to continue. But this practice of thinking on two levels, formal organization and bureaucratic politics—or in some cases thinking of the latter but calling it the former—has done considerable damage to intelligent discussion of foreign affairs organizational problems. To the extent that formal organizational language is accepted as the "proper" means of discussing such questions, many will take it at face value. Thus will be perpetuated the myths that require its use in the first place. As long as political rationales for organizational changes remain *sub rosa,* devoid of testing and refinement in open debate, understanding of how reorganization can affect the politics

48

of decision-making is likely to remain at a primitive level.*p*

It is fortunate, then, that while not fully rejecting the broad framework and assumptions inherent in the formal organizational tradition, recent reports tend more and more to bring in bureaucratic political considerations on a frequent if *ad hoc* basis. Thus the 1968 report sponsored by the American Foreign Service Association (AFSA) describes the Foreign Service as "scrambling just to maintain its position" vis-à-vis entrenched agencies, which believe that State can be "handled." These competitors, while accepting the Secretary of State as *primus inter pares*, tend to "emphasize the *pares* and play down its *primus*"; hence the need for management and personnel policies which recognize the "special conditions and requirements of competing in Washington directly with other agencies in their home bases." Similarly, the Institute for Defense Analyses report prepared the same year recognizes that "Procedures in this field [national security policy] are, in practice, built around particular men rather than abstract organizational theory; hence, this study is not a blueprint of machinery for churning out decisions."[39]

Yet the proposals of even relatively sophisticated reports like these provide only infrequent rationales explaining why proposed reforms should be expected to work out in practice. They are not completely free from the formal tradition, and this doesn't require such

p A long-time official of the Bureau of the Budget writes that the ritual of Presidents' proposing reorganizations only for "orthodox" efficiency reasons has "contributed materially to congressional failures, both in hearings and floor debates, to expose to public view the basic political questions posed by reorganization proposals. The more knowledgeable members of Congress and the executive branch are generally quite well aware of what these issues are—and they seldom have anything to do with economy and efficiency. But the real issues are openly discussed, if at all, by indirection and in a language which only insiders can understand." (Harold Seidman, *Politics, Position, and Power*, Oxford University Press, 1970, pp. 10-11.)

rationales since it treats the formal as equal to the real. And they are not altogether free of the tradition which holds that "politics" is a bad or unacceptable element in decision-making (or at least one that shouldn't be publicly acknowledged) and which thereby makes reformers reluctant to discuss their proposals in the political terms such rationales would require.

In fact, none of these three ways of treating the role of formal organization requires or even encourages the reformer to explain how his reforms should affect the politics of decision-making. If organization's influence on politics is indeterminate though presumably important, it is discussed as it would have been in the formal tradition. If its aim is to supersede politics, then to analyze in terms of its political impact would be to admit failure. If its aim is to mask politics, one will certainly not expose the "political" connotations of organizational changes.

Thus all three approaches avoid the critical question —how organization can influence the real world. The first two also strongly encourage an exaggeration of formal organization's importance. It is, after all, the thing that they are concerned with. Deprived of a framework for thinking about organization which could put formal factors in perspective, they offer no check, aside from common sense, against pushing a particular approach beyond what is possible or desirable.

And it is precisely this which characterizes the main thrusts of the organizational proposals which we have discussed. It is important to have competent professional personnel in foreign affairs assignments; therefore, as many high-level posts as possible should be filled from the career service. Broad "policies" should shape day-to-day operations; therefore there must be an intricate formal system of policy planning and operational coordination. High officials lack sufficient ability to control foreign affairs activities; this can be remedied by giving them authority commensurate with their responsibility. There is no one in our government short of the President (or the Secretary of State) who can effectively integrate broad foreign policy, and he doesn't have time; therefore we should create a First Secretary of the Government (or an Executive Under Secretary of State).

The fact that such arguments are still taken seriously today can only be explained in terms of our legacy of mistaking the organizational form for the policy-making reality, or treating the reorganizer's intention as the predictable result. Although *ad hoc* practical insights can and often do rescue us from the worst dangers of this type of organizational thinking, we cannot hope for general improvement unless we develop an approach which forces the organizational reformer to consider explicitly how the changes he proposes will affect the decision-making process. Nor is this likely to be achieved unless we can develop a set of concepts which provide a useful general view of the real policy-making world, and can compete effectively with the discredited, but far from extinct, formal concepts.

It will not have escaped the reader that the set of concepts to be advanced here is one that treats policy-making as a bureaucratic political process. To describe what this means in greater detail is the purpose of Chapter Three.

CHAPTER THREE

Organization and Bureaucratic Politics

BUREAUCRATIC POLITICS is the process by which people inside government bargain with one another on complex public policy questions. Its existence does not connote impropriety, though such may be present. Nor is it caused by political parties and elections, though both influence the process in important ways. Rather, bureaucratic politics arises from two inescapable conditions. One is that no single official possesses either the power, or the wisdom, or the time to decide all important executive branch policy issues himself. The second is that officials who have influence inevitably differ in how they would like these issues to be resolved.

The best general introduction to the bureaucratic politics view of government is still Richard Neustadt's *Presidential Power*. His demonstration that the power of our highest official is basically just "the power to persuade," and that "the power to persuade is the power to bargain" highlights the need for a President to work very hard building support within the government for what he wants to accomplish. "Command," he emphasizes, is seldom enough. And his pungent quotations from Truman[a] dramatize the plight not only of Presidents, but of all high government officials who learn how limited their ability to control their subordinates can be.[1]

Logic suggests that executive branch relationships would be political, bargaining relationships even if the

----

[a] Truman on his own problems: "I sit here all day trying to persuade people to do the things they ought to have enough sense to do without my persuading them. . . That's all the powers of the President amount to." On Eisenhower's: "He'll sit here, and he'll say, 'Do this! Do that!' *And nothing will happen.* Poor Ike—it won't be a bit like the Army." (*Presidential Power*, p. 22.)

executive branch were impervious to influences from Congress and the larger society. As Frankel puts it, "In the course of a single day the important decisions made by government are too large in number and varied in content to be made by any small group of men, or any ten small groups. So power spreads out."[2] It is impossible to control all these decisions with a few general guidelines. So the President would need the aid of others if they were to be decided the way he felt to be right. He would require even in this self-contained government a relationship of *mutual* dependence with his Cabinet members, for example. For if the latter were to be effective in getting others in the government to carry out Presidential objectives, they would need Presidential support in battles with bureaucrats who had other ideas. But the need to support a man competes with the capacity to order him freely; a Secretary very often overruled loses credibility with his colleagues and subordinates, and thereby usefulness to his boss. Thus the President would necessarily end up in a sort of alliance with his chief officials, and the junior partners in such alliances can develop considerable leverage vis-à-vis the senior.

These officials in turn would have to work hard to influence *their* subordinates. For the latter bring to issues their own constraints and values and priorities, their own narrower responsibilities and interests. Not only would they be affected by these in exercising their inevitable discretion or in passing information and advice upward. They would also be tempted to delay in implementing explicit high-level decisions because of disagreement, difficulties in carrying them out, or hopes that the boss would change his mind or forget the matter entirely. Max Weber wrote of an ostensibly absolute monarchy: "All the scornful decrees of Frederick the Great concerning the 'abolition of serfdom' were derailed . . . in the course of their realization because the

53

official mechanism simply ignored them as the occasional ideas of a dilettante."[b] Dean Acheson said of the job he once occupied: "The Secretary's role is one in which command is not an important function. It is one of guidance and influence."[3]

But of course the process is not so self-contained, and persons outside government affect it as well. Even though most important foreign policy decisions tend to be made within the executive branch, they are influenced by members of Congress, public figures, the press, and the way key Administration figures assess the likely public reactions to alternative courses of action. All of this affects not only the range of people directly involved in decisions, but the positions that individual executive officials take in their bargaining with one another.

The notion that intra-executive branch relationships are political in this sense is not a new one. In the years following World War II, many scholars of government and public administration highlighted the complexity of actual relationships within and among large government departments, and the inadequacy of formal authority as a means of controlling them. Yet their main interest was the domestic government, and until recently the foreign affairs bureaucracy received little similar treatment. Graham Allison could still write in 1969: "Occasional memoirs, anecdotes in historical accounts, and several detailed case studies to the contrary, most of the literature of foreign policy avoids bureaucratic politics. The gap between academic literature and the experience of participants in government is nowhere wider than at this point."[4]

[b] Weber suggests that the king's control problem is actually greater the more closed the system: "The constitutional king can control these experts better because of what is, at least relatively, the public character of criticism, whereas the absolute monarch is dependent for information solely on the bureaucracy." (*Specialists and Generalists*, p. 44.)

Fortunately, several foreign affairs scholars have recently undertaken to analyze this process in considerable detail. They have been concerned not primarily with organizational issues, but rather with explaining actions taken by governments in the international arena.[c] Yet their work is highly relevant to the problems of foreign affairs organization. It offers, of course, no direct alternative to traditional maxims like "making authority commensurate with responsibility." Indeed, treating government as bureaucratic politics brings one closer to the position of one anti-traditional book—that "practical rules simply do not exist which can be applied in an automatic or mechanical fashion to actual organization problems."[5] But it provides an invaluable antidote to thinking of government as formal organization. For it centers attention on the critical question of what influences government actions, thereby compelling the would-be reformer to face the question of what he is seeking to change, and how his proposals would actually change it.

What specific insights does the bureaucratic politics view of government have to offer? How does it depict the actual workings of the foreign affairs bureaucracy? The basic concepts[d] can be grouped under four general headings—

1. Power and Perspective
2. Issues as a Flow
3. Constraints, Channels, and Maneuvers
4. Foreign Policy as Bureaucratic Political Outcome

1. *Power and Perspective*

Power is spread unevenly among many individuals in different governmental positions.

[c] They have also been interested in predicting such actions, and to some extent in suggesting how particular bureaucrats might proceed if they wish to influence the behavior of their own and other national governments.

a. The "Diversity of Values and Goals and of Alternative Means and Policies"[6]—Rational policy-making may be salutary as an ideal, and reasoned analysis may be able to improve policy-making at many points. But there is no way for reason alone to overcome the diversity of goals and means that are inevitable among participants in foreign policy-making. Goals are based on value preferences as well as rational analysis. And even differences as to means of achieving common goals cannot be resolved by reason. Our understanding of the likely consequences of particular policies is very poor, since they involve complex chains of human interaction with each step very hard to predict. Even if men agree to promote a negotiated peace in Vietnam, we know so little about decision-making in Hanoi that any conclusions about whether invading Cambodia will help or hinder negotiations must involve considerable conjecture. After all, Washington was quite surprised when, in April 1968, North Vietnam agreed to preliminary peace talks in response to the partial bombing halt. Thus it is unrealistic to hope men would reason their separate ways to common policy conclusions even if they approached the problems from the same vantage point and possessed the same information.[7] But they don't.

b. Perspective: Men in Positions—More than one sage has been credited with the maxim, "Where you stand depends on where you sit." While officials' views and actions are not predetermined by the positions they hold, they are greatly influenced by them. For each official has a separate job to do, whether it be President or Air Force Chief of Staff or Turkey desk officer in

[d] As the notes will show, the pages that follow draw heavily on the general work of Neustadt, Hilsman, Huntington, and Warner R. Schilling, and on the more elaborate recent efforts by Allison and Morton H. Halperin. There is no intention here to present a formal conceptual model like those of Allison. What is sought instead is to give the reader both the flavor of the bureaucratic politics view and an introduction to its basic concepts.

56

State. Each receives a different mix of information. Each is subject to a different mix of pressures. Each must maintain the loyalty of a different group of subordinates, the respect of a different group of peers, the confidence of a different boss. Thus each views a problem from his own particular "perspective."

Men's perspectives grow narrower the further down in the hierarchy they sit. Even on a matter as critical as the Cuban missile crisis, the Chief of Naval Operations' determination to run what he judged a militarily sound blockade and protect his ships against possible encounters with Russian submarines conflicted with the President's broader need to avoid provoking the Soviets and give them "time to see, think, and blink." And not only do men in positions tend to see issues in terms of their positions. They also tend to press for their resolution in the direction that will most strengthen their ability to do their particular jobs. The State Department was concerned in the early sixties about McNamara's frequent trips to Vietnam, fearing that "visits by so highranking an official . . . would get United States prestige hooked too tightly to the roller coaster of events in Vietnam in spite of the fact that we had only limited influence on those events." But according to Hilsman, McNamara felt he had to see for himself in order to support the policy, and the President felt he had to support the Secretary who was his instrument to keep the services in line. McNamara may in turn have felt he needed the trips to keep one-up on the military. For Hoopes reports that McNamara continued to use such trips as leverage to trim requests for more troops until the end of his tenure.[8]

c. *Bargaining Advantages: Who Influences What How Much*—Differences among men sharing power can only be resolved by bargaining. Thus officials strive to be *effective* in influencing their colleagues. But they are not equally successful, and they do not come to the battle

57

equally armed. Nor does the fight necessarily go to the swiftest of tongue, the man with the best rational arguments. For persuasion requires not just logic but a hearing, and some are more listened to than others. To influence particular issues bureaucrats need "bargaining advantages," sources of influence which make others take them seriously. Allison lists these as "drawn from formal authority and obligations, institutional backing, constituents, expertise, and status." Hilsman cites as "sources of power" within the executive branch "the confidence of the President," "position and title," "representing a particular constituency," "institutional backing," and "statutory or designated authority and responsibility."[9]

This list can be lengthened to include involvement in regular action processes, such as budget review or cable clearance; access to or control over information; alliance with foreign government counterparts or domestic constituencies; the confidence of other important officials as well as that of the President; and the capability to produce "good staff work." Moreover, the advantages of different officials will vary markedly on different issues, depending on such factors as what office has "the action" (primary responsibility) and the relevance of the issue to the official's job.

Nor is it just what advantages a man has. Important, as Allison argues, are both "skill and will. . . . Power wisely invested yields an enhanced reputation for effectiveness. Unsuccessful investment depletes both the stock of capital and the reputation."[10]

For most critical to any official at any one point in time are his relationships with others whose influence is important to him. To play the game well, he must develop a subtle blend of insistence on his right to be involved and recognition of the problems of others where they sit. He must also develop the reputation of one who is likely to win the tough fights, and who remembers who his supporters and adversaries were. He must treat any issue with an eye to how it affects his bargaining advantages for battles yet unknown or unfought. He will therefore tend to see any issue heavily in terms of his personal "stakes," what he is likely to gain or lose from alternative outcomes.[e]

2. Issues as a Flow

The discussion thus far treats "issues" as if each arose separately, and as though bargaining took place over the issue in its entirety. But officials usually consider issues not as whole but one piece at a time, with decisions on many "pieces" adding up to "policy" over time. Also, each piece must compete for their attention with pieces of many other issues. And issues tend to be broader than particular individuals' jurisdictions, so that lateral bargaining becomes a critical element.

a. *Issues as Bits and Pieces*—Issues generally arise not all at once or once and for all, but bit by bit. So while bureaucrats *may* be thinking in terms of the larger question, battles tend to be fought over how to handle today's problem—how to respond to a possible "signal" from Hanoi, what bombing targets to hit next week, whether and how a particular part of the Saigon AID Mission should be reorganized. And the combination of players involved will differ for different pieces of the problem, as will the bargaining advantages they bring to the table. The Assistant AID Administrator for Vietnam, for example, would usually not be at all involved in the first two but would be in the center of the third. Our Ambassador in Saigon would be particularly concerned that we did nothing vis-à-vis Hanoi which weakened the government in Saigon, but he might be less worried about what bombing targets we hit unless a major

---

[e] Neustadt writes: "For every player, any move toward action brings an element of personal challenge wrapped in a substantive guise. Of these his stakes are made." (*Alliance Politics*, p. 78.)

shift were contemplated. Both would be deeply involved in deciding whether we should press Saigon to raise its procurement price for rice.

b. *Issues as Simultaneous Games*—"Players" involved in foreign policy-making, particularly top officials, have "a full plate," a diet of diverse problems in the form of memos, orders for their signature, Presidential recommendations requested. This diet is so rich and varied that it is difficult for them even to taste all the problems set before them, let alone digest them. They are fighting on a number of issues simultaneously, so they must weigh in on one and quickly move on to the next. They must also consider each policy game not entirely on its own terms, but also for its relationship to other games.

In the Johnson Administration, for example, the Secretary of Defense was reportedly not sympathetic to the biological weapons development program. Neither were the Navy and Air Force particularly enthusiastic. Furthermore, elimination of the program could be strongly recommended from both a moral and an international political point of view, and would bring cost savings as well. Yet the Secretary of Defense was fighting with the Joint Chiefs on many other issues, above all Vietnam, and he did not feel he could do battle with them on this one too. Similarly, the Navy and Air Force Chiefs had little interest in bucking the Army on the issue, preferring to trade their support of the Army biological weapons effort for Army backing of programs important to them. So nothing was done.

c. *Issues as Overflowing Jurisdictions*—In testifying before the Jackson Subcommittee, Robert Lovett complained that "the idea seems to have got around that just because some decision may affect your activities, you automatically have a right to take part in making it."[11] But looked at from the official's vantage point, this "idea" is inescapable. Can a Secretary of the Treasury charged with improving the U.S. balance of payments avoid seeking to reduce the net dollar outflow from AID programs? Can a Secretary of State ignore the foreign policy implications of a Skybolt decision? Can the Arms Control and Disarmament Agency fail to raise questions about deployment of MIRV, even if its place in the bureaucratic pecking order may make the odds of its reversing this weapons decision very unfavorable? Can a Secretary of Defense seeking to keep a lid on military involvement in Vietnam stay out of the broader foreign policy aspects of our involvement there, when these are probably the main reasons why he feels such a lid is necessary?

The concept of foreign policy-making as bureaucratic politics does not *depend* on issues being interdepartmental. If they were not, bargaining would still take place, both up-and-down and laterally between offices within particular departments. But the interdepartmental character of practically all important issues complicates the game considerably by increasing the number of players and the range of perspectives involved. It reduces the number of issues where a decision can be worked out under the general authority of any one official short of the President. Conversely it increases the number which must be resolved by lateral bureaucratic compromises, or by "escalation" to higher levels.

3. *Constraints, Channels, and Maneuvers*

Like any political system, the foreign affairs policy-making process is characterized by shared beliefs and allegiances, "rules of the game" affecting who has a chance to influence what issue when, and a set of relatively standard maneuvers for influence.

a. *Common Commitments and Perceptions*—There is a widely shared conviction in the government that the United States should have a strong and effective foreign policy, and that positive actions should be taken to further this aim. Thus, as Halperin notes, "Senior participants in the process . . . by and large believe that they should, and do, favor support of policies which are in the national interest."[12] Partly because of this belief, even those with narrower aims generally feel they can win only by framing their cases as plausible arguments for the broader national interest.*f*

A related factor encouraging agreement is what Halperin calls "widely shared values and images of the world." These tend to determine which proposals will be taken seriously and which considered unreasonable. They may at times diverge rather far from reality. For example, a player suggesting the existence of anything but a solid Russia-China alliance at the time of the 1958 Quemoy crisis would have undercut his credibility and his ability to influence that issue, since he would be contradicting the conventional bureaucratic wisdom of the time.

b. *Rules of the Game Structuring Bureaucratic Politics*—There will always be, at any given time, a set of "rules" about the channels through which particular types of issues move, the people entitled to be consulted or to "clear" proposed documents, the individual or office having "the action" or primary responsibility, etc. Some of these are informal understandings relying heavily on personal relationships. Some are more formal and result from the need for standard operating procedures to handle regular phenomena—rules for routing and answering cables, channeling budget and planning documents, signing off on foreign aid agreements, moving issues up for Presidential or Secretarial action. The influence of such formal procedures is both real and limited. The most critical issues tend to jump

f This phenomenon of treating interest conflicts as substantive, analytic issues goes beyond the foreign affairs government. Write March and Simon: "We predict that almost all disputes in the organization will be defined as problems in analysis . . . and that bargaining (when it occurs) will frequently be concealed within an analytic framework." (*Organizations*, p. 131.)

the bounds of regular channels, above all because of the involvement of top officials who seek to handle things their own ways. But their ability to influence these issues effectively can be strongly affected by the involvement and leverage such procedures provide them and their underlings.

c. *Maneuvers for Influence*—Officials seeking approval or disapproval of particular policy courses or actions will engage in maneuvers designed to make their viewpoints prevail. Not only will they seek to structure their proposals for maximum appeal to others whose agreement is needed or desired. They will also seek on occasion to change the composition of the relevant group of people, shutting some out because "security" requires it, bringing others in by placing the issue in a broader context or raising it before a broader forum, redefining the issue in order to transfer the action to someone else, eliminate the need for certain concurrences, etc. Other standard maneuvers include leaking to the press (for example, to publicize certain information that will create pressure on top officials to act, or to kill a proposed change by premature exposure leading to official disavowal); altering the channels through which important documents must move or getting top officials to pull a particular issue out of channels; and employing a variety of negotiating tactics—trading, conciliating, threatening, etc.

Such tactics may be linked to a broader strategy of "consensus-building" in support of a particular broad course of action. The advocate of such a course will require "the active co-operation and support of some, the formal or informal approval of others, and at least the acquiescence of still others."[13] Those who wished to reverse the trend toward escalation in Vietnam not only built a network of active skeptics and sympathizers based in the Office of the Secretary of Defense, but also sought and found sympathy from the Under Secretary of State and his staff and from Harry McPherson in the White House. When this threatened to prove insufficient, Secretary Clifford widened the field of battle by encouraging the President to call together the "Senior Advisory Group on Vietnam," thereby bringing McGeorge Bundy, Dean Acheson, Douglas Dillon, and Cyrus Vance into the coalition urging the President to change policy.[14]

4. Foreign Policy as Bureaucratic Political Outcome

What results from this bureaucratic political system is, of course, foreign policy. But it is not necessarily "policy" in the rational sense of embodying the decisions made and actions ordered by a controlling intelligence focusing primarily on our foreign policy problems. Instead it is the "outcome" of the political process, the government actions resulting from all the arguments, the building of coalitions and countercoalitions, and the decisions by high officials and compromises among them. Often it may be a "policy" that no participant fully favors, when "different groups pulling in different directions yield a resultant distinct from what anyone intended."[15] Any year's defense budget offers innumerable good examples. Often it is difficult to determine where and when in the system a particular policy direction was decided upon.

Moreover, policy is not usually the outcome of any particular battle, but the cumulation of outcomes of a number of battles fought over time. "Rather than through grand decisions on grand alternatives," Hilsman has written, "policy changes seem to come through a series of slight modifications of existing policy, with the new policy emerging slowly and haltingly by small and usually tentative steps, a process of trial and error in which policy zigs and zags, reverses itself, and then moves forward in a series of incremental steps." "Incrementalism," or step-by-step, trial-and-error policy-making, can be the most rational strategy when the

64

impact of policy changes is hard to assess in advance. Lindblom has made this point with particular persuasiveness. But as it occurs in bureaucratic politics, incremental policy-making reflects more the internal dynamics of decision-making than any conscious design to maximize our ability to cope with an unruly world.[16]

Two Possible Pitfalls of the Bureaucratic Politics View

Any generalizing set of concepts tends to bring certain phenomena to prominence, risking an exaggeration of their importance and a neglect of other factors.[g] Thus, even if one accepts the foregoing description as a generally valid picture of "the way things are" in foreign policy decision-making, one must guard against its possible pitfalls. Two are of particular importance to those concerned with foreign affairs organization. The first is the danger that concentrating on what happens within the executive branch may lead to neglect of the broader national politics of foreign policy-making. The second is the emphasis which analysts of bureaucratic politics have tended to give to certain types of bureaucratic motivation, and the danger that this might blind one to other types of behavior of considerable importance to organizational reformers.

Hilsman depicts the politics of policy-making as involving all politically active and interested groups in our society, with executive branch decisions the primary focal point toward which efforts at influence are directed. The more elaborate analyses of Allison and Hal-

---

[g] Analysts of bureaucratic politics do not generally claim to have escaped such dangers. Allison, for example, presents the bureaucratic politics interpretation as one of three alternative conceptual models. Model I, "Rational Policy," assumes that national states act rationally, as units. Model II, "Organizational Process," emphasizes certain characteristics of large organizations. Model III, "Bureaucratic Politics," is the one on which our discussion has drawn. Allison is clearly most interested in the latter. But he recognizes that "each concentrates on one class of variables, in effect, relegating other important factors to a *ceteris paribus* clause." ("Conceptual Models," p. 716.)

perin, however, focus their attention largely on officials and relationships inside the executive branch. Such a focus has a considerable practical basis. It makes sense in many ways to see foreign policy-making, at least on national security questions, as primarily an intra-governmental process, with the major persons and interests seeking to affect it centered in the executive branch. The frequent genuine need for secrecy, combined with its even more frequent use by officials to increase their influence; the broad and flexible authority the President has for dealing with major crises; the lack of strong political feedback on overseas actions comparable to that in the domestic policy area from directly affected governors, mayors, or other national or regional politicos; the unamenability of many of the most important foreign policy activities to budget or legislative controls —all of these conspire to place within the executive branch much greater influence over foreign policy than it could possibly exercise over domestic.

But concentrating on the bureaucracy can be misleading. For though career bureaucrats may deal largely with others within the government, Presidents and Cabinet members must operate in a wider arena. In particular, if our foreign policy goals and means cease to have broad general support in the larger society, the opportunities and channels for outside influence multiply. The President and his top officials must then become effective persuaders in this broader public arena or see important elements of policy slip from their grasp. Thus President Nixon, relatively successful in taming the foreign affairs bureaucracy on the major issues, has suffered far stronger Congressional challenges on national security matters than any predecessor since the pre-war Roosevelt.

Hilsman offers a useful compromise, one that allows concentration on the executive branch while taking broader influences into account. He describes the policy-making arena as a number of "concentric rings," with the "innermost circles" being entirely within the executive branch. It makes sense for a study of foreign affairs organization to concentrate on these "innermost circles," analyzing organizational reforms and strategies heavily in terms of their impact on intra-executive branch decision-making. But it is important not to forget that the politics of the federal bureaucracy is, in the words of one authority, a "subsystem of the American political system" as a whole.[17]

Problems of Interest and Motivation

A more complicated problem for those applying the bureaucratic politics approach, however, is the question of the interests and motivations of individuals and their organizations. Politics is often characterized as the interplay of individual and group interests. Yet it is not by accident that nowhere in our description of the fundamentals of bureaucratic politics is the question of individual interest directly discussed, except as it relates to players' perspectives and their needs for effectiveness. Due to the limits of rational analysis and the impact of particular perspectives, bureaucratic politics is a logical outgrowth of the nature of government and foreign policy even if the only interest of each official is to do his own job effectively. The bureaucratic politics view need not assume that officials are inordinately self-seeking, or committed only to the interests of their organizations. In fact, as noted by Schilling, Allison, and Hilsman, one considerable reason why battles are often so heated is that men have strong convictions about what the "right policy" is.

. . . When in the late 1950's, for example, intelligence officials leaked secret information foreshadowing an upcoming "missile gap" to Democratic senators and sympathetic members of the press, it was not because they were disloyal, but because they were deeply convinced that the nation was in peril. They had tried and failed to convince the top levels of the Eisenhower administration of the validity of their projections, and they felt completely justified in taking matters into their own hands by going over the President's head to Congress, the press, and the public.[18]

But men do of course have more selfish interests as well. They may seek power for its own sake, or financial reward, or prestige, or personal advancement, or a larger role for their agency programs. Sometimes they pursue these goals unabashedly, recognizing them as self-interest. More often, probably, they grow to equate the importance of their function and the strength of their organization with the broader national interest and welfare. Admirals are generally sincere when they urge a stronger navy as vital to America's security. Foreign Service officers genuinely believe that the nation benefits when the great majority of Ambassadorships are filled from their ranks.[h]

However, because analysts of bureaucratic politics are concerned primarily with explaining what influences foreign policy, they tend to portray officials who actively seek to affect that policy and strive to build up their bargaining advantages in order to accomplish this aim.

[h] A provocative "typology" of government officials and their motives, developed by Downs, illustrates the mixture of bureaucratic types. Downs suggests two varieties of "purely self-interested officials": "climbers," who seek increased power, income, and prestige almost exclusively; and "conservers," who are similarly devoted to convenience and security. In addition there are three types of "mixed-motive officials": "zealots," who are "loyal to relatively narrow policies and concepts" and promote them with "implacable energy"; "advocates," who tend to promote activities under their jurisdictions; and "statesmen," whose loyalty is primarily to "society as a whole." (*Inside Bureaucracy*, pp. 88-111.) Zealots are comparable to what Frankel calls "hedgehogs." He quotes a Greek poet via Isaiah Berlin, "The fox knows many things, but the hedgehog knows one big thing." (*Foggy Bottom*, p. 151.) Foxes are presumably "climbers."

Such officials are aggressive about getting involved in issues which relate to their responsibilities. They tend to see this relationship broadly, jumping into matters well beyond those where they have primary action responsibility.[i]

But often men seek not to plunge aggressively into what others see as none of their business, but rather to draw lines separating their jurisdictions so as to minimize conflict. After all, classical economic theorists usually placed more value on competition than business practitioners. The latter often sought protection and security from the buffeting of market forces. Similarly, many officials seek not to expand the range of their jobs but to cut them down to manageable size. Secretary Rusk put the problem succinctly in 1963: "There are those who think that the heart of a bureaucracy is a struggle for power. This is not the case at all. The heart of the bureaucratic problem is the inclination to avoid responsibility."[19]

And in contrast to the "serious bureaucrat" which bureaucratic politics descriptions tend to emphasize, there is that opposite stereotype—of the man who takes refuge in nit-picking rules, refuses to give a straight answer or make a clear decision, lives in a world rather narrowly bounded by his own particular agency and program, and reserves his greatest interest for the annual unveiling of the new government pay scale. His behavior might be described as a flight from bureaucratic politics.

There is, of course, no reason why the foreign affairs government cannot be thought of as a political system

---

[i] It takes just one further short logical step to assume that officials pursue issues and develop strategies for influencing them in a rather systematic and calculating way. Neither Allison nor Halperin makes this assumption in general. Halperin, in fact, distinguishes between the "serious bureaucrat," the man who "develops and pursues a strategy designed to bring about a desired change in policy or patterns of action," and the official who does not. Much of his analysis, however, is directed toward the former.

without assuming that all participants are equally power-oriented or politically motivated. We certainly think this way about our larger national political system, and our citizens show a wide variance in political interest and effectiveness. But to balance and deepen the basic picture developed so far, it is useful to highlight two important ways in which men tend to be more concerned with protecting the inner life and existence of their organizations than with building broader policy influence. One is the tendency of organizations to develop their own subcultures. The second is the tendency to give priority to a parochial piece of policy "territory."

Organizational Subcultures

Many men spend the major part of their working lives in one large government organization or career service. How they relate to those inside the organization may well become more important to both their psychic well-being and their personal advancement than how they relate to those outside. It is not surprising, then, that organizations develop their own informal subcultures, which—like the broader national culture within which they develop—both prescribe certain patterns of belief and behavior and penalize those who do not conform to them.

Probably the most important example of this phenomenon in the international affairs bureaucracy is the State Department's Foreign Service. In a notable effort to describe this subculture, Andrew Scott argues that most Foreign Service officers share an "ideology" composed of various "prevalent beliefs" which are "perfectly plausible" but, like those in most ideologies, contain " a mix of truths, half-truths, and errors." A typical belief is that "the really important aspects of the foreign affairs of the United States are the political ones—the traditional ones of negotiation, representation, and reporting." One critically important aspect of this ideology, Scott holds, is the "extent to which it encourages officers to become inward-looking and absorbed in the affairs of the Service."[20]

A related characteristic of these prevalent beliefs is the placing of highest value on what *has been* the organization's most important role in the past, traditional diplomacy. Similarly, writes Halperin, Navy men believe "that the Navy's business is to man combat naval ships and that their mission is to maintain control of the seas," but "have tended to view the Polaris missile-firing submarines as . . . extraneous to the Navy's 'essential' tasks."[21]

"An important question about any administrative system," suggests the Jackson Subcommittee staff, "is whether the qualities which enable an individual to survive and advance in the organization are the same as those which will enable the organization to survive in a competitive environment." In this sense, the pattern Scott describes is "dysfunctional," since it tends to provide protection from that environment. "Order and discipline within the service," he concludes, "are purchased at the cost of imagination, flexibility, and organizational drive."[22]

Parochialism and Jurisdictions

Organizations, like individuals, have parochial perspectives and priorities. Anthony Downs has developed the concept of "territoriality," suggesting that bureaucracies—like animals and nations—tend to "stake out and defend territories surrounding their nests or 'home bases.'" Certain parts of "policy space" comprise a bureau's *heartland*, where it is sole determinant of policy; surrounding this will be the *interior fringe*, where the bureau's interest is primary but where other agencies have some influence. Outside of this is *no-man's land*, where no bureau dominates but many have influence.

71

Territorial boundaries are never absolutely clear; "the inherent dynamism of human life" prevents jurisdictional lines from ever reaching an equilibrium. Because policy issues often cut across any possible allocation of jurisdictions, "Every large organization is in partial conflict with every other social agent with which it deals." But "the basic nature of all such struggles is the same—each combatant needs to establish a large enough territory to guarantee his own survival."[23]

The last quotation hints at a broader phenomenon. For, contrary to what certain elements of the bureaucratic politics view might lead one to assume, organizations tend to choose clear primary responsibility for a narrow policy area over the opportunities and dangers inherent in contesting for influence across a broader policy range. They will give primacy to fortifying the heartland. Members of the Joint Chiefs of Staff do not go out of their way to challenge the pet proposals of other services—rather, they trade support of these for reciprocal support of their own services' priorities. Foreign Service officers seldom make hard-nosed challenges of military tactics. They prefer to confine their involvement to the "political" aspects, and hope the military will reciprocate by staying out of "diplomacy."

Even an apparent opportunity to expand one's organizational role may be spurned if it involves too great a threat to existing territorial arrangements. Halperin notes, for example, that though the Gaither Report of 1957 "recommended across-the-board increases" in military spending, there was "no support forthcoming" from the services. For they saw a danger that, given tight Budget Bureau restraints on total spending, the report would not result in higher total outlays but might change the way present money was allocated. The services were "reluctant to commit themselves to what was in effect a new, more 'rational' method of splitting up the defense pie," since they feared they would not be

72

able to control it. Similarly, as a high departmental official recently put it, the reaction of the State Department to the rapid post-war expansion of government foreign affairs activities was to "protect its exclusiveness and high standards."[24]

Implications for Foreign Policy-Making

The nature of the bureaucratic political process seems to contradict almost the very notion of our government even pretending to make coherent, purposive foreign policy. And further investigation does nothing to brighten the picture. In fact, when one draws on other analyses of organizational behavior, the problems become even more complex, and even less susceptible to clear-cut reform.

"Pluralists" describing the politics of domestic policy-making have sometimes gone beyond *description* to *prescription*, to asserting "confidence in the capability of the political process to produce the right results."[25] Such faith in political competition finds its parallel in Adam Smith's notion of the "invisible hand," a guiding principle whereby the sum of economic actions taken by individuals for their own selfish purposes would lead to the best possible outcome for society as a whole. But is the outcome of the *internal* competition of bureaucratic politics the kind of policy that will be successful in dealing with a troubled *outside* world?

Huntington feels he can answer this question with "qualified optimism." He sees one major virtue as stability: "the forces of pluralism correct and counterbalance the instabilities, enthusiasms, and irrationalities of the prevailing mood." Hilsman carries such optimism a step further. "In spite of the untidiness and turmoil of the politics of policy-making in Washington," he writes,

. . . such an open process of conflict and consensus-building, debate, assessment, and mutual adjustment

73

and accommodation can be solidly effective in the assessment of broad policy alternatives if the conditions are right. The conditions are, first, that the subject is one on which the competing groups are knowledgeable. Second, both the participating constituencies within the government and the "attentive publics" outside must be well informed. Third, all levels of government, those who will carry out the policy as well as those who decide it, must be responsive to the decision and persuaded by it. Under these conditions, the chances are good that the policy will be wise, that the effort and sacrifice required will be forthcoming, and that the work of carrying out the policy will go forward intelligently and energetically.[26]

But without denying that wise policy may emerge "if the conditions are right," it seems doubtful that the results will always, or even usually, be so reassuring. The central danger is inherent in the notion of policy emerging from bureaucratic competition, responsive more to the internal dynamics of our decision-making process than to the external problems on which it is supposed to center. As Schilling has noted, the bureaucratic political process can produce "no policy at all," stalemate; "compromised policy," with the direction hardly evident; or "unstable policy," where "changes in the ad hoc groupings of elites point policy first in one and then in another direction." It can result in "contradictory policy," where different government organizations pursue conflicting courses; "paper policy," officially promulgated without the support needed for effective implementation; or "slow" policy, since competition and consensus-building take time.[27]

Moreover, just to influence policy, officials need to apply inordinate attention to internal conflict, thereby limiting the time they can focus on the overseas situation toward which policy is ostensibly directed. As Stanley

74

Hoffmann has noted, "There inevitably occurs a subtle (or not so subtle) shift from the specific foreign-policy issues to be resolved, to the positions, claims, and perspectives of the participants in the policy machine. The demands of the issue and the merits of alternative choices are subordinated to the demands of the machine and the needs to keep it going. Administrative politics replaces foreign policy."[28]

The troubling logic of policy-making by bureaucratic politics is taken one step further by Halperin. He depicts bureaucrats who are so deeply engrossed in intra-governmental maneuvering that the actions which result are seldom clear signals to other countries. Foreign bureaucrats in turn receive and interpret these signals selectively since they are looking for evidence to support them in their own internal bureaucratic battles. Thus "communications" between nations tend to become dialogues between the largely deaf and dumb. Similarly, Neustadt's analysis of the Suez and Skybolt crises in *Alliance Politics* emphasizes how American and British officials concentrating on their own intra-governmental games regularly misinterpreted the motives and constraints of their allied counterparts.

Furthermore, if bureaucratic politics causes officials to shift their focus from substantive policy issues to "the positions, claims, and perspectives of the participants in the policy machine," organizational subcultures can cause a further shift, turning men away from the inter-agency bureaucratic competition and toward concern primarily with relationships within their own organizations. This can lead to strikingly inappropriate, unresponsive behavior in relation to those outside the organization.

Resistance to Change

If the inward-looking nature of the bureaucratic political process seems its most dangerous fault, it is hardly its only one. A closely related problem is the bias against change. Superficially one might expect the opposite. Classical economists thought that competition would cause a steady surge of new ideas, from men seeking the rewards that would come from "building a better mousetrap." More recently economists have had doubts, noting that industries which most closely approximated the free enterprise model of many competitive firms (like housing construction) tend to be particularly backward in developing new techniques.

Bureaucratic politics seems to bias policy outcomes against change for not dissimilar reasons. A small businessman cannot afford to innovate because the rewards are uncertain and delayed and because he must survive in today's market. Similarly the bureaucrat seeks effectiveness in today's government, and this generally means moving with prevailing policy tides rather than challenging them.[j] As Roger Fisher writes, a Washington official seeking a quick response to an overseas problem knows that "if the cable can be worded so that it is simply an application of a prior decision or a prior statement by the President or another high official, the cable will be more difficult for others to object to, it can be cleared at a low level, and it can be dispatched more quickly."[29]

More generally, the problem is what Schilling has called the "gyroscopic" effect. Policies once adopted tend to become self-perpetuating because, in Henry Kissinger's words, "An attempt to change course involves the prospect that the whole searing process of arriving at a decision will have to be repeated." Galbraith's offspring, Dr. Herschel McLandress, had a slightly different explanation.

To increase the number of men working on a foreign policy problem—Berlin, Castro, Viet Nam—is to in-

---

[j] One official interviewed described the "bureaucrat's instincts" as "to ask for the minimum you need and explain the minimum; otherwise you lose."

crease the number of men whose agreement must be obtained before action is taken. The more men whose agreement must be obtained, the more time required.

If the number at work on a given job is large enough, action, it would seem to follow, will be indefinitely postponed. Although this tendency does exist, things work out somewhat differently in practice. In many foreign policy situations, action is often unavoidable. Accordingly, while no new step can command agreement, something must still be done. So opinion will eventually coalesce on whatever has been done before.[30]

Resistance to change also arises from certain inherent problems of large organizations. One is the need for routines to structure an organization's response to particular events. To make possible coordinated and effective action by large numbers of people, organizations devise standard operating procedures or programs prescribing the roles of individuals and units in dealing with recurring events or predictable threats. Such "routines" can range from the standard procedures for processing and funding of technical assistance requests to contingency plans to cope with a Soviet ground invasion of Western Europe. An organization can have only a limited number of such routines in its repertoire; these constitute the organization's coordinated action capabilities at any one time. They are also difficult and time-consuming to change. Those for dealing with crises are necessarily "precooked," plans devised in advance for contingencies as defined by the organization. When an actual event comes, the organization can only respond to it by doing what it has already established procedures for doing. For example, one FSO working on indepartmental Berlin contingency planning in the early 1960's was impressed with how inflexible he and his colleagues

77

found the military instrument which they would have liked to think of as capable of being tailored to specific circumstances.[31]

It is not surprising, then, that such general routines are likely to be very inappropriate in the special circumstances of a particular military crisis. One example is the already-cited conflict between the Navy's standard blockade plans and the President's needs during the Cuban missile crisis. Another, slightly more complicated, is our military's efforts in the 1950's and early 1960's to train the South Vietnamese army to fight a conventional war. It was what our army "knew how to do," even though the conflict did not become anything like a conventional war until our massive intervention in 1965.

Resistance to Control

In the end, all of these problems are part of the largest one of all. Running through both our criticism of traditional approaches and our discussion of bureaucratic politics is a common theme—the limits of high officials' control over what the foreign affairs government is doing. Some writers have suggested the problem is insoluble. Gordon Tullock, for example, argues that distortions in the flow of communications, information, and orders up and down the hierarchy lead after a certain point to "bureaucratic free enterprise," with activities by bureaucrats on the firing line essentially unrelated to what bosses want. Others, like Downs, are more moderate, but still argue that "no one can fully control the behavior of a large organization," and that "the larger any organization becomes, the weaker is the control over its actions exercised by those at the top."[32]

John C. Ries highlights one aspect of this problem, summarizing the findings of several organizational analysts to paint a rather bleak picture of the information problems facing top officials.

Where the hierarchy is used as an information network, each step in the communication chain acts as a screening point to decide how much information will flow upward. This happens because subordinates cannot pass up the line all the details available to them. In order to reduce communications to tolerable size, a subordinate must synthesize and summarize the facts available to him. Facts, then, are transformed into judgments. If the chain of communications is very long, each link must take the judgments of lower echelons and use them as facts.

This process of substituting inferences or judgments for facts has been called "uncertainty absorption." . . . Furthermore, through this process, communications moving upward tend to get sugar-coated. A subordinate is much more likely to report improvements and successes than failures. . . .

As the above comments show, the higher up the pyramid one proceeds, the more difficult rationality becomes. Judgments replace facts; the specific becomes abstract; the definite becomes vague. Improved communications promise to offset some of this, but there is little evidence that it can overcome all. . . . The individual who occupies the top position in a hierarchical structure is much more isolated, powerless, and dependent than the advocates of the hierarchical model believe.[33]

A further insight into top-level control difficulties stresses the dependence of modern organizations on group processes. In striking contrast, perhaps contradiction, to his condemnation of group decision-making in State, Galbraith argues in *The New Industrial State* that the increasingly complex technical underpinnings of corporate production decisions have forced the real

79

power of decision out of the hands of top management and deep into what he calls the "technostructure." There it is exercised by committees of experts, and topside interference is likely only to upset this process without any compensating constructive achievement. Warren Bennis has similarly suggested that, as the tasks of organizations grow "more technical, complicated, and unprogrammed . . . adaptive, temporary systems of diverse specialists . . . will gradually replace bureaucracy as we know it." But this adds even greater complexity to the control problem of those at the top. It is easy to sympathize with John F. Kennedy's terse remark when a U-2 plane strayed over Siberia at the high point of the Cuban Missile Crisis: "There is always some so-and-so who doesn't get the word." It is harder to assure that something similar won't happen again.[34]

Implications for Organizational Reform

The implications of all this for those who seek to organize for purposive and coherent foreign policy are obvious and unfavorable. The system as it seems to operate directs men's attention more to intra-governmental matters than to the overseas situations policy must influence; clings to old policies because of the difficulty of changing them; and resists efforts to control it from the top. Though competition may sometimes have positive effects, there is no reason to believe that these will be the rule rather than the exception. And if bureaucratic politics turns men's energies inward from the substantive policy problem to the bureaucratic political one, organizational subcultures can narrow attention still further, encouraging a flight from inter-agency bureaucratic politics to an emphasis on intra-agency relationships.

The danger which the existing system poses for coherent and purposive foreign policy may explain the allure of the sorts of reform proposals which have been recurrent in the post-war period. One is tempted to urge that policy-making be "rationalized," or authority be joined to responsibility. Yet politics and large organizations are not evils to be exorcised by the proper mix of admonition and formal restructuring, but basic, persistent "facts of life." The reformer faces a world, to borrow two of Neustadt's characterizations, of "intractable substantive problems and immovable bureaucratic structures," of "emergencies in policy with politics as usual."[35] And he must extend to the entire government Neustadt's depiction of a President who feels the urgent need for wise policy but recognizes that our arrival at such policy is anything but automatic.

For if there is no reason to deny the perils of bureaucratic politics, no more can one ignore its pervasiveness. So the organizational reformer must begin by dealing with the government as it is, not as he would like it to be. The bureaucratic political view is particularly valuable because it forces attention to leverage. If, for example, one proposes to increase policy coherence by establishing a new central official, it makes sense to ask first whether he can achieve the leverage, the "bargaining advantages" to make his role effective. But one must ask also whether the person being placed in such a position will be one with, in Rusk's words, "the inclination to avoid responsibility." For giving a man all of the bargaining advantages in the world is of little use if he will not use them. Interestingly, then, part of organizational reform inevitably involves not the banishment of "politics" from decision-making, but rather an effort to assure that officials upon whom one's strategy depends can play the game effectively.

Not only can the bureaucratic political view make us treat proposed reforms in terms of their effects on how decisions are actually made. It can also perform a more traditional function—to highlight what some of the problems are. One cannot think of bureaucratic politics as something to be abolished. But one can look for organizational means to affect the "rules of the game," or alter the bureaucratic balance of power, so as to mitigate some of its more dangerous tendencies. If, as this study has indicated, a serious look at our policy-making system suggests that decisions tend to be reached as compromises between men with narrow perspectives; that issues tend to be resolved piecemeal, with policy evolving in incremental fashion; that officials are dangerously diverted from focusing on the international environment by the attention they must pay to intra-governmental politics; that our overall system is biased against change, resistant to central control and coordination, and often clumsy in responding to unique situations—if all these things are true, then organizational reformers must seek ways to reduce these problems to less threatening size. This will not, of course, be easy. Particularly tricky is an effort to reconcile the strengthening of coherence, which requires strong officials dealing effectively with intra-governmental political phenomena, with the need for our foreign policy to have a sufficiently "outward-looking" orientation to be relevant to the overseas problems toward which it is directed. Moreover, any attack on such "biases" in the present system must recognize and fight that all-too-human distaste for viable partial solutions, the temptation of more sweeping cures which ignore "the way things are." In government organization, also, the best is often the enemy of the good. But a skepticism about attaining the best should be joined with a determination to seek the better.

CHAPTER FOUR

What to Do? The Need for an Organizational Strategy

THE bureaucratic politics view of government suggests considerable modesty about just how much coherence and central purpose can be brought to foreign policy. Yet it equally underscores the urgent need to try. It allows refuge neither in solutions that do not solve, nor in faith that the forces at work will produce happy policy results. A serious approach to the foreign affairs organizational problem must therefore combine the realist's recognition of the motives that move men within the system, with the militant cry of reformers and protest movements, "Business as usual won't do!" And it will require, in Max Weber's words, "both passion and perspective."

Effective reform cannot come from efforts to transcend the bureaucratic political system. Rather, it must be based on a strategy which copes with the patterns of politics and tries to turn these patterns to its advantage. This must be mainly an intra-governmental political strategy, one explicitly shaped to affect the bureaucratic politics of foreign policy decision-making.

The logic of bureaucratic politics makes the basic element of such a strategy simple, unoriginal, and inescapable. The only way to counter the strong centrifugal forces in the bureaucracy is to build up the influence of central officials, men who are more likely to think broadly about foreign policy and be oriented toward "national interest" objectives. We are back to what Kaufman calls one of the three "core values" of twentieth century public administration, the goal of "executive leadership."[1] This was likewise the goal of those who advocated such solutions as the joining of authority and responsibility, and the creation of a new central official. But these were inconsistent with how the foreign affairs government actually works. Is there another strategy which offers greater promise?

The first question in devising such a strategy is whose influence one should seek to strengthen. Around whom should coherence be built? Once the question is put in this way, there is but one choice. Only the President has sufficient legal authority, prestige, and other bargaining advantages—plus sufficient motivation—for carrying out coherent and purposive policy.

Post-war studies have generally talked in terms of strengthening the President and enhancing his capacity to choose. The Hoover task force cited the Constitution in stressing the President's "ultimate responsibility for the conduct of foreign affairs." The AFSA report of 1968 "believed it is necessary to start with the role of the new President." The IDA study reflects this emphasis in both its title and its contents. And though the Herter Committee focused more narrowly on the State-AID-USIA group, it stressed that "Whatever the Department of State does in exercising leadership and coordination, it must do as an agent of the President."[2]

But combined with this general endorsement of Presidential leadership has been concern that it not get out of hand. In particular, high officials have tended to see strengthening the President as synonymous with helping them do their own jobs. There was a particularly strong reaction to Franklin Roosevelt's methods of dealing with (or around) his top officials. The Jackson Subcommittee noted that "the National Security Council was chiefly the inspiration of James Forrestal, who wanted to enhance the defense role in peacetime policymaking and especially to insure regular consultation by future Presidents with their principal civilian and military advisers. The purpose was at least as much to make the Presidency serve the needs of the departments as to make the latter serve the former." The Hoover Commission task force similarly inveighed against FDR, characterizing Presidential participation in the conduct of foreign affairs as "marked with many pitfalls," stressing that "the President should consult his foreign policy advisers in the executive branch before committing the United States to a course of action."[3]

Many academic analysts praised Roosevelt's handling of the bureaucracy. But more recently the scholarly community too has turned somewhat sour on the Presidency. General distaste among intellectuals for the last chief executives, the failure of "Great Society" legislation to ameliorate social problems, the Vietnam war, a more general gap between the hopes Americans have vested in the Presidential office and the achievements that have come from it—all of these have led to second thoughts among many one-time advocates of enhanced Presidential power. Symbolic was the sudden Washington visit of 13 Presidentially-oriented Harvard scholars in the wake of the Cambodia invasion, to express alarm to old colleague Henry Kissinger and offer aid and comfort to the enemy on the Hill.[4]

Insofar as the "revisionist" critique reflects a more tempered view of what Presidential leadership can actually accomplish, or how much it can "rise above" other political forces, the new skepticism is entirely salutary.[5] Certainly a foreign affairs organizational strategy based upon an illusion of Presidential omnipotence or unique virtue would be as useless as one based on the myth of the magic of formal structure. But recognizing the limits of the Presidency does not lead us to any alternative man or institution around which foreign policy coherence can be built.

The legislative branch can hardly be a force for foreign affairs leadership and coherence. Congress can at most be a restraint on the President—sometimes for good, sometimes for ill—or the source of useful but sporadic initiatives. To the extent that Congress can impose specific restrictions like the Cooper-Church amendment prohibiting a return of our troops to Cambodia, or affect actual foreign policy by general legislation, it can have undeniable effect. But this influence is limited primarily to constraining, modifying, or supplementing Presidential and executive branch aims and actions, not imposing a coherence of its own. The Constitution and 180 years of tradition give foreign affairs primacy to the President. Congress itself is not remotely a unified organization; it is more a complex of semi-autonomous power centers. Even in as unusual a case as Cambodia, Congressional opposition quickly became cautious once it seemed as if the President might prevail with the public. Sam Brown could write by August 1970: "The initial spurt of enthusiasm in the Congress, especially in the Senate, has largely ebbed. Regular meetings of anti-war Senators have ceased, and there is little evidence of the cooperation or initiative necessary to effect a strategy to end the war."[6]

But if the possibility of coherent Congressional foreign affairs leadership can be dismissed as impractical, more sobering is the increasingly accepted idea that the Presidency itself is becoming an "irrational" institution, with a built-in isolation which makes "the most important, and least examined problem of the Presidency" that of "maintaining contact with reality." Former Johnson aide George Reedy suggests that the heady atmosphere of the White House "dulls the sensitivity of political men and ultimately reduces them to bungling amateurs in their basic craft—the art of politics." He likens the President to a monarch, treated with such deference and so insulated from the political give-and-take which once served to sharpen his political judgment and sensitivity that he is almost bound to blunder badly on critical issues. And no sooner had the book come out than Nixon's Cambodia decision seemed a frightening confirmation of the isolation thesis, with the solitary totting up of plusses and minuses on yellow pads and the explanatory speech not seriously discussed with responsible advisers before it was given.[7]

This is a serious problem, and to base a strategy around the President is not to argue for running the government the way Nixon seems to have come to: seeking to center all important matters in an augmented Presidential staff, dealing mainly with and through a very few individuals on that staff, keeping most of the permanent government (and the Congress) at more than arm's length. There are, however, countervailing forces against insulation. Presidents certainly have strong incentive for effective political performance, since so much of what they can accomplish depends upon it. Lyndon Johnson's political achievements through 1965 did not evidence any dulling of his political sensitivity. His later tendency toward isolation may have been more a reaction to attack than the result of insulation from it. Even the Cambodia crisis can be used as a counterexample. It forced the President to make an explicit, public effort to reestablish communications with dissenting groups, suggesting that isolation carried too far brings corrective forces into play.

None of this implies that the President even approaches the rational ideal of the wise, unbiased central decision-maker. For in addition to the pull toward isolation, Presidents seem to have other recurrent tendencies not necessarily conducive to wise foreign policy. One is toward activism. Presidents want to make names for themselves in history, whether it be a Kennedy seeking to build a new Atlantic relationship of "interdependence" or a Johnson yearning for a summit conference in the closing months of his tenure. They may therefore tend to press too hard for immediate gains visible during the current term, neglecting the frequent need for patience in waiting until "the time is ripe," or in allowing broad trends and forces to have their gradual effects.

Finally, Presidents are partisan politicians. They are concerned with building up the party, and even more with strengthening their own personal political positions. They may well take action on a foreign policy matter not for reasons of international relations, but because there are partisan gains to be had at home. Elie Abel properly opens his account of the Cuban missile crisis with reference to the fall election campaign debate over weapons and the Castro problem. Thomas E. Cronin criticizes McGeorge Bundy's recent book calling for a stronger Presidency because it tends to "lightly dismiss the highly partisan and political nature of presidential transactions."[8]

Yet here also there are mitigating forces. Presidential activism can be a useful antidote to bureaucratic immobilism. Regarding partisan politics, one should not ignore the eye cocked toward the next election, nor the way the overall national political system and the President's sense of his place within it affect all of his actions. As Sorensen has noted:

> Politics pervades the White House without seeming to prevail. It is not a role for which the President sets apart certain hours. It is rarely the sole subject of a formal Presidential meeting. It is instead an ever-present influence—counterbalancing the unrealistic, checking the unreasonable, sometimes preventing the desirable, but always testing what is acceptable.[9]

Yet few today would argue that our foremost foreign policy official should be someone not responsible to what we call public opinion. Partisan politics is our crude way of trying to enforce such responsiveness. Nor are there any easy criteria for determining how much of a role "domestic political" considerations should play in "foreign policy" decisions. One can argue endlessly about whether the Kennedy-Johnson Vietnam escalation resulted from fear of losing the Cold War or fear of losing the next election, and whether increased or decreased sensitivity of national leaders to partisan politics might have prevented it. But it is hard to see the logic of centering a strategy for coherent and purposive foreign policy on any official who isn't compelled by his position to weigh both international and domestic politics.

Ultimately, however, one comes back to the fact that there is no other choice. An alternative might theoretically be the Secretary of State, who shares the President's motivation for a purposive and coherent policy and has responsibilities both to the President and to Congress. But any Secretary who wishes to be strong is overwhelmingly dependent on Presidential favor and support. His basic Congressional grant of authority is to "perform and execute such duties as shall from time to time be enjoined on or entrusted to him by the President of the United States." In practice the critical importance of the relationship is confirmed by the experience of two of the strongest post-war Secretaries. Acheson has written of the critical importance of the President-Secretary relationship, especially the need that "from first to last both parties to the relationship understand which is the President." Concerning Dulles it has been noted that "few Secretaries of State have ever been more conscious of dependence on the President, and none has been more careful of his White House credit."[10]

One may, of course, still argue against enhancing Presidential influence because of mistrust of a particular oval office occupant, or a more general belief that the potential dangers of executive power outweigh the benefits it can bring. But to do so would, for all practical purposes, be to renounce the aim of coherent policy altogether. Even in this age of disillusion, Rossiter's summation still holds: "Leadership in foreign affairs flows today from the President—or it does not flow at all."[11]

Basing foreign policy coherence on the President seems, then, to be the only serious choice. Yet the President is only one man. And if policy is seen as emerging from what thousands of officials do day by day, he has an immense personal control problem. In trying to shape its actions to his central purposes, he must be able to get a handle on activities well down in the bureaucracy. To achieve this he must have men who can help him do his work.

And just as the President needs the aid of others, men in the government who aspire to major influence need Presidential support. As Dean Rusk said after eight years as Secretary of State, "The real organization of government at higher echelons is not what you find in textbooks or organization charts. It is how confidence flows down from the President."[12]

Presidential "confidence" includes at least two elements. One relates to *competence*—all of the factors that lead a President to believe that a subordinate is doing a strong, capable, effective job. The second, at least as important, involves *alliance*—the President's belief that a man is *his* man, *responsive* to him and *loyal* to him. It is hard to think of any close, lasting relationship between a President and a top foreign affairs official which did not include both elements.

Thus the needs of both the President and other high officials point to a strategy of building foreign policy coherence around a group of related individuals who support and supplement the President in carrying out his foreign policy responsibilities, *and* who depend on his confidence for much of their own influence. This is the only way to build central organizational strength in the foreign affairs government. These men cannot in the nature of things see matters exactly as the President sees them. They may be his men, but they are not he. But they must be so chosen and so placed in the government that they will combine a high order of responsiveness to his needs with involvement in the important daily actions of the foreign affairs bureaucracy. The very fact that the President must see and act partly through other men means, of course, some dilution right at the start of the kind of "coherence" which is achieved only by an individual working unaided. Being unavoidable, this cost must be accepted.

To build central organizational strength means to build up the bargaining advantages of the President's men so that their influence is increased. At the same time, it requires care that they not become too fortified with bargaining advantages usable against *him*. Both the words of Rusk and the general experience of recent high foreign policy officials suggest, however, that the higher men are placed in the government, the more they feel dependent on the flow of Presidential confidence for their own influence. A strong President ought, then, to be able to keep them in tune with his priorities.[a]

Assuming such a strategy, with what official should it begin? And how far down in the government should it reach? Is it enough for the President to have one trusted agent supported by an able staff? Or does he need a number of agents? If the latter, should they be based in the White House or include men in departmental positions? Should they be a relatively loose group of persons dealing individually and somewhat *ad hoc* with the President, or should they be more structured in terms of rank and substantive responsibility? And isn't there a limit to the number of "President's men" there can be? Doesn't a law of diminishing returns come into play

[a] He will find this harder to do, however, if a man has an outside political base, as Secretary of State William Jennings Bryan had under Wilson, and as Adlai Stevenson would have possessed had Kennedy followed liberals' urgings and appointed him to the senior Cabinet post.

91

after one passes the number who can easily remain in contact with the President's personal priorities and proclivities?

How the first of these questions is resolved tends to shape the answers to the others. The main choices are the standard ones. The first is to lean primarily on the White House staff and the Assistant to the President for National Security Affairs.[b] This is the path taken by President Nixon. The second is to rely on the Secretary of State, as Truman did substantially on Acheson and Eisenhower on Dulles. There can of course be a mixture —the Roosevelt system of depending on various men at various times for various purposes; the Kennedy and Johnson approaches, which relied more regularly on the senior foreign policy officials but allowed for no official with clear primacy. But what such a mixture gains in flexibility it tends to lose in coherence, since it deprives the President of any man short of himself with the clear and recognized responsibility for bringing Presidential purpose to foreign policy activities across the entire government.

If the President does choose to begin with one man, he must weigh the advantages and disadvantages of the principal candidates. Partly these relate to their individual positions. The Assistant is a White House aide, with virtually total dependence on the President for his effectiveness. The Secretary has something of an independent power base as head of the senior Cabinet Department, but his dependence is still great. The Assistant is freed from the encumbrances of a public role—obligatory time spent on the Hill, in foreign capitals, in explaining policy to the public. But this in turn limits the use of him as a "front man" who articulates and de-

---

[b] Under Nixon the title was changed from "Special Assistant" to "Assistant." Henceforth the latter will be used when discussing the office in general, with whichever title is appropriate employed for treating particular periods and incumbents.

fends policy in the domestic and international political arenas.[c] It also deprives him of the added understanding and potential influence that can accrue to a man with a public role. An Assistant enjoying Presidential favor can develop wide influence in the bureaucracy. But it is not identical to that of a Secretary of State who can combine Presidential confidence with formal authority over the major foreign affairs department. Yet to the degree that the Secretary is seen as the spokesman for one Cabinet agency among many, the Assistant will have the advantage of appearing as an "honest broker" with no departmental axe to grind.

The choice of the primary foreign affairs official is intimately tied to the other critical questions—how far down in the government central strength should be built, how many "agents" the President should have on his foreign policy team, and in what relationship to him and to one another. If confidence "flows down from the President," it will tend to flow through this central official rather than around him. He, in turn, will tend to place confidence in the men who are most clearly responsive to him. Thus, one might assume that reliance on the Assistant would tend to make such confidence flow to key members of the White House staff which he heads.[d] By contrast, Presidential confidence in a system centered on the Secretary of State would be more likely to flow to *his* key subordinates, such as regional Assistant Secretaries. So another major consideration in deciding what official should have primacy would be whether regional Assistant Secretaries or White House aides with area responsibilities were better placed in the foreign affairs government political system to fight for coherent, Presidential policy.

[c] And giving the Assistant primacy undercuts any other man who tries to play this public defender and explainer role, as evidenced by Secretary Rogers' credibility problems on Capitol Hill.

[d] In fact, however, there seem to be strong pressures which mitigate against this, as discussed in Chapter Five.

This question need not arise, however, if sufficient coherence could be gained through using one agent supported by staff. If there are organizational means to extend this man's personal reach, so that he and the President can be assured of making the decisions which will basically shape what the bureaucracy actually does, then the need for Presidential confidence to extend beyond him is much less. Thus an organizational device like a "policy planning" process might serve as an alternative to the existence of "President's men" in the bureaucracy, provided the system was really effective in shaping government actions. The Nixon Administration seems to have placed much of its hopes for coherence in such a system. Kennedy, by contrast, eliminated such formal processes and depended almost entirely on personal relationships to tie the foreign affairs government to his purposes.

To illuminate these issues further, however, it will be necessary to review at some length the experience of recent Presidents and their Administrations. That is the purpose of Chapter Five.

CHAPTER FIVE

The Strategies of Presidents:
Foreign Policy-Making under Kennedy,
Johnson, and Nixon

IF COHERENCE in foreign policy must be built around
the President, a realistic approach to the problem requires a look at what specific Presidents have done. On
what officials have they relied to control the executive
branch foreign affairs agencies? Have they sought to
build coherence around one subordinate, or several? To
what extent have they sought enhanced influence
through formal policy-making processes? Through informal personal relationships? To what extent did they
pursue explicit foreign affairs organizational strategies
at all?

The decade ending in 1970 is a particularly fruitful
period for seeking answers to these questions. It featured
three very different Presidents, who handled foreign
policy in three very different ways. It was also the period
when the National Security Council staff became a
strong Presidential instrument for foreign affairs management and control.

Two of the Presidents of this period saw foreign
policy as their field of primary competence and interest.
While Lyndon Johnson emphasized domestic matters in
his brilliantly improvised early months, John F. Kennedy and Richard M. Nixon gave top priority to foreign
affairs from the moment they entered office. And while
Johnson's methods of handling foreign policy developed
mainly from his personality and his experience in office,
Kennedy and Nixon entered the Presidency with rather
strong ideas of how they wanted to run the show. Their
ideas were quite different. Kennedy was attracted to in-

95

formality and a loose, highly personal style of operating; Nixon has emphasized thoroughness, regular channels, relatively formal procedures. Kennedy sought to develop productive communications and relationships with as many high officials as seemed possible and fruitful. Nixon has preferred to deal with and through a very small number of intermediaries. Yet each seems to have tried quite consciously to develop an approach which maximized his own influence over the foreign affairs government. Those concerned with foreign affairs organization in the future must seek lessons from both their successes and their failures.

The Kennedy Approach

Kennedy inherited a highly structured formal system of national security policy-making and coordination which had come under increasing attack as Eisenhower's term drew to a close. The Jackson Subcommittee reflected both its own investigation and a broader consensus among experts when it urged the new President to "deinstitutionalize" and "humanize" the NSC process, and to rely more on the Secretary of State for policy leadership.[1] More important, its approach to policy-making problems was highly consistent with Kennedy's predispositions, and in his first months the new President acted toward both of these ends.

The negative organizational effort, dismantling the Eisenhower machinery, was the more successful. Less than a month after his inauguration Kennedy abolished the Eisenhower-created Operations Coordinating Board, with the announced aim of "strengthening the responsibility of the individual departments" for operational coordination. Other interdepartmental committees were also abolished in an effort to center responsibility in individuals rather than leaderless groups. National Security Council meetings became less frequent. And, as noted by Special Assistant for National Security Affairs

McGeorge Bundy, the Administration ". . . deliberately rubbed out the distinction between planning and operation which governed the administrative structure of the NSC staff in the last administration. This distinction, real enough at the extremes of the daily cable traffic and long-range assessment of future possibilities, breaks down in most of the business of decision and action . . . especially . . . Presidential action."[2]

Bundy also stressed "increased reliance on the leadership of the Department of State."

> . . . the President has made it very clear that he does not want a large separate organization between him and his Secretary of State. Neither does he wish any question to arise as to the clear authority and responsibility of the Secretary of State, not only in his own Department, and not only in such large-scale related areas as foreign aid and information policy, but also as the agent of coordination in all our major policies toward other nations.

But there is room for question about the extent to which primary reliance on the State Department was a serious Kennedy objective. Many, such as Hilsman and Schlesinger, have argued that it was, and without doubt State was handed a ball it could have carried much farther than it did. But if Kennedy no doubt wished he had a stronger State Department, he does not seem to have been all that serious about it, in the sense of carrying out a deliberate, systematic strategy designed to make it so.[a] His initial appointments to key State posts were

[a] Some have suggested that Kennedy's real aim was the opposite—a weak Secretary of State so that he could run things himself. David Halberstam, for example, has characterized "the Kennedy Administration in foreign affairs" as a "deliberately structured group," with the Rusk, McNamara, and Bundy personalities admirably suited to the President's designs. But this gives Kennedy credit for considerable perspicacity, given his very brief personal contact with both Rusk and McNamara prior to their appointment. And it does not explain

aimed at getting good people, recognizing political prominence and service, and cultivating the foreign policy establishment. They certainly were not designed to produce a team of men responsive to the lead of a strong Secretary. McNamara accepted his post on condition he would have a free hand in naming subordinates. Rusk was offered his after Under Secretary Chester Bowles, U.N. Ambassador Adlai Stevenson, and Assistant Secretary for African Affairs Mennen Williams had already been selected.[3]

Kennedy did exhort State to try harder. He told the American Foreign Service Association on May 31, 1962, "This is the great period of the Foreign Service"; echoing Harry Truman, he asserted that "the place to be is in the kitchen, and I am sure the Foreign Service Officers of the United States feel the same way." But the first two foreign affairs task forces he appointed had Defense Department chairmen, though their subject matters (Laos and Cuba) would have naturally called for State leadership were the Department seriously expected to "take charge." Kennedy's May 1961 letter to Ambassadors was a milestone in strengthening their authority; ironically, the initial draft was reportedly written by White House aide Ralph Dungan. His November 1961 reshuffling of State personnel (the "Thanksgiving Day Massacre")[b] improved things on balance. Yet even here the aim of strengthening State was not unalloyed. The transfer of Walt Rostow to State's top planning position,

---

Kennedy's later unhappiness with Rusk. ("Education of McGeorge Bundy," p. 29.)

[b] The "Massacre" involved several high-level changes, the most important of which was the replacement of Chester Bowles as Under Secretary of State by George Ball. Bowles was given the title of "Special Representative and Adviser to the President for African, Asian, and Latin American Affairs." George McGhee was named to the number three post, Under Secretary for Political Affairs; Averell Harriman became Assistant Secretary for the Far East; and Walt W. Rostow became Chairman of the Policy Planning Council.

for example, seems to have reflected in part a desire to get him out of the White House, since Bundy didn't work well with him and Kennedy was wary of the "dangerous" ideas he tended to produce.[4]

So whatever Kennedy might have liked to see happen, his inauguration did not usher in a golden age of leadership for the State Department. His major organizational contribution lay elsewhere—in the White House basement. It lay in the creation of a strong personal foreign policy staff, and in the way he used that creation.

Central to the Kennedy Presidency was a loose, open, dynamic operating style, reflecting a desire to reach out and grab for issues and a sense that overly formal policy machinery might victimize the President it was supposed to serve. In his January 1960 speech to the National Press Club, Kennedy argued that the President must be "the vital center of action in our whole scheme of government," a man "who acts as well as reacts." In the pre-inauguration period he was concerned about "free access" to the idea market, saying, "I simply cannot afford to have just one set of advisers." Kennedy grew to practice what he had preached. Said Sydney Hyman one month before the assassination: "He does not rely merely on the information that reaches his desk through official channels. The President has many auxiliary lines of communication within the Government, so that he can get different views on the same subject and allow subsecretaries to reach the ear of the White House by out-flanking their departmental chiefs. And he still seeks information from many independent sources outside the Government. . . ."[5]

Kennedy also disliked formal, fixed committee meetings. Sorensen noted in 1963 that, on important issues, "President Kennedy prefers to invite only those whose official views he requires or whose unofficial judgment he values." As Kennedy himself put it in 1961, "We have averaged three or four meetings a week with the

Secretaries of Defense and State, McGeorge Bundy, the head of the CIA and the Vice President. But formal meetings of the Security Council which include a much wider group are not as effective. It is more difficult to decide matters involving high national security if there is a wider group present."[6]

By 1963 the National Security Council had become, in the words of one staff member, "little more than a name."[7] It continued to meet but seldom was the place for serious discussion of serious issues. Still, the name conveyed a legitimacy which was important at times—hence the dubbing of Kennedy's personally-chosen Cuban missile crisis group as the NSC "Executive Committee."

The Council also served as an umbrella under which Kennedy could create a strong Presidential foreign policy staff. His predecessors had had highly valued individual foreign affairs aides. But until 1960 the NSC staff was manned primarily by career officials, with the Special Assistant to the President for National Security Affairs (an office created by Eisenhower) supposed to link the career group to the President's needs. Kennedy made the staff a personal staff, with most of its members recruited specifically for his administration. It numbered about ten, and its chief—McGeorge Bundy—was able to bring onto it several exceptionally talented men, who came mainly from outside of government and owed no allegiance to any agency within it.

Kennedy did not want the staff to become a layer separating him from the line departments. It reviewed and commented on papers reaching the President from the departments, and this role gave it an important bargaining advantage. But he kept in close communication with his key Cabinet officers and other agency heads, and dealt periodically with officials at the Assistant Secretary level. Unlike Franklin Roosevelt, Kennedy was not inclined to treat his Cabinet officers as "natural enemies."

100

To the extent that he could get personal, staff-type support from them, he was more than willing to do so. Inside the White House, relationships were likewise fluid. Kennedy abolished the hierarchical system of the overall White House staff, where Sherman Adams had once reigned as *the* Assistant to President Eisenhower. Bundy had a more specific substantive mandate than the other senior Presidential advisers, and his subordinates were organized mainly on regional lines. But access to the President was not limited to the top man. Personal secretary Evelyn Lincoln guarded a door to Kennedy's office, armed with a list of staffers permitted to walk in and talk to the President during his free time. Bundy was one of them, of course, and he was clearly the major foreign affairs staff official. But also on the list, reportedly, were Carl Kaysen, Robert Komer, and Michael Forrestal of his staff. And Sorensen, Dungan, Jerome Wiesner, and Schlesinger from the larger White House also dealt directly with the President on foreign policy matters, as did of course his brother Robert.

Because the President sought involvement in so many current issues, "the [Kennedy] staff concentrated heavily on what was happening at the moment."[8] There was a corresponding lack of a comprehensive planning process such as the Eisenhower Administration had developed. The Eisenhower system tended to assume that decisions setting broad objectives or guidelines could and would shape specific actions. The Kennedy people doubted this, believing that day-to-day involvement in events brought more results than top-level statements of purpose and general direction. Rostow tried unsuccessfully to interest Kennedy in a comprehensive policy formulation system, but the President and his top officials felt they had more important uses for their time.

The staff was expected, according to Schlesinger, "to become the President's eyes and ears through the whole area of national security," and "to uncover in the middle

101

levels of government ideas which deserved a hearing at the top before they had been diluted or choked off by interbureau or interagency rivalry."⁹ Thus the flow of both information and policy ideas received priority. Bundy insisted that the White House receive the most important cables and intelligence reports "raw"—before they had been pre-digested by the line agencies. And a continuing effort was made to avoid the Eisenhower tendency to have "agreed recommendations" subscribed to by all major agencies and officials presented for Presidential ratification. Instead, the aim was to discover and illuminate alternative courses of action which would allow real Presidential choice among them.

One important Kennedy innovation was the creation of interagency task forces to help manage important current issues. They were responsible for both current action and forward planning, and were intended to serve the President rather than the agencies represented. Responsibility was generally centered in the task force chairman to avoid decision-making by committee. To relate the various *ad hoc* groups to one another and to broader Administration policy objectives, they usually included one White House staff member.¹⁰

The Bundy staff tended to concentrate far more on "State" than on "Defense" problems. There were exceptions, notably Kaysen's involvement in arms control issues. But Kennedy and Bundy were more interested in international politics than in weapons management systems. McNamara encouraged this emphasis by demonstrating that he could handle defense matters to the President's satisfaction.

Moreover, as the staff developed in fact into the President's prime "agent of coordination" for foreign affairs, it was inevitable that it would relate most intensively to State, which had the formal coordination mandate and necessarily played a role more central than any other department. And often State was *the problem,* supposed to lead in theory but sluggish in fact. Thus, as Moose has written, "In those instances where the Department of State's response did not measure up to the President's expectations, the NSC staff moved in."[11] There was serious resentment of White House "interference." Moose suggests, moreover, that Kennedy's staffing procedures purchased "direct responsiveness and immediate feedback" at the cost of diminishing State initiative and disturbing "its already none-too-strong internal organization." This was no doubt true. Yet "moving in" meant anything but taking over exclusive jurisdiction. It meant working with officials of various departments, bringing them together, seeking resolution of issues in directions consistent with Presidential wishes, communicating to bureaucrats a sense of Presidential priorities and working to make their activities reflect these priorities. As Schlesinger put it, the staff was "helpless without allies throughout the permanent government." And much of the influence of Bundy and the staff came precisely from their ability to connect circuits, to link related individuals and groups and activities with each other. Sorensen reports that Bundy "made certain that no responsible officer or point of view was omitted from meetings on foreign policy," and if major officials did not always cherish being "coordinated" on matters they preferred to handle their own ways, they valued the assurance of "having a shot at" issues which came up for Presidential attention.[12]

This does not mean that had the staff not existed line bureaucrats would have found it necessary to invent it. The staff certainly needed bargaining advantages to play a serious substantive coordination role, including personal Presidential confidence, independent access to cables and intelligence reports, the right to clear particular messages to the field, and the all-important role of handling the President's daily foreign policy business. But if departmental officials did not originally want the staff, they did learn they could live with it, and they often found it useful. There was a common interest among top officials who had to work closely together whether they would have wished it or not, an interest in an honest broker, a means to get attention paid to issues, and a link to influence in their resolution. One of Bundy's signal achievements is his recognition that service to this widespread interest could bring both power to himself and the President and benefit to the entire system. He proved to be the master at "keeping the game going."[13]

Changes under Johnson

Lyndon Johnson did not plan to be President. Once President, he did not plan to emphasize foreign policy. But Vietnam was a problem he could neither avoid nor resolve. In the course of dealing with this and other challenges, he made the foreign affairs government a far different place from what it had been in the Kennedy era.

There were some strong similarities. Johnson kept Kennedy's three top foreign affairs officials, and two of them served him longer than they did his predecessor. And his penchant for informality and operational flexibility made inconceivable any restoration of a formal policy-making system of the sort Kennedy dismantled. As Bill Moyers noted in 1968, Johnson found the NSC to be "not a live institution, not suited to precise debate for the sake of decision." He found it more useful "to call in a handful of top advisers, confidants, close friends."[14]

Johnson's one important procedural innovation likewise followed the Kennedy pattern: it gave formal emphasis to State Department leadership in a way that had little real effect. In March 1966, at the urging of General Maxwell Taylor and Deputy Under Secretary of State U. Alexis Johnson, he established a system of interdepartmental committees designed to strengthen the Secretary's foreign affairs leadership. Interdepartmental Regional Groups (IRG's) chaired by Assistant Secretaries of State were to coordinate policy at their levels and report to a Senior Interdepartmental Group (SIG) chaired by State's Under Secretary. Included at both levels were representatives of the Secretary of Defense, the Joint Chiefs of Staff, CIA, AID, USIA, and the White House. But neither Johnson nor Rusk gave the committees enough support to make the system work effectively on important issues.

Yet despite these parallels, Lyndon Johnson was very different from his predecessor, and his handling of foreign policy reflected the differences. Kennedy had felt quite at home with both the substance of foreign policy and the community of men who influenced it. Johnson was comfortable with neither. His long Capitol Hill experience had given him confidence about his feel for domestic policy issues and the people who sought to affect them. But he tended, in the words of one official of his Administration, to view foreign affairs as a sort of "black art," its substance alien to him and its Eastern establishment practitioners even more so.

Lacking confidence on international matters, feeling that his strengths and his opportunities lay in the domestic policy arena, Lyndon Johnson did not seek to duplicate Kennedy's comprehensive global involvement in international issues. Yet he seems to have seen foreign policy as an area that could get him into serious trouble. To avoid this, he leaned heavily on the men Kennedy had bequeathed him, above all Rusk and McNamara. If he could be sure of their loyalty to him and their commitment to his Administration's major policy decisions, he apparently thought, their talents and establishment credentials would make it easier for him to navigate in the dark and dangerous international waters.

Facilities and procedures developed under his predecessor gave Johnson access to a broad flow of foreign affairs information, which he consumed voraciously. He also acted on the considerable number of issues referred to him for decision. But on only a few matters did he seek continuing personal control. Some of these were in areas like foreign aid, where he could press hard for stronger agricultural "self-help" measures in countries like India without upsetting the East Coast establishment the way a similarly forceful initiative in European matters would have. Others were problems that he couldn't avoid, like Vietnam. Once he did move into an area, however, Johnson was likely to insist on very close control over details. He ordered procedures requiring every food aid agreement—and every development loan over $5 million—to come to him personally for approval, and he sometimes held up aid to India for months at a stretch. And his involvement in Vietnam matters, from bombing targets to letters from servicemen, became a legend in his own time.

✓Johnson kept the personal Presidential foreign policy staff. But while it grew somewhat in size—to perhaps sixteen substantive officers in 1967—it diminished in influence. The Special Assistant continued to have dealings with the President "more frequent than those of any Cabinet officer,"[15] and his work continued to have a "here and now" orientation.[c] But being less confident

[c] Moose lists the basic functions of the Special Assistant under Johnson as six: (1) coordinating the flow of information and intelligence to the President; (2) managing the flow of decision papers to the President and assuring adequate background information; (3) following daily government operations to assure proper coordination and responsiveness to Presidential interests; (4) communicating Presidential decisions and instructions to departments and agencies; (5) acting as liaison with Cabinet officers; and (6) serving as personal adviser to the President, providing substantive analysis where needed. (IDA, *President and National Security*, pp. 85-6.) This is also a good description of the functions of the Assistant and staff under Kennedy and Nixon, though under the latter it has added management of the new national security studies program. For a more extended analysis of the work of such staffs, see Chapter Eight.

than Kennedy had been of his own judgment on foreign policy, Johnson was less inclined to encourage staff questioning of ongoing policies, and less interested in maintaining channels through which sub-Cabinet officials could get their ideas to him without going through their bosses. Bundy had been adept at encouraging a flow of ideas and alternatives to the President. On Vietnam, Bill Moyers had performed a similar function. But after their departures, bureaucrats pressing for policy changes found the White House staff less and less receptive to their efforts.

Particularly important was the appointment of Walt W. Rostow to Bundy's position in early 1966. Johnson emphasized he was not "replacing" Bundy, and while his successor in fact performed many of the same functions—managing the flow of information to the President, communicating Presidential wishes to the bureaucracy, providing policy analysis and advice—Rostow seems not to have had as strong a mandate as Bundy under Kennedy. He was also a very different type of person. Bundy was a pragmatist who seldom allowed his personal views on policy to prejudice his presentations of alternative viewpoints and balanced analyses to the President. He was also an exceptional administrator-operator. Rostow, by contrast, was primarily a thinker and more than a bit of an ideologue, who tended to view particular events in terms of the broader theoretical constructs he was most adept at developing.[16]

Rostow proposed the bombing of North Vietnam early in Kennedy's administration and remained a committed "hawk" to the end. And because of this tendency to treat information and issues in terms of strongly held policy convictions that others did not always share, departmental officials were much less likely to trust him to represent their views objectively to the President. This was true even regarding activities like development aid, for which Rostow had long been a determined and

107

influential advocate. On the other hand, his absolute conviction that we were doing the right thing in Vietnam could only reassure a President who felt increasingly under siege, and Rostow's personal relationship with Johnson was apparently much closer than Bundy's had been.

But just as Kennedy's strong trust in McNamara had limited NSC staff involvement on defense issues, Johnson's confidence in Rusk reduced staff influence on those foreign policy problems which were clearly within State's sphere. In areas like aid, where Johnson was personally involved and Rusk was indifferent, or in the international monetary field, where a strong White House role was important to balance Treasury influence, staff members like Edward Hamilton, Francis Bator, and Edward Fried were able to play strong personal roles very much in the Kennedy staff pattern. So also were interdepartmental task forces like the "Deming Group" on monetary problems. But generally the use of task forces with broad mandates declined, and the staff role became more liaison than leadership. Rostow tended to save his influence for Vietnam, and the lack of bureaucratic confidence in him as an "honest broker" made him unable to act as an across-the-board coordinator or circuit-connector in the Bundy manner. Fewer members of his staff had personal relationships with the President, and "fewer memorandums went to the President on the responsibility of individual staff members." Most of the exceptional Bundy group departed well before the end of the Johnson era, and the staff, in Moose's words, "dwindled to a rather small group of officers, most of them detailed from the departments and agencies."

It was neither a highly structured staff organization like that existing in January 1961, nor the assertive and highly personalized staff inherited by President Johnson. It was, instead, a staff which largely limited

108

itself to monitoring the national-security process from the President's perspective, making sure that the various elements of the process were in touch with each other when other means proved insufficient, and providing the President with whatever in-house advice and support he felt he needed.[17]

To the extent that any institution served as a Presidential focal point for foreign policy-making during the Johnson Administration, it was the "Tuesday Lunch" held weekly with the Secretaries of State and Defense and the Special Assistant for National Security Affairs.[d] It dealt largely with current Vietnam issues, reflecting top officials' overwhelming preoccupation with the war from 1965 on. It reflected also Johnson's organizational approach to the conduct of the war—what Cooper terms "a mixture of tight personal control and loosely structured organization"—and what James C. Thomson, Jr., has characterized as ". . . the 'closed politics' of policy-making as issues become hot: the more sensitive the issue, and the higher it rises in the bureaucracy, the more completely the experts are excluded while the harassed senior generalists take over (that is, the Secretaries, Undersecretaries, and Presidential Assistants)."[18]

For the President and his key advisers, the Tuesday Lunch was a highly useful institution. It gave the top officials a chance to discuss Vietnam and other hot issues directly and at length with the President, and provided them a better sense of his and each others' feelings, problems, and priorities. It also made available to their aides a forum where they could seek to have important issues surfaced for top-level consideration.

But it caused their subordinates great difficulties. Staff officials who sought to support the principals and carry

---

[d] In the later Johnson Administration, the CIA Director, the Chairman of the Joint Chiefs of Staff, and the President's Press Secretary were also regular participants.

out their decisions went to considerable lengths to develop a regular agenda so they could get major issues raised and assure that the top men were adequately briefed. They were not always able to do this, and even when they could they had serious problems finding out whether the issues were actually discussed and what decisions if any were made. Rusk and McNamara were reluctant to discuss the content of Tuesday Lunch discussions with their senior subordinates. Up to a point this was understandable: Presidents need to be able to discuss matters in a context where not every word of theirs is taken as law and promulgated. But the Secretaries appear to have been much more sensitive to the President's right to confidentiality than to their subordinates' need to know enough to give top-level decisions operational meaning. The top men grew to live in one world, having loyalty primarily to each other, and seeing problems in a context that their subordinates could not understand because they were outside the charmed circle. Not only did the latter find it hard to translate "the policy" into daily action. They also found it difficult to know when a particular issue was being discussed so that they could bring to bear their own information and analysis and advice.

So the problem went beyond the banishment of expertise, to a deep communication gap between "that tight little group of desperate men"[19] at the top and the underlings who were supposed to be serving them. It was exacerbated by the President's compulsion about secrecy, and by a personal operating style which sought to maintain tactical flexibility for the President by keeping others in the dark about his intentions. Presidential "options" were kept open, at the cost of not conveying to those below a sufficiently coherent and detailed sense of what the President and his top officials wanted. So the options of those below remained open also, and agencies

110

were able to "interpret" Presidential wishes in ways consistent with their own predilections.

Recognizing the weakness of Vietnam coordination at levels below the Tuesday Lunch, Under Secretary of State Nicholas Katzenbach convened a series of interdepartmental meetings at his level. The group he invited was virtually identical to the SIG (which had no mandate to get involved in Vietnam), and its members sought to improve Vietnam operations by sharing information and analyses with one another. But the existence of this *ad hoc* committee was so closely held that it was dubbed the "non-group." Thus it could hardly provide subordinates with regular policy guidance.[20]

Of course there were reasons for such close handling of the Vietnam issue which went beyond the idiosyncrasies of Lyndon Johnson. In some cases battlefield security may have been at stake. More often, one suspects, it was security against a different enemy. The President's innate tendency to sniff treason within government walls was, by 1967, exacerbated by increasing indications that many subordinate officials -who had doubts about the Vietnam policy were regularly unburdening themselves to the press. Such unhappiness below solidified the top group's sense of being embattled, both strengthening their loyalties to one another and their separation from the rest of the government. Apparently, in Johnson's view, McNamara ultimately proved not quite loyal enough. But it was not until Clark Clifford broke into the charmed circle, and until the Tet Offensive shattered the Administration's base of national support, that Vietnam policy took a significant shift in course. It is unrealistic to suggest that a different foreign affairs organization or operating style would have averted the unfortunate decisions of early 1965. Establishment of an organizational focal point below the Tuesday Lunch, however, could surely have improved

111

the coordination of government Vietnam operations and the implementation of Presidential decisions. And a greater Presidential receptiveness to alternative analyses might have encouraged serious reassessment sooner than it finally came.

The Kennedy and Johnson Approaches—A Broader Assessment

The Kennedy approach to foreign policy had strong virtues. It put the President in daily touch with a wide range of information and opinions, notably reducing the danger of his capture by any one. It gave him the service of a number of exceptionally fine staff aides, and their access to him maximized both their influence with the bureaucracy and their incentive to stay on the team. It recognized the futility of mechanical solutions to the problem of Presidentially-based policy coherence, such as the Eisenhower NSC system. It recognized that foreign policy-making is inherently a political process, and that the President's influence can be stretched through a network of personal relationships which he and those who work on his behalf can use to their mutual advantage.

But it was more effective in recruiting a strong team of bureaucratic players than in placing them in the particular positions where they might do the most good. Kennedy made his major State Department appointments—Rusk, Bowles, Ball—with little if any concern about whether they could work well together as a top-level team. Once he took these actions, his subsequent efforts to improve things had the nature of patchwork. The "Thanksgiving Day Massacre" of 1961, and the elevation of Averell Harriman to the number three State Department position in 1963, raised to higher positions individuals with whom Kennedy could work. But neither did much to strengthen the management of the department as an institution. Instead, Kennedy took the

112

route of Roosevelt before him, creating a new institution (the personal staff) to perform a needed role rather than seeking to reform the existing one (State). As long as he was determined to keep Rusk he had little choice, since the Secretary tended not to concern himself very much with how his organization actually operated, and it is unlikely that a President could reorganize a department effectively going around the top man. But by all reports he was not satisfied, and by some he intended to begin his second Administration with his Cabinet headed by Secretary of State Robert S. McNamara.

The NSC staff did evolve into a good team, its informal operating style suited to the President's preferences. But though Bundy was strong and effective, and probably was more broadly responsive to the President's foreign policy priorities and preferences than anyone else in the government, his job as both he and Kennedy saw it made it necessary for him to defer to Cabinet officers, and to avoid making himself too open a rallying point for the Kennedyites in the foreign affairs government. Thus while the system provided a useful locus of coordination and Presidentially attuned initiative, it included no primary policy leader short of the President himself.

It did, however, make things very hard on the Secretary of State. Rusk resented it when "people like Sorensen and Kaysen with no responsibility were making academic comments,"[21] and his regional Assistant Secretaries had to cope regularly with White House counterparts who were sometimes both more aggressive and on better terms with the source of power. Some of the Assistant Secretaries, like Hilsman and Harriman, solved this problem by cultivating their own Presidential relationships. But this put the Secretary a bit more to one side even when amicable relations were maintained. Given Rusk's personality and highly individual approach to his job, no other pattern was likely or even possible if Kennedy was to be President as he saw the meaning of the office. But there is the more general question of whether the type of White House staff that evolved would have been compatible with a strong Secretary of State. The excellent relations between Bundy and super-Secretary McNamara, and the frequent productive interchanges and alliances among their subordinates, suggest that it might have been. But the operative word is "might." Given the President's strong interests, such a Secretary would have required very, very close attunement to the President's priorities. His staff would probably have had to provide much of the support which Bundy's men ended up giving the President. But even so, he could not generally have been successful with the McNamara technique of providing such thorough staffing and analysis of issues that the President needed no further White House input. The President would have been just too interested, and too likely to have special insights of his own.

The fate of whatever intention Kennedy had to strengthen the State Department provides another insight: that foreign policy-making systems tend to "happen," to evolve as a result of what Presidents and other top officials find helpful and necessary as they face daily problems, and to gain whatever viability they have from their role in these processes. It is not necessary to assume that Kennedy secretly planned the central White House staff role which finally evolved. The other explanation is more plausible: State did not provide him what he wanted, while Bundy and Co. were both able and willing to do so in its stead.

If coherence was damaged by State's weakness, the Kennedy regime has also been criticized for its overconcern with the hot issues of the present, resulting in a lack of comprehensiveness of coverage or concern for integrated longer-term foreign policy planning. Skybolt is the most cited example, where no person or process "coordinated" the systems-management proclivities of the Secretary of Defense with the urgent if dubious desire of the British to prolong the life-span of their nuclear deterrent. This critique was in fact misleading, since Skybolt resulted not from failure to foresee a potential problem, but rather through mutual miscalculation by American and British officials concerning how their counterparts across the ocean would act.[e] But Joseph Kraft's criticism of the Kennedy staff style was more to the point.

The Staff operation, like many other aspects of the Administration, works to put all matters on a pragmatic, case-by-case basis. It does not contribute to the systematic elaboration of coherent programs expressing broad and easily identifiable public policies. A sense of inner purpose may—no doubt does—exist in the White House. But in part because the operation is so casual, so laconic, so frictionless, the purpose and direction of the Administration, its intrinsic character,

[e] Neustadt's account indicates that Kennedy, McNamara, Rusk, and Bundy were all aware of the problems that Skybolt cancellation would cause the British, and McNamara personally warned both Ambassador Ormsby-Gore and Defense Minister Thorneycroft before the final Presidential decision was made. The crisis was more subtle. It was bureaucratically very hard for McNamara to press for a U.S. government decision to offer Polaris to Britain as an alternative, due to strong opposition to the independent British deterrent in State's Bureau of European Affairs. Thus he awaited British initiative in asking for it to solve his own bureaucratic problem. Thorneycroft, meanwhile, was "too weakly placed" in the British government to take such initiative, so he took comfort that "a man as smart as McNamara would not trouble to consult if he intended but to snatch away one missile without offering another." Thus: "Each thought he would be taken off his own hook by the other's initiative. . . . Each waited for the other: Thorneycroft for McNamara's offer, McNamara for Thorneycroft's request."
It is unlikely that strengthened formal procedures for long-range planning or operational coordination would have made much difference here, though a strong central foreign affairs official with a broad Presidential mandate might have helped. (*Alliance Politics*, pp. 107, 45, 109.)

so to speak, have not made themselves felt outside the White House. To that extent at least, the work of the White House Staff, excellent as it may be on an *ad hoc* basis, does not yet serve the President's desire that his administration achieve historic stature.[22]

Kraft was writing mainly of the overall staff operation, and when applied to foreign policy this critique is not entirely fair. Kennedy was able to articulate "the purpose and direction of the Administration" on a broad range of issues—the Alliance for Progress, greater general sympathy for new nations and the developing world, a "Declaration of Interdependence" with Western Europe, a policy of toughness and military build-up vis-à-vis Russia in 1961, a policy inviting detente and re-examining our attitude toward the Cold War in 1963. What was harder was to make these general intentions effective. But Kraft's point remains very important. Due to both its *ad hoc* style and its "multi-polar" power structure, an informal policy-making approach like those of Kennedy and Johnson depends singularly on the President's ability both to conceive in his mind and to convey to the government and the nation a clear sense of direction and priorities. It is not only, as Halberstam rightly emphasizes, that it is dependent "on the President himself to set the guidelines for foreign policy."[23] It also requires exceptional informal lines of communication downward to transmit such "guidelines" from the President to the bureaucrats on the firing line.

The combination of Kennedy's broad world view and the Bundy staff operation met both of these needs in a reasonably effective way, though failure to do much about the State Department meant that the bureaucracy would often be sluggish in responding to Presidential wishes. But Johnson's foreign policy-making "system" met neither. He could not convey "the purpose and direction" of his Administration because he was not sure

116

of it himself on many issues and because he used secrecy as a tactical tool on others. On Vietnam, where his general objectives were clear from 1965 to 1968, his method of handling day-to-day problems achieved maximum uncertainty in the bureaucracy about what officials were expected to do. Yet while it thus stimulated interagency infighting on day-to-day issues, the Tuesday Lunch phenomenon discouraged consideration of important dissenting viewpoints at the Presidential level. Thus the Johnson Administration combined the drawbacks of an informal, *ad hoc* policy-making system—confusion about who is doing what on which issue, lack of a foreign affairs official with a broad mandate short of the President— with a blocking of communications up and down the hierarchy that overreliance on line officials can foster.

Nor did Secretary Rusk exercise the sort of leadership even within his own department that Johnson's confidence in him made possible. He may have progressed, in Halberstam's words, "from being Kennedy's liaison with the Hill to being a Secretary of State." Yet he remained, as one of his Assistant Secretaries put it, "a superb staff officer," one who knew how to serve those above him but not how to lead those below. He neither supported subordinates who sought to exercise strong policy leadership nor communicated his policy preferences to them in areas where the President had not unambiguously spoken.*ᶠ* Lacking such leadership and such support, the SIG and the IRG's began with two strikes against them.²⁴

It was this legacy of non-coherence in policy-making

ᶠ Stewart Alsop reported a common observation during the Secretary's tenure: "Rusk's subordinates, even at the Assistant Secretary level, complain that they never know what he thinks, what policies he favors. . . . Rusk himself defends this lack of communication with subordinates as a matter of conscious policy. A Secretary of State who is known to feel strongly on one side or another of a major policy decision, he contends, inevitably influences the direction of the decision before all factors are weighed. Thus the Secretary should make his views known only to the President, and then only after all the options have been thoroughly examined." (*The Center*, p. 121.)

which President Nixon inherited from a divided and demoralized administration in January 1969. The Johnson Administration had not been without positive achievements in foreign policy. It had stepped down from the unrealistic effort to build a multilateral force, negotiated a nuclear non-proliferation treaty, successfully prodded India to act on her food crisis, and moved forward markedly in the international trade and monetary fields. But its policy-making institutions, formal and informal, had little that would recommend them to its successor.

The Nixon System

Like John F. Kennedy, Richard M. Nixon considered foreign affairs to be his field of special competence. Like Kennedy, he was determined to "call the turn." But if the end was the same, the means he proposed were very different. He promised to "restore the National Security Council to its preeminent role in national security planning," and even attributed "most of our serious reverses abroad since 1960" to its abandonment in favor of "catch-as-catch-can talkfests between the President, his staff assistants, and various others."[25]

Nixon promptly showed that this was more than campaign rhetoric. One month after his election, he named as his Assistant for National Security Affairs the noted Harvard professor of international politics, Henry Kissinger, and ordered him to establish an "Eisenhower NSC system," but "without the concurrences." He also sought the advice of General Andrew J. Goodpaster, who had served President Eisenhower as coordinator of day-to-day national security intelligence and operations. Kissinger quickly assembled a staff and developed a set of formal institutions and procedures built around the NSC for coordinated management of foreign policy issues. These were established by the President on the

118

afternoon of Inauguration Day, and announced to the public two-and-one-half weeks later.[26]

The White House statement stressed the role of the Council as "the principal forum for the consideration of policy issues" requiring Presidential decision. It was to convene "regularly," with "one meeting [to] be held each week for the next few months." To facilitate its work and to "handle more immediate operational problems within the context of the NSC system," "a series of supporting NSC committees and groups" had been organized. And the President had "assigned to the supporting NSC bodies a comprehensive series of studies covering the principal national security issues now confronting the Nation."[27]

The White House made it clear that the enhancement of the Council was not all that the President was seeking: "As important as the regularity and strengthened structure of the Council and its projected policy studies is the approach prescribed by the President for the examination of issues. The guidance to NSC study groups seeks to assure that all pertinent facts are established and all options presented—complete with pros, cons, and costs—so that decisions can be made with a clear understanding of their ramifications."[28]

A year later, in his comprehensive foreign policy message, the President stressed once again his determination to avoid the Eisenhower fate of being confronted with "agreed papers" for his ratification. The aim was what Dean Acheson once called "disagreed papers": "The new NSC system is designed to make certain that clear policy choices reach the top, so that the various positions can be fully debated in the meeting of the Council. . . . I refuse to be confronted with a bureaucratic consensus that leaves me no options but acceptance or rejection, and that gives me no way of knowing what alternatives exist."[29]

119

The "options" sought by the President, moreover, were not supposed to reflect competing agency interests, but rather alternative ways of dealing with a problem which all agencies recognized as reasonable even if they did not support them. As Kissinger explained it in a letter to Senator Jackson, "Formal agency positions are taken only at the level of the Council itself, and are argued out in front of the President."[30]

But if the Eisenhower "concurrences" were scorned, the new approach shared with that system the stated belief that broad, careful planning and analysis could lead to wise general Presidential decisions which would then shape bureaucratic operations. In fact, the President's justification of his procedures had the ring of older calls for a "rationalized" policy process. "American foreign policy must not be merely the result of a series of piecemeal tactical decisions forced by the pressure of events," he said. "If our policy is to embody a coherent vision of the world and a rational conception of America's interests, our specific actions must be the products of rational and deliberate choice." Thus, he explained, "In central areas of policy, we have arranged our procedure of policy-making so as to address the broader questions of long-term objectives first; we define our purposes, and then address the specific operational issues."[31]

In addition to such rational policy-making, the system sought thoroughness and dependable relations with the larger government. As Kissinger explained it, "The more *ad hoc* approach of the 1960's often ran the risk that relevant points of view were not heard, that systematic treatment of issues did not take place at the highest levels, or that the bureaucracies were not fully informed as to what had been decided and why." And the President suggested that a relatively formal system could give officials a sort of administrative due process, a right to their day in court:

120

The NSC system also insures that all agencies and departments receive a fair hearing before I make my decisions. All Departments concerned with a problem participate in the groups that draft and review the policy papers. They know that their positions and arguments will reach the Council without dilution, along with the other alternatives.[32]

In several respects the Nixon-Kissinger system restored the planning-operations distinction that the Kennedy-Bundy approach had "rubbed out." Most fundamental have been the apparent assumptions that planning could effectively shape operations in the major policy areas, that operations could wait for planning and not be forced by unanticipated crises (which the system has gone to great effort to avert), and that policy-making is something that can basically be directed from one place —the top. But in one important respect a separation of planning and operations was consciously avoided. The new national security studies were not assigned to a special planning staff or staffs, but to committees of officials from the offices that would do the implementing. The goal, as one participant in the system put it, is not just analysis to develop the best possible options, but to get the bureaucracy to endorse the various alternatives as "real" ones capable of implementation, so that the President could make a "real" choice.[33]

To support the NSC and strengthen central management of foreign policy issues, a network of general inter-agency committees was established. The Johnson Administration's IRG's were renamed IG's (Interdepartmental Groups), with AID and USIA removed from regular membership but State's Assistant Secretaries remaining as chairmen. Similarly, the SIG was replaced by the Under Secretaries Committee (USC) headed by the Under Secretary of State. But unlike under Johnson, these State-chaired groups reported not one to another, but both to the Kissinger-chaired NSC Review Group (on which the same agencies were represented). State officials vociferously protested this breach of their departmental chain of command. But the subordination of the committees to the Review Group and the Council did resolve one serious problem in the SIG-IRG system —its lack of any strong link to the Presidency. Another change was that the main role of the regional groups was not operational coordination, as it was intended to be under Johnson, but overseeing the preparation of NSC policy papers. These were then examined by the Review Group, "to insure that the issues, options, and views are presented fully and fairly."[34] After appropriate revision, the most important papers were presented to the President and the National Security Council.

The role of the Under Secretaries Committee was to consider policy issues referred to it by the Review Group (presumably of a lesser order of importance than those referred to the NSC), and to provide operational coordination on issues where Presidential policy decisions had already been taken. The committee network also provided flexibility by authorizing appointment of "NSC *Ad Hoc* Groups" to deal with specific problems, and a number of studies have been handled by these rather than in the IG framework.

On balance, the formal policy-making system was a rather sophisticated one, profiting from the experience —and the mistakes—of several administrations. But what most impressed Washington in early 1969 were the people brought to the White House to run it. Nixon might better have expressed his wishes as "an Eisenhower NSC, minus the concurrences, plus the personal staff." For Kissinger and his supporting cast clearly comprised a critical element in Nixon's foreign affairs organizational strategy. And by early February the

White House was able to release a list of 28 professionals under the National Security Assistant's wing, only two of them holdovers from the Rostow group. The staff was quickly labeled "a real powerhouse."[35]

The typical staff members were not too different from the Kennedy period—relatively young, mobile, aggressive men, combining substantial background in the substance of foreign affairs with primary allegiance to the White House. They boasted greater bureaucratic experience than the Kennedy men, however, and a number had formidable reputations for operating effectiveness. And several were known to be critics of Johnson Administration policies, particularly on Vietnam.

The System in Practice—Kissinger as Prime Official

Nixon apparently meant what he said about emphasizing the NSC, for the promise of weekly meetings in the Administration's early period was largely fulfilled. The Council convened 27 times in the six months after the inauguration, compared to 16 for the parallel period in the Kennedy Administration.[g] In regular attendance at Council meetings have been the statutory members (the President, the Vice President, the Secretaries of State and Defense, and the Director of the Office of Emergency Preparedness), Kissinger, the Under Secretary of State, the CIA Director, the Chairman of the

[g] Neither matched the Eisenhower record. "During 1953 . . . the Council met 51 times and considered 305 items, whereas the highest previous number in one year was 34 meetings and 192 items." (Timothy W. Stanley with Harry H. Ransom, "The National Security Council," reprinted in Jackson Subcommittee, *Organizing*, Vol. II, p. 196.) According to Stanley L. Falk, "the Council met 145 times and took 829 policy actions" during Ike's first three years, "as opposed to 128 meetings and 699 policy actions in its more than five years under Truman." ("The National Security Council Under Truman, Eisenhower, and Kennedy," *Political Science Quarterly*, September p. 423.) The Nixon total—now 63 meetings in 2¼ years—is likely to fall far short of Eisenhower's, and probably below Truman's as well.

Joint Chiefs of Staff, the NSC Staff Secretary as recorder, and Attorney General John Mitchell at the President's request. Others are invited when appropriate, such as the AID Administrator, the Secretary of the Treasury, or the appropriate regional Assistant Secretary of State or White House staff specialist. But in general the presence of subordinates has been strongly resisted, and the number in the room is reportedly much smaller than was the case under Eisenhower.[36]

The effort to keep the meetings small is aimed at two problems which afflict formal, fixed-membership groups —the danger of leaks to the press and the inhibition to frank discussion posed by the presence of a crowd. Leaks seem to have been rare. But though the sessions have performed a useful role in giving agencies a chance to be heard (one official called it "knowing what game is being played where"), and while discussions may have been more lively and relevant to serious business than was apparently the case in Johnson's less frequent NSC sessions, there is little evidence either from published sources or interviews to suggest that the Council meetings themselves are the place where the primary "serious business" of sorting out issues is carried on. And as the Administration has grown older, the Council has convened less frequently. There were 37 meetings in 1969, but only 21 in 1970, and only 7 in the six months ending in April 1971.[37] Many problems are now apparently resolved by Kissinger's Review Group. And on critical issues like Cambodia, Nixon—like his predecessors— has discovered the uses of "catch-as-catch-can" gatherings, preferring to meet with a smaller group outside of the NSC framework.

NSC meetings seem to have provided Nixon with some useful argument and a perhaps more useful feel for the views of his top subordinates. In turn, their attendance has helped them get a feel for how he looks at

124

issues. But on balance the Nixon NSC has looked more and more like the Kennedy NSC, like a *pro forma* body which symbolizes a serious approach to policy-making and legitimizes staff work done in its name. For what came clear very quickly was the central role being played by the chief of the NSC staff, Henry Kissinger. Unlike the situation in the Kennedy era, when State had the official coordination assignment however much it failed to cultivate it; and unlike that in the late Johnson years, with the Tuesday Lunch above and relative chaos below—foreign policy in the Nixon Administration is White House-centered both in form and in fact. The *New York Times* of February 19, 1970, accurately reported "stronger, more centralized White House direction of foreign policy than ever before."[38] And the only surprising thing about Symington's speech a year later was that he would state the plight of the Secretary of State in so undiplomatic a way.

Kissinger's strength derives partly from Nixon's preferred operating style. As everywhere noted, the President prefers to work with and through a handful of people: *Time* compared the three direct telephone lines from his office in 1970 (to John Ehrlichman, Harry Haldeman, and Kissinger) to the 60-button console of which Johnson used to boast.[39] It suits Nixon to deal with the foreign affairs government principally through one man, and his trust in Kissinger grew very strong very early. Thus, by contrast with the Bundy era, he is the only NSC staff member with significant Presidential access. Also unlike the Bundy era, the larger White House contains no Sorensens or Dungans who are involved in particular foreign policy issues on a continuing basis.

In addition, President Nixon finds the way the system presents specific options to *him* very nicely suited to his preference for making decisions in private, like a judge who weighs evidence and alternative courses of action in lonely splendor.[h] And solo decision-making reinforces a system in which the NSC can be the prime visible institution but the Assistant and staff the more influential one. Kissinger has emphasized that "the NSC remains an advisory body," and that the President does not usually decide on issues at the meetings but "after further private deliberation."[40] Thus not only does the President protect himself from undue pressure to base his decision on the sense of the discussion; he also makes it impossible for any outsider, and for most insiders, to tell clearly whether the "principal" influence is the NSC discussion, the analyses presided over by his staff, or some other source. His flexibility is well preserved. And so is Kissinger's influence, since he is the man most important in formulating issues for Presidential decisions.

To support him, Kissinger has assembled by far the largest NSC staff since Kennedy and Bundy transformed it into a Presidential institution in 1961. From 28 professionals (excluding Kissinger) as of February 1969, it has grown to 38 in September 1969, 44 in August 1970, and 52 as of April 1971. This last number is about triple the Rostow staff at its peak.[i]

Internal staff organization is also more elaborate. Slightly less than half of Kissinger's men serve on the "Operations Staff," which is organized mainly by region

[h] Of course, solo decisions can go too far. Nixon reportedly "never submitted" his first television speech justifying the Cambodia invasion "for editing by his main Cabinet advisors. All of Mr. Nixon's senior aides still wince at some of his rhetoric." (Hedrick Smith, "Cambodia Decision: Why President Acted," *New York Times*, June 30, 1970, p. 14.) For an account differing in detail but likewise highlighting Presidential isolation, see Rowland Evans, Jr. and Robert D. Novak, *Nixon in the White House* (Random House, 1971), pp. 245-56.

[i] These figures are based on lists provided by the NSC staff. They represent professionals handling substantive staff work, but not clerical, communications, or other support personnel. They include professionals on the NSC Staff Secretariat, but not White House Situation Room officials. Several early 1971 sources put Kissinger's staff at about 110 persons, but less than half of these were professionals.

and parallels most closely its Rostow predecessor. A number of others—seven at latest count—work as personal Kissinger aides in the "Office of the Assistant to the President." A "Staff Secretariat" monitors the formal procedures and performs general operational coordination. A "Program Analysis Staff" oversees a number of elaborate studies of "all U. S. programs in key countries and their interrelationships."[41] It also analyzes and reviews the defense budget. And in the course of the staff's development there have been several groups assigned the function of "planning." This has apparently included work on the regular national security studies, efforts of a more long-range nature, and general service as a sort of "think tank" for Kissinger.

The evolution of the formal system since January 1969 has likewise highlighted Kissinger's dominant role. The State-chaired committees have proved rather weak. The IG's have served not as leadership vehicles for Assistant Secretaries of State, but rather as formal coordinators of national security studies specifically assigned to them. The Under Secretaries Committee has been involved primarily in rather specialized policy questions incapable of resolution at the Assistant Secretary level yet insufficiently important for NSC (or Kissinger) time.

By contrast, there has been a proliferation of new groups chaired by Kissinger himself. In July 1969 the Under Secretary-level Washington Special Actions Group (WSAG) was established to oversee crisis management and contingency planning. The following fall the Defense Program Review Committee (DPRC) was created to review "major defense, fiscal, policy and program issues in terms of their strategic, diplomatic, political, and economic implications."[42] Members of this group included not just the Under Secretary of State, the Deputy Secretary of Defense, the JCS Chairman and the CIA Director—standard officials on other NSC groups—but also the Director of the Budget and the

127

Chairman of the Council of Economic Advisers. And Kissinger also chairs three more specialized groups—the Verification Panel involved in the strategic arms talks, the "Forty Committee" for supervising covert intelligence operations, and the Vietnam Special Studies Group.

Thus the pattern has been increasingly for critical issues to be the formal responsibility of Under Secretary-level interdepartmental committees under Kissinger's direction. How much of their work is actually handled in regular committee meetings is unclear, but since Kissinger's office provides their staff support their existence tends to increase his leverage. And the Review Group, for one, has been particularly active. To conform to the general pattern, it was reconstituted the "Senior Review Group" on September 14, 1970, with the level of departmental representation raised from the Assistant Secretary to the Under Secretary level. Formerly State had been represented on the committee by Planning and Coordination Staff Director William Cargo and Counselor Richard Pedersen, and the regular Defense Department representative was Assistant Secretary for International Security Affairs G. Warren Nutter. But none of these men had proved remotely comparable to Kissinger in either analytical competence or bureaucratic clout, and the change brought onto the committee people who were more able to speak for their departments. The Senior Review Group has met twice as frequently as its predecessor—about once a week in the first four months of 1971—and has apparently played a broader policy coordination role than its publicly stated responsibility for reviewing formal studies would imply.[43]

Operating at the Under Secretary level has important advantages to Kissinger. He and his President are surely sensitive to charges that he has usurped the role of Secretary of State William P. Rogers. Rogers is undoubtedly even more sensitive. To put Kissinger in a position of giving orders to Cabinet members, or chairing a committee on which they served, would be too great a breach of bureaucratic etiquette, and would contradict Nixon's insistence that Rogers is his primary adviser. But Under Secretaries are by Washington folklore and sometime practice "operational." Thus it is less of a threat to anyone's prerogatives if Kissinger manages issues for the President with them or passes down Presidential decisions through them. This is one reason why Kissinger developed an exceptionally close operational and intellectual relationship with Under Secretary of State Elliot Richardson early in the Administration. This relationship does not seem to have been duplicated, however, with Richardson's successor, John Irwin. One reason may be the obvious problems this creates for Rogers.

Thus since January 1969 Kissinger's staff has been enlarged and his formal position enhanced. But what seals his position is the President's personal confidence and operating style; it is this parallel between formal and informal lines which builds real organizational strength and gives the official system a chance for real impact. The closest recent parallel is McNamara in Defense, whose support of new budget procedures buttressed by remarkable Presidential confidence forced the military services to take these procedures seriously. As long as the men at the top who have influence support the system, those lower down who seek influence are forced to deal through it.

On the things Nixon considers most important Kissinger has clearly been the man who counts. All the "chronologies" of the recent Cambodia decision highlight his role as the President's "crisis manager," getting information and pulling together alternatives while the Secretaries of State and Defense gave rather generalized advice.[44] He is likewise the key official on the Strategic Arms Limitation Talks (SALT) and in the movement toward more normal relations with China. His role as

129

the President's prize briefer of newsmen is well known. And on a quite different project also dear to the President's heart, Kissinger and his staff aides basically wrote Nixon's 1970 foreign policy message to Congress, despite a massive previous drafting effort in the State Department. Of all the major Administration policy efforts, only the Middle East peace initiative has come primarily from the Secretary of State and his Department. Rogers has suffered by comparison in both image and influence. Despite Nixon's expressed intent to have "a very strong Secretary of State," Rogers has been an adviser somewhat removed from the central policy-making system. He is enough out of the main stream to cast doubt on his credibility as a spokesman for Administration foreign policy to Congress and the public, a development not only deplored by Symington, but foreseen and protested by Senator J. William Fulbright within a month of the inauguration.[45]

Rogers' problem is not that of Walter Hickel. In an administration where few men deal directly with the President, the Secretary has ready access. He makes use of this access, speaking with Nixon regularly by phone, and seeing him as much as several times a week. His judgment as an old and trusted friend is undoubtedly valued, and on the Middle East he has been able to play an important role. But if Rogers probably talks to Nixon more than any of his Cabinet colleagues, Kissinger probably has more serious communication with the President than any other human being. And both the formal system and the President's informal weighing of issues and options seem to rely predominantly on the Assistant's analyses and operational support.

Thus it has been impossible for Administration officials to offer a credible explanation that denies the competing nature of Kissinger's and Rogers' roles, or implies that Kissinger is not getting much the better of the battle. Kissinger has been quoted as dismissing the much-cited rivalry as "a melodramatic account that doesn't make any sense." Rogers, he has said, "is operationally oriented . . . responsible for conducting foreign policy. I am more conceptually oriented. I help the President set goals."[46] But it is the notion that the Secretary can really direct our disparate foreign operations that "doesn't make any sense" in a system where another man has the leverage that comes from prime Presidential confidence and the central role in the formal policy system.

The President on the other hand, has insisted that Rogers is "the chief foreign policy adviser and the chief foreign policy spokesman of the Administration." Yet he asserted on the same occasion that Kissinger "covers not only foreign policy but national security policy; the coordination of those policies."[47] This seems, intentionally or not, to present a more accurate description of their actual roles—Rogers as publicly and formally the more important in the area of traditional State Department responsibility (diplomatic relations), but Kissinger as central in "national security policy" and overall "coordination," which are what most Presidential involvement in foreign affairs is all about.[j]

For despite Nixon's campaign threat to "clean house,"[48] his general approach to the State Department has been to leave it be and build above it, with perhaps the hope that many of its officials would end up working for Kissinger. Nixon has brought few of his own men into the Department: four of the five regional Assistant

[j] As noted in the opening chapter, this book recognizes no line between "foreign policy" and "national security policy," assuming rather that the former includes the latter. And this seems in fact to be the real Nixon Administration position, Presidential semantics notwithstanding. For the general Nixon Messages to Congress—entitled "United States *Foreign Policy* for the 1970's" (italics added)—are dominated by "national security" issues like the Nixon doctrine, troops in Europe and Korea, strategic arms policy, and the balance of power with the Soviet Union.

131

Secretaries, for example, are career Foreign Service officers. Nor has there been much other constructive White House concern with the State Department as an organization. One might assume, for example, that the President would be well served if the Secretary could organize his Seventh Floor[k] as an instrument to make the Department more responsive to Presidential priorities. But the NSC system designedly undercuts the Seventh Floor by having the regional IG's get their assignments directly from the White House and transmit their studies directly to the Review Group.

In fact, it appears that State officials have managed to limit the impact of this procedure. After the failure of an apparent effort to get a Presidential decision strengthening the Seventh Floor role, Under Secretary Richardson reportedly ordered the Assistant Secretaries to touch base with him during each study for substantive guidance, and to clear the final product through him before it goes to Kissinger. In addition, directives and reports now seem to move physically through the Seventh Floor on their way from and to the White House. With these steps, plus the creation of a Planning and Coordination Staff which monitors and reviews State inputs to NSC documents, State's Seventh Floor has been able to regain some ground on the formal issue of who bosses State's regional bureaus. But its influence over the substance of the documents seems to be far less than that of the White House staff.

The NSSM Program—The Limits of Policy Studies

The "comprehensive series of studies" promised in February 1969 proved to be a major bureaucratic event, an impressive effort to review U.S. policies on virtually all important foreign policy-national security issues.

[k] The seventh floor of the State Department building houses the Secretary, his principal deputies, and their supporting staffs. Hence, the expression "Seventh Floor" is commonly used to refer to those officials and staffs.

Before June 30th of that year the White House had sent out 61 "NSSM's" (National Security Study Memoranda) assigning reviews of particular policies to various departments and inter-agency groups. By April 1971 the total had reached 126.[49] Almost all have been undertaken at White House initiative, though departments and agencies are free to propose them. Subjects have ranged from Vietnam to arms control, from relations with Japan to policy toward southern Africa, from our overall defense posture to the future of the Alliance for Progress.

The aim, of course, has been not research for its own sake, but elaboration of policy choices and their implications. And the procedure has proved useful both in strengthening White House influence and in bringing policy changes. The system gives the staff a means to bring issues out on the table for explicit treatment and to force them up for ultimate Presidential action. It has the primary role in deciding what office or what type of inter-agency committee should conduct a study. And the options device is likewise helpful to the staff, for it is harder for officials to deny agreement to an alternative the staff wants to have considered when they are asked not to endorse it but just to recognize that it is a realistic choice.

The NSSM device made a particularly important contribution to the decision to renounce use of biological weapons. Only the Army really wanted them, and, within the Army, mainly the branch specializing in them. But as noted in a previous chapter, the issue never got to President Johnson for his review because neither the Secretary of Defense nor the Secretary of State was willing to pay the bureaucratic political price of recommending a change. Under the Nixon system, however, once the White House ordered a study, the staff could see to it that the "option" of renouncing biological weapons was presented as one alternative for NSC discussion and Presidential decision.

133

This did not mean, of course, that the President could ignore the position of the Secretary of Defense or the JCS. In this case, the fact that Laird was reportedly satisfied with the decision made the President's choice much easier. For a President cannot really make a "choice" like this in the manner of a judge considering only the substantive issues; there is inevitably a strong element of "striking a bargain" that his top officials can live with.[1] But it was easier all around when Laird did not have to take upon his shoulders the burden of *initiating* the change.

Examples of other decisions directly attributable to the system are harder to find. But it is likely that an action like the return of Okinawa to Japan was less painful because a hardened JCS position did not have to be confronted early in the process, even if this position was well known.[m]

Yet despite promising procedures and real accomplishments, the studies system gives evidence of a number of problems. The number and comprehensiveness of the studies has been sufficient to create a serious bureaucratic logjam. It takes a long time for the bureaucracy to prepare them, it is a heavy burden on Nixon and Kissinger to digest them, and hard to schedule them for

[1] Sorensen expresses it well: "In choosing between conflicting advice, the President is also choosing between conflicting advisers, conferring recognition on some while rebuffing others. He will, consequently, take care to pay more attention to the advice of the man who must carry out the decision than the advice of a mere 'kibitzer.' He will be slow to overrule a Cabinet officer whose pride or prestige have been committed, not only to ease that officer's personal feelings but to maintain his utility and credibility." (*Decision-Making*, p. 79.)

[m] One tribute to the NSSM procedure, probably too glowing, is in Joseph Kraft's "The Nixon Supremacy," *Harper's*, March 1970, pp. 48-50. An antidote is John Osborne's search for "any major decisions or departures in foreign policy that would not have occurred if the Kissinger system . . . did not exist." ("Henry's Wonderful Machine," *The New Republic*, January 31, 1970, pp. 11-13.) Kraft has since modified his view of how much the system can accomplish. ("In Search of Kissinger," *Harper's*, January 1971, pp. 54-55.)

NSC consideration within a period of time which meets the needs of the particular issue. The papers themselves are often very long: one reportedly had a *summary* running 75 pages. There has also been a quality problem. The type of analysis required is very difficult and goes against the usual tendency of officials to write "advocacy" papers supporting specific points of view. Thus alleged "options" are often advocacy in more sophisticated guise, one real choice and two or three straw men, like the Johnson/Nixon tendency to present our Vietnam choices (at least for public consumption) as (1) blow up the world, (2) continue the present policy, or (3) scuttle and run.[n] And departments are hardly willing to concentrate on disinterested analysis of options at the working level and leave consideration of formal agency positions for the NSC meeting. Rogers, for example, has ordered that State officials provide him with a departmental paper—recommending a State position for him to urge on the President—for each issue on which a NSSM is completed.

Many participants argue that the papers are quite good by comparison with parallel policy analysis efforts in previous administrations. They have certainly caused officials at several levels to give broad thought to issues that they might have otherwise considered in a narrower framework. But there has still been continued White House unhappiness with the results. One reason, undoubtedly, is Kissinger's high analytic standards: he is an exceedingly hard man to satisfy. But another must be the great difficulty those at the working level have in sensing the President's perspective, in knowing enough about what he knows and the way his mind ticks to judge what

---

[n] According to one source, an early NSSM paper on U.S.-Soviet relations came from the State Department with three basic "options"— (1) negotiate on nothing; (2) negotiate on anything the Russians want to talk about; (3) be selective in what we are willing to negotiate about. The White House staff reportedly reformulated the issue by eliminating the first two and subdividing the third.

135

facts and arguments he finds necessary or relevant. The fact that the President deals directly with so few people cannot but exacerbate this problem.

Both the logjam and the quality problem would seem to press the NSC staff in the same direction—toward boiling down the papers to a length which can engage the attention of Kissinger and Nixon, redoing the analysis and redrawing the options to meet their preferences and needs. The Kissinger-chaired Review Group provides a useful vehicle for doing this, since it is responsible for assuring the adequacy of the studies. And while it is impossible for outsiders to determine how much such rewriting actually occurs, interviews indicate that it has been at least reasonably common. Nor, of course, would White House staff redoing of departmental papers be at all peculiar to the Nixon Administration. But for the staff to follow this natural tendency to "do the real work" is to eliminate one of the major justifications for dragging papers up through the system—the desire to have bureaucrats help develop and recognize as real the various options from which the President must choose. It is also to deny or water down the "due process" that the system has so loudly promised. The same costs accrue if Kissinger responds to the inadequacy of the papers by using NSSM's less and less on major problems,[o] or by pulling problems on which studies are underway out of the formal channel because they need action before the cumbersome multi-level interdepartmental process can grind out a paper.

The staff has no easy answer to this dilemma. And the dilemma illuminates a broader paradox. As noted earlier, the congruence between the formal system and the informal relationships *can* strengthen the formal system

[o] There was considerable speculation in early 1970 that the NSSM's might fall into disuse because of the problems discussed here. This has not happened. In fact, the rate at which NSSM's have been issued increased from less than two a month in early 1970 to close to four a month in early 1971. This compares to about eleven a month in January-June 1969.

since it cuts out possible alternative channels for those down in the bureaucracy who wish to affect high-level decisions. But the same bureaucratic political situation which denies them the choice to go around the system gives this choice to Kissinger. Moreover, the fact that he is under pressure from all sides on operational matters due to his pre-eminent position means a powerful temptation to handle each issue in a manner that seems most effective in the short run.

At least some of the studies could conceivably result in the worst of both worlds. They may be too important to disregard given the commitment of the principals to (and investment of bureaucrats in) the process, and thus clog the system and take large amounts of staff time. Yet they may not be sufficiently relevant to serve as actual decision documents for the President, thereby creating a malaise within a bureaucracy which had been more or less promised that they would so serve.

One fault may lie in the number of studies called for and the need for virtually all of them to receive attention from Kissinger. Reliance on the Under Secretaries Committee might ease the load. But if papers considered in that forum are options papers aimed at choice, who chooses? Officially the Under Secretary of State has the authority to "decide" USC questions, but he does not have the type of topside backing required to make that authority real. So USC differences can be resolved only by compromises or by appeals to the top.

A larger limitation of the NSSM procedure, however, is that government policy on most important issues cannot be effectively controlled by periodic top-level strategic choices, however sophisticated a system may be in facilitating them.

The Limits of Strategic Decisions

When Kissinger came to Washington he avowed to a number of people his determination to "leave operations to the departments and to devote more time to policy planning." His new boss said upon his appointment, "I don't want him to get down in the situation room in the White House and spend too much time going through cables." By May of 1969, Chalmers Roberts could write in the *Washington Post*: "Few believed it would work that way and, in fact, it hasn't." By 1970, no one was bothering to pretend that it had.[50]

Kissinger may, of course, have simply been making the usual disclaimers of a newly chosen White House staff man. He apparently was deep into operational matters well before Inauguration Day. But much in his writings suggests that his intention to concentrate on broad "policy" was a serious one. He had criticized our government's tendency to treat problems as "isolated cases," "to identify foreign policy with the solution of immediate issues" rather than with the development of a broad strategy for coping with the world over a period of years. He had also decried a bureaucracy where "success consists in moving the administrative machine to the point of decision, leaving relatively little energy for analyzing the merit of this decision."[51]

And while Kissinger's perceptive analyses of the problems of bureaucratic policy-making gave ample attention to the presence of inter-agency bargaining and the difficulty of surfacing longer-term issues, the emphasis was primarily on problems of decision-*making*. He defined the problem basically in terms of the government settling on a wide, inter-connected foreign policy strategy, presumably by Presidential decision, and was slow to recognize the problem of getting the bureaucracy to implement such a strategy once set.[p]

---

[p] Kissinger does recognize, in a talk given in 1968, that the problem of implementing a Presidential decision is "not a negligible issue," in part because in many cases "the execution really depends on certain nuances of application." ("Bureaucracy and Policy Making: The Effect of Insiders and Outsiders on the Policy Process," in Henry A. Kissinger and Bernard Brodie, *Bureaucracy, Politics and Strategy*, Security Studies Paper Number 17, University of California at Los

Yet even as much of a "thinker" as George Kennan had noted long before that "What the foreign affairs segment of the Government needs is not primarily an occasional National Security Council paper but intimate day-by-day, hour-by-hour direction. . . . It needs, in the language of the day, to be ridden herd on."[52]

So if Kissinger did not already know it, he learned quickly that the strategic thinker remains an exclamation point in the margins of foreign policy-making if he does not join the bureaucratic battles to give operational meaning and effect to general objectives. By mid-July 1970 he was emphasizing that getting a decision made was not enough: ". . . the outsider believes a presidential order is consistently followed out. Nonsense. I have to spend considerable time seeing that it is carried out and in the spirit the President intended."[53]

Thus the Assistant to the President found personal involvement in operations critical to his influence and to the central role both the President and he wished him to play. He learned also that Presidents tend to use trusted aides without undue regard for their intended roles. On preparations for the Cambodia incursion, there could be no practical separation between the "policy" judgment of what to do and the decisions about particular military operations, and the President inevitably wanted the same man to handle both. Hence the need to create the Washington Special Actions Group for detailed operational management of crises. And because he is the key man, Kissinger is under enormous operational pressure from below as well, since "getting to him" seems to many others their best hope for effective influence.[q] This operational pressure, in turn, shapes in a major way the demands and pressures on his staff.

Angeles, 1968, p. 2.) But the overwhelming emphasis in his major writings is on the problems of getting wise strategic decisions made.

[q] As Kraft has written of the Nixon system of governing in general: "The few staff men who do have regular access are subject to enor-

None of this is to deny that broad planning-type activities have been of some importance. The staff's geographic officers have been deeply engaged in the NSSM process, making them less able to stay on top of day-to-day bureaucratic developments than their Rostow predecessors. The elaborate country program evaluation studies being managed by the Program Analysis Staff are a definite departure from anything previously attempted by the White House. And Kissinger's desire to devote considerable staff time to relatively long-term issues is evidenced by his repeated efforts to establish a special planning group relatively free from day-to-day concerns.

But the very fact that the staff's planning components have been repeatedly reconstituted illustrates the problem of carrying out this intention in a meaningful way. For the pull of operations remains powerful, as does the difficulty of relating broader planning to them effectively. Thus the geographic officers seem to be expected not only to do everything their predecessors did but also to place top priority on the studies/planning effort. And whatever decline there has been in the time they must devote to the latter as the Administration has grown older cannot help but be offset by the growing job of pressing for implementation of the policy decisions the system helps the President to make.

Once it is recognized that day-to-day involvement in operations is essential to shaping policy, the problem of organizing for coherence assumes far larger dimensions. Those in top positions cannot limit themselves to shaping broad decisions; they must engage in continuing bureaucratic combat. This takes vastly greater amounts of time and energy. It limits the number of issues one

---

mous pressures. Because they are known to have the President's ear, everyone in the Administration and the Congress and the Press is after them." (*Washington Post*, September 16, 1969, p. A21.)

man can effectively influence, however great his leverage. Consequently, it increases the number of men a President requires to fight his battles if he is to make the foreign affairs government his own. Thus the question becomes whether building strength in the White House is enough, even if Kissinger can dominate the issues on which he can concentrate. The need would seem rather to go beyond this, to have other officials at key places in the foreign affairs government who are responsive to the President's perspective and priorities, and who are armed with the leverage and the staff support to influence policy in Presidentially preferred directions.

Looked at in this light, the successes of the Nixon-Kissinger system appear less impressive, the deficiencies more serious. For it has generally failed to build centers of strength responsive to the President in other parts of the foreign affairs government. As already noted, State's Seventh Floor has been treated less as a potential ally than as an encumbrance. The system seems designed to reduce its effective influence by going around it. The regional Assistant Secretaries, who do play an important role in the formal system, owe allegiance less to the President than to the career service, and the IG's they chair have not become vehicles for Presidentially attuned leadership.

The situation at Defense is worse. Secretary of Defense Melvin Laird appears to view his role as that of a shrewd adjudicator of service interests, rather than as a McNamara-type leader seeking to bring defense programs into closer accord with Presidential priorities. Laird has encouraged the weakening of two key OSD staff offices whose role had been to challenge service interests in the name of such wider priorities. The Office of International Security Affairs (ISA) has become a home for a group of right-wing officials under Assistant Secretary Nutter, its influence far less than in the McNamara-

141

Clifford days. The Systems Analysis Office has lost its main source of strength—a Secretary who uses its analyses as an important factor in his decisions.

The cost of such weakness to the President has apparently been considerable. Just as it took Kennedy two years to get our diplomats to "indicate discreet sympathy" for Italy's opening to the left, Nixon's similar failure to make the State Department a Presidential instrument meant an unavailing effort to get State to do more about Biafran relief. The weakness of ISA may not be entirely unrelated to the delays in implementing as seemingly straightforward a directive as that of ordering the destruction of biological weapons stockpiles. And the lack of a strong OSD ally has undermined the White House staff's efforts to bring analysis to bear on the defense budget. Thus, as noted by William Beecher in the *New York Times*, the role of the Defense Program Review Committee, established to enhance White House control over military programs, has been limited to "broad budgetary guidance, and little else."[54]

And not only has the Nixon system failed to build strength beyond the White House. In the way it has operated, it has tended to limit the influence of men on the NSC staff itself.

The Attrition of the Staff

In February 1969, Washington was awed by the strength and depth of the Kissinger staff. By September, it was talking about how many were leaving. Ten of the 28 men on the February 6th list were absent from the one issued September 25th, not counting one person who decided not to come on board at all. And as impressive as the number of men who left was their quality —Morton Halperin, a widely respected foreign policy analyst and operator, and former Deputy Assistant Secretary of Defense; Richard Sneider, a leading State Department Asia expert; Richard Moose, the highly respected author of the chapters in the IDA study on White House foreign affairs organization; and Surgeon Keeny, a long-time specialist in arms control. May 1970 brought five more important resignations, three of them Cambodia-related. By April 1971 only nine of Kissinger's original 28 were still on board.

Just as attracting impressive staff men had been a major success, the inability to hold them was a major failure. Kraft's diagnosis at the peak of the first exodus, while probably exaggerated, pinpointed several problems. Because of the Nixon-Kissinger method of operating, he suggested, "some of the brainiest members of his staff found that they were where the action wasn't."

They saw the President only rarely. They had trouble getting to see Kissinger. They were taken far less seriously throughout the bureaucracy than former members of the National Security Council staff under Kissinger's predecessors—McGeorge Bundy and Walt Rostow. They even found themselves denied what they thought were regular perquisites of the White House—notably the mess.

In these circumstances, there developed a situation practically unique in the annals of the White House staff—a situation in which other pastures began to look greener.[55]

The root problem was that though Kissinger's personal influence was virtually unassailable, his staff members found themselves operating from positions of substantially lesser strength. They were denied direct access to Nixon; they could not aspire to become Kaysens, Komers, or Bators, men whose personal relationships with Kennedy and Johnson gave them strong leverage with the bureaucracy. Moreover, many found it difficult

143

to get to Kissinger, so preoccupied was he with fending off multiple pressures and meeting the President's considerable demands. The problem of lack of contact with the boss reportedly came to a head in late summer 1969, and regular meetings with senior staff members were instituted that fall.

But the problem was not just contact. The most important senior staff people apparently *could* get to him the same day if they had an urgent problem, though they often had to wait until late evening. More serious still was the matter of support, the degree to which staff members could act in Kissinger's name, the extent to which he wanted them to act and would back them up. Even if denied the bargaining advantages that come only from direct dealing with the President, staff members could hope for substantial if lesser leverage if they were known to speak for Kissinger, or at least if his relationships with them included a recognition of the importance of giving them support.

It seems clear that in general they have not received such support. This grew to be recognized rather widely in the bureaucracy. It may not have undercut their effectiveness too much on matters (like national security studies) which would ultimately rise to the White House, but it has hurt them rather seriously in efforts to influence ongoing bureaucratic activities. One official not in the White House discussed the Kissinger staff in terms of what he called "the law of delegation and escalation." Men who have delegated authority from a strong boss are in an impressive bargaining position because their adversaries cannot reverse them by appealing to the next level. Exceptional men will work on staffs only where the boss is a good man, tied to power, and willing to delegate. Kissinger met the first two qualifications, but time showed he did not meet the third. So some good men left him.[56] And while others have replaced them, they have increasingly been career officials on detail rather

144

than independently recruited men owing prime allegiance to the White House.[r]

Obviously much of the problem was personal. Kissinger himself has noted that "the qualities rewarded in the rise to eminence" are seldom "the qualities required once eminence is reached."[57/s] And like many who achieve "eminence" in the academic world, Kissinger is a strong-minded, independent individual whose whole life has taught him the virtues of relying overwhelmingly on himself and his own judgment. In addition, life in the academic world requires, at least for the man who has made his reputation, considerably less attunement to the needs and the feelings of one's colleagues and subordinates than life in most other modern organizations. What are virtues in one situation may become vices in another. So just as it was not surprising that a Bundy, whose independent academic work had been modest and who had made his mark by winning the cooperation of obstinate professors he could never hope to "boss," should see power as something enhanced by encouraging and influencing the initiatives of others; so also was it not entirely unpredictable that Kissinger, whose academic work was far more extensive and original, would think of power as tied directly to the work he did personally, himself. Nor should it be startling that his dealings with White House subordinates have generally lacked those touches of sympathy and occasional gratitude with which a necessarily demanding boss can make life much more bearable for his underlings at very little cost to himself.

A related factor is the apparent difference between the ways the two men and their bosses have viewed their

---

[r] Between February 1969 and April 1971, the proportion of Kissinger's staff comprised of career military or State Department officials rose from 36 to 48 per cent (author's calculation based on NSC staff lists).

[s] Kissinger would not have applied this insight in this way, however. In fact, his meaning was close to the opposite: he argued that rising usually required "administrative and technical skills," whereas "vision and creativity" were what were "needed for leadership."

roles. Unlike Bundy, Kissinger seems to see himself as responsible for making individual foreign policy proposals and actions consistent with an explicit global strategy which he, working for the President, has the central intellectual role in shaping. This makes his work much more personal, and even to some extent "private," than that of Bundy, the informal system operator.

One should not overdraw the picture. Obviously the White House continues to be "where the action is" on the most important issues, and Kissinger's pre-eminence cannot help but rub off to some degree on his staff. Also, most of the bureaucracy has only a fuzzy notion of intra-White House relationships, and from this ambiguity an able staff man can build considerable leverage. Yet the problem remains a very serious one. For whatever reasons, the Nixon "system" has brought about the loss of some of its best staff members and sharply limited the impact of those who remain. The cost is not just to staff men seeking influence, but to an Administration which badly needs more strong, "Presidential" agents to do battle with the bureaucracy.

Can the National Security Assistant Be Foreign Affairs Coordinator?

Thus, despite its impressive start and an unusually serious and systematic approach to the problems of foreign policy-making, the Nixon system has developed some very serious troubles. Policy studies have tended to clog the path from the bureaucracy to the NSC policy-making "summit," and to be judged insufficiently responsive to Presidential needs when they are reviewed. The pivotal policy official is inundated with pressures from all directions to do things that no one else in the system has the influence to do. Short-run pressures to serve the President responsively encourage Kissinger and his staff to handle things more and more in-house, thereby increasing the gap between the bureaucracy and the

146

President that the system was calculated to bridge. There is a lack of centers of Presidential strength outside the White House staff. Yet even the staff finds itself on weak ground.

To all of these problems there seems a simple answer: delegate! Problems that cannot be postponed seek the level at which they can be resolved. The overloading of the system reflects the fact that no one seems to be really trusted by Nixon and Kissinger but Nixon and Kissinger. One is therefore tempted to attribute the whole problem to personalities and suggest that (in theory at least) it could be resolved by the replacement of one or both.

But the problem probably goes deeper. Kissinger's failure to support his staff reflects not just a regrettable but widespread personal trait found in eminent men. A careful look suggests that he is being asked to play two roles that are incompatible. Kissinger's role as *personal* staff adviser demands that he place top priority on meeting the President's immediate, daily needs, on handling the President's own personal foreign affairs business. Not only is this what the President wants; Kissinger's overall influence is inescapably tied to his performing this job to the President's satisfaction. But this means subordinating his *institutional* role as kingpin of the NSC system and director of the largest White House foreign policy staff in history. For the latter requires not just service *ad hoc* on immediate Presidential priorities but comprehensive management of a broad range of issues, not just responsiveness upward but responsiveness downward, so that by such responsiveness he can confer on those who must wage many daily battles on his behalf sufficient leverage to have a fighting chance of prevailing.

Why should the two conflict? A major reason is time. Kissinger's attention to the personal needs of the President leaves him markedly less time to support staff members or other bureaucratic allies in their battles and

147

assure that *their* needs for effectiveness are met. But the problem seems more fundamental. The Assistant to the President must protect his boss's flexibility; to do this he must guard his own. But a staff needs authoritative guidance and the presumption of support. Without such support it cannot help the Assistant make his effectiveness truly comprehensive. Ten years ago the Jackson Subcommittee warned that the institutional responsibilities of a foreign affairs "super-Cabinet" official could "mitigate against the maintenance of his close, confidential, personal relationship with the President."[58] The Nixon system seems to have produced the converse—a man whose unavoidable decision to give priority to this personal relationship weakens his institutional role.

When considering the problem of building strength outside the White House, moreover, there is the question of whom Kissinger might "delegate" authority to even if he could. Strong, Presidentially-minded regional Assistant Secretaries of State would be immensely helpful to a President seeking to control the bureaucracy. Yet they do not work for Kissinger in form (except as chairmen of the IG's), and it is not difficult for a Secretary of State sensitive about his own authority to find ways to limit their doing so in practice.

The system then tends to divide issues into two types —those where Kissinger can be effectively engaged, and those where he cannot. The former may receive the broad, high-quality analysis that Kissinger is eminently capable of giving them, and may be resolved in the way the President would wish. But the latter will tend to drift and be governed by minimal, temporizing decisions, since no one will feel he has a sufficient power base from which to press for more serious action without threat of an embarrassing reversal. Centralization is purchased at the price of exacerbating bureaucratic tendencies to handle second-order issues by individual agency determinations, minimal compromises, or continued infighting.[t]

And because Kissinger must involve himself so deeply in issues like Vietnam or China or the SALT talks, the list of "second-order" issues neither he nor others can master for the President has grown quite large. The system's failure to deal effectively with economic issues has been recognized in the establishment of a new Council on International Economic Policy which parallels the NSC and is run by a new Assistant to the President for International Economic Affairs.[u] The fact that Kissinger

[t] This analysis is strikingly corroborated by Elizabeth Drew's description of the Nixon system's handling of Biafran relief. All the elements are there: a President "generally inaccessible"; a Kissinger well-informed but overworked; an NSC staffer who pressed for a stronger relief effort, but who was in a position where "it was not entirely clear to the State Department to what extent he was speaking for Kissinger"; a State Department "influenced by the traditionalists," "more than it had been for some time," because "the Administration made very few appointments from the outside to key State Department jobs." (*Atlantic*, June 1970, pp. 21-8.)

One obvious area where there have been more than "minimal, temporizing decisions" despite Kissinger's limited role has been the Middle East. The key here seems to have been an unusual Assistant Secretary of State—Joseph Sisco—who has been able to respond effectively to two masters (Rogers and the White House) while aggressively moving the peace initiative forward. Also important has been Rogers' increasing concentration on the problem as the one where he has the best chance of making a major contribution and redeeming his reputation; and Kissinger's apparent reluctance to get involved too deeply since he is a Jew. Since his department has clearly gotten the initiative on the problem, Rogers has apparently been able to exploit his access to the President to handle it in considerable measure outside of the NSC system and around the NSC staff.

State Department officials discussing Sisco's bureaucratic skill often note that he is one of the few Foreign Service officers who have never had an overseas assignment.

[u] At this writing the new Council has only been in existence a few months, so it is too soon to assess how effective the new approach will be. The Council itself appears quite unwieldy as a forum for serious business, including as it does not only the President as Chairman and the Secretary of State as Vice Chairman, but the Secretaries of Treasury, Agriculture, Commerce, and Labor; the Director of the

has more important business has contributed to the rather slow bureaucratic progress in following up on the Peterson Task Force recommendations for aid reorganization. The effort to control the defense budget through a Kissinger-chaired committee has proved but a paper solution to that large problem. And our policies toward major African and Latin American countries seem to have received very little Presidential treatment.

These gaps would not necessarily arise if the foreign affairs government problem were solely, or even mainly, that of making what Nixon has termed "rational and deliberate" Presidential choices, and if these could rather easily shape actions on "operational issues." In that case, service to the President's need for options would be equal to bringing what Kissinger has called "coherence and design" to the bureaucracy. Management of the system would be a relatively routine matter, and the costs of weakness outside the White House acceptable. Put otherwise, if decisions on "first order,"

Office of Management and Budget; the Chairman of the Council of Economic Advisers; the President's Special Representative for Trade Negotiations; the director of Nixon's Domestic Policy Council, John D. Ehrlichman; and Henry A. Kissinger. The real question is whether strong staff coordination work can be performed from the White House under the Council umbrella.

The foreign economic policy area is, however, something of a "natural" for a strong White House role. It involves a range of agencies none of which has clear primacy, though State and Treasury both lay claim to it in certain areas. It involves reconciling a mix of domestic and foreign policy interests. And particularly in the trade and monetary fields, much of the most important U.S. government activity involves international negotiations for which continuing interagency negotiations are required. If the new Assistant to the President for International Economic Affairs, Peter G. Peterson, were to emerge as a strong White House aide dealing directly with the President and Cabinet members on these matters, he would parallel the role of the Deputy Special Assistants under Kennedy and Johnson.

(In fact, President Nixon's August 1971 foreign economic policy initiatives grew primarily from the advocacy of Treasury Secretary John Connally. But the absence of both NSC staff and State advisers from the early decision-making seems not unrelated to the apparent damage done our long-term relations with Japan and Western Europe.)

"policy" issues really can predetermine "second order," "operational" matters, then the system would handle best what is most important. Apparently Nixon and Kissinger believed this when they entered office, and the scarcity of foreign affairs crises in 1969 may have strengthened such a conviction.

But Kissinger's heavy involvement in operational matters suggests the opposite. It corroborates, rather, one of the basic insights of the bureaucratic politics view: the inherent limits of any effort to have general decisions or guidelines control actions taken and commitments made day-to-day at the "working level." For power is inevitably dispersed through the foreign affairs government because officials at various levels have bargaining advantages, created in part by the sheer limits on the time and attention of those at the top. Schemes to centralize power can, if wisely developed, strengthen the influence of those at the top, and this has certainly happened under Nixon and Kissinger. But much policy will still be made at lower levels. Unless, therefore, a system seeks to develop centers of strength at several hierarchical levels and to make them responsive to top-level influence and priorities by the sharing of authority, communication, and confidence with them, power will not all rise to the top but simply become even more diffused throughout the government. Top officials will lack "handles" for issues being dealt with at these levels because there seems no one with strong influence with whom they can deal.[59]

The Assistant to the President for National Security Affairs is singularly ill-placed to concentrate on building such centers of strength below him in the government. He is dominated by the immediate demands of the President. He lacks the advantages of a position of official authority such as that of the Secretary of State. He lacks a general hierarchy of line subordinates to whom to delegate authority and confidence, even if such delegation

151

did not conflict with his role of personal Presidential adviser. He is a poor man on whom to build an institutional system for the overall coordination and management of foreign policy.

Dean Rusk after eight years at State described "the real organization of government at higher echelons" as "how confidence flows down from the President."[60] Henry Kissinger after much less time in the White House learned that much of his energy had to be spent not on broad policy objectives, but on influencing bureaucratic operations which in the end add up to policy. If one combines Rusk's observation with the fact which confronted Kissinger, that policy is influenced by many men at a number of bureaucratic levels, it follows that only a system which allows confidence from the President to flow down strongly to a number of individuals and offices at key points in the system has much chance of achieving coherent foreign policy. Ironically, in Rusk's State Department, Presidential confidence was not felt to flow through him. Under Kennedy it flowed around him; under Johnson it flowed to him but stopped there. He did not "delegate confidence" to subordinates, nor does Kissinger today.

One might suggest, then, that if the Nixon Administration was correct in its conclusion that the United States government had not been making coherent and purposive foreign policy in the 1960's, its diagnosis of the disease which produced these symptoms was only in part correct. Nixon officials, as reported in the *Washington Post* early in the Administration, felt that the Kennedy Administration " 'overreacted' to the formality of the Eisenhower paperwork and ended up with something far more 'chaotic.' "[61] But the cause of chaos—at least in the Johnson period—may not have been primarily the absence of properly developed papers. Extreme informality in policy-making did create real problems. But more important, perhaps, was the situation, typified in the Tuesday Lunch, where the President and his top group of senior officials were unwilling to share power and confidence and communication downward. Not recognizing that this was the central problem, the Nixon Administration exacerbated it by tending to limit the charmed circle to one man. The result must be one of the shorter "lines of confidence" in bureaucratic history.

If a major cause of the problem was the decision to build coherence around the National Security Assistant, this suggests renewed attention to the "other" choice for an organizational strategy—building around the Secretary of State. But is this approach any more promising? A consideration of whether it might be will require first a look at his Department's relation to the President, and a more general analysis of its management problems and efforts at reform.

CHAPTER SIX

Problems with State: Presidential Dissatisfaction and Efforts at Reform

THE expanded White House staff role in foreign policy did not come mainly by design. Though certainly premeditated in its Nixon-Kissinger phase, it grew earlier more as a cumulative response to State Department inadequacies as seen from the White House. Thus, any consideration of the possibility of reversing this trend, of moving away from a White House-centered foreign policy system and leaning instead on State for leadership, requires an explicit look at why Presidents have been so regularly dissatisfied with the Department.

Dissatisfied they have been. Franklin Roosevelt enjoyed repeating the advice of one veteran FSO: "You can get to be a Minister if (a) you are loyal to the service (b) you do nothing to offend people (c) if you are not intoxicated at public functions." John Kennedy, of course, called the State Department "a bowl of jelly," with "all those people over there who are constantly smiling." So Richard Nixon was only following tradition when he promised on the 1968 campaign trail to rid State of "the routine men who have been the architects of the policies of the past. . . . I want a Secretary of State who will join me in cleaning house in the State Department. We are going to clean house there. It has never been done."[1]

Kennedy and his administration may have begun with a more affirmative view. Bundy described the role of the Secretary of State as "agent of coordination." The OCB abolition order stressed State's enhanced responsibilities. And Dean Rusk issued the challenge to Departmental policy-making officers one month after the inauguration:

Power gravitates to those who are willing to make decisions and live with the results, simply because there are so many who readily yield to the intrepid few who take their duties seriously.

On this particular point the Department of State is entering, I think, something of a new phase in its existence. We are expected to take charge.[2]

But according to Sorensen, Kennedy "was discouraged with the State Department almost as soon as he took office. He felt that it too often seemed to have a built-in inertia which deadened initiative and that its tendency toward excessive delay obscured determination. It spoke with too many voices and too little vigor." He concluded, wrote Schlesinger, that "Bundy and I get more done in one day in the White House than they do in six months in the State Department." He "used to divert himself with the dream of establishing a secret office of thirty people or so to run foreign policy while maintaining the State Department as a facade in which people might contentedly carry papers from bureau to bureau." In his understated but indisputable critique before the Jackson Subcommittee in March, 1963, Richard Neustadt concluded: "So far as I can judge, the State Department has not yet found means to take the proffered role and play it vigorously across the board of national security affairs."[3]

The Nixon Administration has not yet produced its memoirs, but the informal White House complaints are strikingly similar.

State in turn has its frustrations with Presidents. When asked by Kennedy what was wrong with "that goddamned department of yours," career diplomat Charles Bohlen replied, "You are."[4] Similarly, the Nixon regime meant for State a rebuff in its early tangle with Kissinger and Co., and a failure of the American Foreign Service Association's new "Young Turk" leaders to win acceptance of their major reform proposals. Consequently, many residents of Foggy Bottom once again became first resentful, then philosophical about Presidents and their preferred ways of doing business. Each, they pointed out, is likely to develop his own arrangements based on his own habits and preferences, the personalities of his top officials, and the passage of time. But this attitude reflects an unfortunate idea that Presidential behavior is somehow random, that there is no pattern to the frustrations of various Presidents with State, and that therefore there is no rational State response to the Presidency but short-term adjustment.

The evidence suggests the opposite, that there is a pattern to White House complaints about State which cuts across several Administrations. It can be gleaned from both written and off-the-record comments by White House staffers and men otherwise close to the last three Presidents. It reflects also a pattern of *needs* related to the President's involvement in foreign policy, needs that State has failed to fill. And if an assessment of such failures can be adequately provided, it becomes a basis for considering the type of reforms which might help State gain greater Presidential confidence.

The Central Ill—Lack of "Responsiveness"

To say State has failed to satisfy Presidents because it has not been responsive to them is, in one sense, merely to restate the problem rather than to explain it. But the concept of "responsiveness" highlights the frequent observation that State is not very much oriented toward the President's needs. Galbraith complained to Kennedy of "a widespread feeling" within State "that God ordained some individuals to make foreign policy without undue interference from Presidents and politicians." A Kennedy NSC staffer has similarly remarked on the inclination of Statesmen to see the President as "a transient meddler in their business."[5]

But the White House indictment of State is far more

156

specific than this. It centers around six largely consistent complaints—that State produces "bad staff work," and that it is slow to respond, resistant to change, reluctant to follow orders, unable to lead, and incapable of putting its own house in order.

Bad staff work refers partly to *quality*. Schlesinger's statement is once again the classic: "Whether drafting memoranda, cables or even letters or statements for the President, the Department fell into full, ripe, dreariness of utterance with hideous ease."[6] Most White House staff members since him seem to have shared this complaint. And quality means not just good English but sound analysis. An equally serious criticism of State staff support of the President has been the tendency to provide "*only one option*, the preferred policy"—as one former staff man described it—instead of analysis which would illuminate alternatives and enlarge Presidential choice.

Disappointment with the papers sent from State to the White House has survived several administrations. Moose reports a consensus through the Kennedy-Johnson period that "the State Department generally lacked sufficient top-echelon staffing to review memorandums with . . . thoroughness or breadth of perspective" comparable to that applied by the NSC staff. And back in 1959 Paul Nitze asked whether "the staff work available to the Secretary of State" was "adequate to enable him" to play a broad foreign affairs leadership role on behalf of the President. He concluded, "A strong case can be made that it is not."[7]

If the product is generally considered bad, it is also felt to be *slow in coming*. "Kennedy had expected a quick American response" to the *aide-memoire* on Berlin presented him by Khrushchev in Vienna, but it took nearly six weeks for State to produce something that Richard Rovere considered "like the kind of speech Andrei Gromyko might make if he were on our side."

157

Nixon's national security studies are, of course, supposed to take more time, but much NSC staff exasperation has been expressed at the slowness with which they move up the line. Frequently cited as causes are what Galbraith has called the "elephantiasis" of the department and the number of clearances and consultations required before final State action is taken.[8]
Resistance to change and new approaches is high on the list of complaints. We would expect this from our earlier discussion of large organizations. And we get it. What Adlai Stevenson called a "tremendous institutional inertial force" in his pre-inauguration task force report to Kennedy, Thomson later dubbed the "_curator mentality_ in the Department of State. . . . At State, the average 'desk officer' inherits from his predecessor our policy toward Country X; he regards it as his function to keep that policy intact—under glass, untampered with, and dusted—so that he may pass it on in two to four years to his successor. And such curatorial service generally merits promotion within the system."[9]
Both slowness to act and reluctance to change contribute to the fourth fault, _inadequacy in carrying out Presidential decisions._ As has been amply noted, Kennedy ordered removal of our short-range missiles from Turkey two months before the Cuban missile crisis, but implementation efforts apparently stopped when the Turks indicated resistance.[a] Also well known is Schlesinger's account about State's resistance to Presidential orders to "indicate discreet sympathy for the opening to the left" in Italy.[10] A White House staffer of later years characterized the problem as: "When you give State an order, they don't obey it."

a This was not just a State lapse, since Nitze of Defense was also involved. The non-implementation, however, was for diplomatic reasons—Turkey's objections—rather than military ones. And if Abel reports correctly, neither was it just a verbal order. The instruction had been issued as a National Security Action Memorandum. (_Missile Crisis_, pp. 169-71).

A quite different criticism, but one only superficially inconsistent with refusal to obey, is *failure to lead.* Much of the public record on this issue reflects Kennedy's frustrations with Rusk. But several criticisms relate as much or more to the career bureaucracy: a tendency to smother rather than take initiatives; a predisposition toward seeing one part of a problem, the "diplomatic" or "political," rather than the whole; a reluctance to challenge the expertise of others—the CIA on the Bay of Pigs, the military on Vietnam—though such challenges are indispensable to taking a broad view; an operating mode tending to "exclude" other agencies from issues rather than "including" them in discussions; a failure to exploit numerous opportunities to "take charge" in interdepartmental issues, notably the limited effort in most regions to build up the IRG's (now IG's) and their staffs.

Admittedly the White House tends to be ambivalent on State leadership. The Nixon regime has given little evidence of wishing it. And—as Mosher and Harr have reported at length—the Budget Bureau (part of the extended White House, at least) chose to fight one of the major leadership initiatives which came from State in the mid-1960's, the Foreign Affairs Programming System.[11] But if there is room for disagreement on how wholeheartedly the White House has wanted true State leadership, there is little doubt that the Department has not seized the leadership opportunities it has had.

Finally, there is a strong White House feeling that *State does not have control of its own house.* It was never clear to President Kennedy, said Sorensen, "who was in charge, who was clearly delegated to do what." A White House staff paper written in 1966 described State in particularly colorful prose: "The State Department is not an organization in the usual sense. It is a constellation of small power centers—some moving, some stand-

159

ing, some competing, some hiding, some growing, some decaying, a few coalescing, but more breaking apart into smaller fragments which soon develop all the organs and physiology of their parents."[12]

All of these problems reflect to some degree State's internal politics. This includes the competition and compromise required to resolve issues in-house before responding to the President, and the tendency to use its bargaining advantages—provision of analysis to the President, responsibility for handling diplomatic relations—to bend both Presidential decisions and ultimate implementation in State's preferred direction. More generally, however, State's pattern of behavior can be seen as the common bureaucratic one of shunning the opportunity for a large policy role for the security of a safer if smaller one.

For in many ways, the State Department is quite similar to other large governmental organizations which put their own functions and programs first and broad policy issues second. Like them, State has sought the security of a dominant role in a limited sphere rather than the chancier challenge of broad policy leadership. It has undertaken to secure a narrow though important piece of turf—"diplomacy," communications with Embassies, international "political" questions—and to "exclude" other agencies from this turf. It has shied away from broad, "inclusive" coordination of foreign affairs despite a fairly strong traditional and Presidential mandate.

In bureaucratic political battles, State officials could seek to depend primarily on one of two general "bargaining advantages." One is the prospect of Presidential support for a comprehensive policy role. The second comes from State's responsibility for "international relations"—communications with Embassies, negotiations, a network of relationships with foreign officials. Like domestic government bureaus that lean mainly on client groups, State has built on the second bargaining advantage, that arising from relations with Embassies and foreign countries. It has not built on the stronger but (at least in the short run) riskier reed of the Presidency. The Department's tactics in interdepartmental dealings have tended to be *defensive* and *protective*. Life is made easier by tacit nonaggression treaties—State steers clear of military tactics so the military will keep out of diplomacy.[b] State is remarkably unassertive even on programs like AID which have less capacity to fight back. State's token involvement in aid to India in the mid-sixties is notable, especially since the food crisis there involved strong Presidential interest and action, and strong U. S. pressure on the Indians.

But the problem is that any narrow area of foreign affairs ground is very hard to secure and protect from intruders. It is virtually impossible if the area that State seeks to make its heartland includes something that is potentially very broad—"international relations."And in any case foreign affairs issues—particularly the most difficult and important issues—tend inevitably to be interdepartmental.

Efforts to resolve these two problems can bring only limited success. "International relations" can be narrowly defined as "political" relations, whatever that may mean. If stress is put on "diplomacy" separated from "operations" that other agencies run anyway; if concern is focused on "political" (distinct from economic? military? development?) policies, and attention riveted to communicating with Embassies about these "political" problems, inter-agency conflict is reduced. And the States-

[b] Lest one think this was a particular feature of the Rusk-McNamara period, the Woodrow Wilson Foundation study group reported during the term of Dean Acheson that "the basic error of the State Department is its wholly unwarranted disposition to limit narrowly the area of its interests, especially where there is a question of possible conflict with the Department of Defense." (Elliott, *et al.*, *U. S. Foreign Policy*, p. 100.)

161

man can hold the comforting belief that his own business is primary, too important to be compromised by such activities as aid, information, etc.

To the extent that problems just aren't separable into jurisdictional categories, the ancient device of the bureaucratic compromise can be brought into play. Issues can be resolved by allowing each agency the dominant voice in areas of its interest or expertise. Opening or reopening of large issues can be avoided, since this threatens intra-governmental treaty arrangements.

But the more aggressive bureaucrats do not always reciprocate. The lure of foreign policy is strong in Washington, and State's self-denial about jumping into the spheres of others may not be returned in kind. So— to look fondly back at the sixties—the Joint Chiefs and the CIA make policy toward Cuba in 1961, Orville Freeman pressures the Indian government during the 1965 food crisis, and ISA is everywhere. State tends to end up with the worst of both worlds—neither the lead role nor a secure piece of turf.

But the crowning blow is that if State fails to exercise broad policy leadership, the President must have others who do. White House "interference" becomes inevitable, even in spheres State considers its private preserve. The pattern of behavior becomes, in sociological jargon, highly "dysfunctional," achieving neither the type of environment the Department as a whole tends to want nor the satisfaction of others (in and out of State) who wish a more comprehensive, more responsive overall State policy input.

But it is important to stress not only the ways State is consistent with a more general model of organizational behavior but also its uniqueness. Here it is notable how the "prevalent beliefs" cited by Scott in his analysis of the Foreign Service subculture tend to reinforce these tendencies toward insulation, glorification of traditional functions, and conflict avoidance. Three such beliefs are particularly relevant here:

> The only experience that is relevant to the activities of the Department of State is experience gained in the Foreign Service.
>
> The really important aspects of the foreign affairs of the United States are the political ones—the traditional ones of negotiation, representation, and reporting.
>
> Overseas operations of the kind conducted by DOD, AID, USIA, and CIA are peripheral to the main foreign policy task.

It all adds up, concludes Scott, to a system of widely-shared beliefs and behavioral norms which "satisfy short-term needs of the career service and individuals in it but which do not necessarily satisfy the long-term needs of the Department of State nor the requirements of American foreign policy."[13]

The President's view of State may be shaped by how effectively it responds to him and how well it deals with the bureaucratic and overseas environment. But individual FSO's, like members of any career system, tend to be judged and rewarded more on the basis of how well their behavior accords with the internal values of the subculture. The felt lack of an alternative employer and the circumstances of overseas life reinforce this loyalty and mutual dependence. It is but one step further to become more concerned with their status and position within the service than with what they can accomplish in relation to the world outside it. As one young officer who resigned put it, "The trouble with most FSO's is that they are too concerned about *being* something or *becoming* something—being a DCM or becoming an Ambassador—and not enough with *doing* anything."[14]

163

There are, of course, many FSO's who are interested in "doing something." But working against such tendencies are norms of personal behavior stressing accommodation rather than the open and aggressive facing of differences of interest and view. In a study based on three management conferences attended by 60 senior Foreign Service officers, Chris Argyris concludes that "the living system of the State Department in general, and of the Foreign Service in particular, is so constructed that it predisposes the State Department to managerial ineffectiveness. It contains norms that inhibit open confrontation of difficult issues and penalize people who take risks." This phenomenon led Scott to conclude: "As long as the norms of the subculture prescribe organizational accommodation rather than combat, and caution rather than venturesomeness, and as long as the ideology assumes that members of the subculture are doing a good job, it is vain to expect bold and innovative policy from the Department of State. [This would require] prolonged and disruptive debate . . . precisely the kind of disruptive behavior that the norms of the subculture are designed to eliminate."[15]

Another characteristic working against foreign affairs leadership is a strong traditional preference for service overseas. Stewart Alsop, a strong defender of the "elite" Foreign Service concept, is one of many who have noted that "almost all Foreign Service officers assigned to Washington can hardly wait to get abroad again."[16] It is worth noting that State's *Biographic Register* provides helpful information on particular officers' overseas backgrounds, but often only useless personnel-type descriptions—"int rel off," "for aff off"—for Washington tours. This reflects, in the view of one former White House staff official, a "fundamental misperception" of where the serious foreign policy business is carried out. This perception is changing, spurred by the fact that the majority of FSO's are now stationed at home for the first

time. But how fundamental the change has been is open
to question.

These handicaps in terms of Washington bureaucratic
effectiveness are exacerbated by certain effects of the
personnel system. A central one, seldom stated in this
exact form, is that the system tends to discourage officers
from being overly committed to outstanding performance in today's job. "Curiously," observe Mosher and
Harr, "in those career personnel systems where the lifetime commitment is strongest—the Foreign Service and
the military—the post commitment is likely to be the
weakest." Daniel Lazorchick points out that "a disap-
pointingly high number of [Foreign Service] officers" do
not "give their all" in Washington assignments, because
"the investment of time and effort brings too little in
return." The problem is not the oft-cited brevity of
tours—relatively few of the officials with whom they
deal most at the White House and Defense, for example,
hold their positions longer—but a promotion system
which rewards what is judged to be a satisfactory mix
of assignments more than spectacular performance in
any one of them.[17]

When there is added to this the fact that rapid upward mobility is virtually impossible[c]—mobility which
in other professional spheres is the reward for outstanding achievement—it is perhaps inevitable that the Department ended up with a system where, in Schlesinger's
words, "the risks always outweighed the opportunities."
A White House staff paper prepared in 1967 pungently
described the effects of "mid-career malaise."

[c] A recent task force of FSO's and other departmental officials reports
as follows: "Practically speaking, it is not possible, no matter how
brilliant one's performance, to acquire a significant degree of individual
responsibility, particularly in the area of policymaking and policy implementation, before the latter stages of a career. . . . These conditions
inevitably move the Foreign Service officer . . . to think twice before
taking possibly disquieting initiatives, to interpret his responsibilities
narrowly and to develop a defensive reflex against obtrusive outsiders."
(State, *Diplomacy for the Seventies*, p. 381.)

The Foreign Service looks upon the mid-career period as a time for the maturing and seasoning of officers who, in their early careers, have usually been exposed to several geographic areas and functional specialties. Professor Richard Neustadt sees it differently. He concludes from his observation of FSO's, in Washington and at overseas posts, that there is a 15-year gap between the time an FSO is "ready for power" and the time he attains sufficient rank to exercise power. On the average, this would be the period from age 35 or 40 to age 50 or 55. . . .

Neustadt's observation is self-evident to FSO's and has not been challenged, but his implicit assumption that FSO's, in general, seek power, as distinct from status, is open to some question. . . . But regardless of whether the FSO is waiting for power, or responsibility, or just a respectable amount of status, fifteen years is a long wait. It is a period during which most officers will make at least a small blot on their copy books. The trauma of a bad (or mediocre) efficiency report is ordinarily enough to impress upon the recipient the value of caution and patience. Mid-career officers come to appreciate that the use of the word "abrasive" once in an FSO's file can be enough to counteract repeated appearance of words like "creative" and "resourceful" . . . so the art of being unabrasive becomes a part of the FSO's stock in trade.[18]

By contrast, the effective White House staff officer finds it almost essential to be "abrasive" from time to time, to press particular questions very hard, to issue tough-minded challenges to the expertise of others, to write the sort of staff papers that draw issues in ways which "threaten" many officials' pet ideas and perhaps their reputations as well. Those who seek to make State

166

the center for foreign affairs leadership in the name of the President, then, must not only face the evidence that the Department is now strikingly "un-Presidential." They must also face the evidence that the Department's major personnel system tends to perpetuate a Foreign Service "subculture" which has its own disqualifying traits insofar as "Presidential" leadership is concerned: the internal, guild loyalties reinforced by a self-run promotion system, which inevitably compete with loyalty to the President; an overly narrow view of foreign policy; a value system prizing overseas service and downgrading Washington bureaucratic effectiveness; an assignment sequence which usually deprives men of responsibility while they can still grow in its exercise. To these can be added what Yarmolinsky (and many others) have characterized as "detachment from domestic realities," particularly national politics; and the shortage (cited by Yager and many others) "of good executives, well-trained economists, specialists in political-military affairs, and officers able to bridge the fields of foreign policy, science, and technology."[19] These characteristics constitute a formidable problem for those who would make State *the* central foreign affairs agency.

But they are not the whole story. For there have been several recent thrusts toward reform: the broad management innovation program initiated by Deputy Under Secretary William J. Crockett; the takeover of the American Foreign Service Association by a group of "Young Turks" with values markedly at variance with the traditional subculture; the recent efforts at "reform from within" being pressed by State's present top "administrative" official, Deputy Under Secretary William B. Macomber. This "new reform movement"—as we shall call it—has been an important and growing contestant for influence within State, and an assessment of both its accomplishments and its limitations is in order.

167

The New Reform Movement

The opening gun was sounded by the Herter Committee, a high-level study group sponsored by the Carnegie Endowment for International Peace and encouraged by Secretary Rusk. It sought ways to adapt foreign affairs personnel and management practices to what Kennedy men called the "new diplomacy." This "new diplomacy," said the Committee, was characterized by an "arsenal of instruments" which included not only "traditional diplomacy," but "international law; intelligence; political action; technical assistance and various types of foreign economic aid; military aid programs; informational and psychological programs; monetary policies; trade development programs; educational exchange; cultural programs; and, more recently, measures to counter insurgency movements." To employ these effectively, the foreign affairs government required action-oriented officials with "a high level of executive talent," a variety of "specialized competences," and a "zeal for creative accomplishment."[20]

Leaving aside its detailed personnel proposals and the advocacy of a "National Foreign Affairs College," the Committee made three basic recommendations. The first was the creation of "a new post of Executive Under Secretary of State," whose "primary responsibility should be to make sure that the resources of the Department of State and the other principal foreign affairs agencies are giving maximum support to the Secretary of State in his role as leader and coordinator." To aid him in performing this function, the Committee recommended establishment of a foreign affairs programming system "whereby foreign policy objectives are translated into programs of action to be undertaken in each area of foreign affairs activity." To "provide a rational personnel framework for the conduct of foreign affairs activities at home and abroad," the third basic proposal was that the personnel systems of State, AID, and USIA "should be organized and administered as a family of compatible systems reflecting substantial uniformity in personnel policies and coordinated personnel operations."[21]

These three proposals were to recur in future reform efforts. So would the Herter Committee's emphasis on State leadership and its tendency to define the leadership problem mainly as a need for better "management." The Secretary and other top departmental officials made no major effort to carry out these reforms, or even to deal in any systematic way with the problems which they highlighted. But a serious effort was undertaken by William J. Crockett, who in June 1963 was appointed Deputy Under Secretary of State for Administration, the department's fifth-ranking post. Moreover, the Crockett effort went well beyond the Herter Committee proposals.

Crockett saw his mandate as much broader than had most previous occupants of his office; indeed, he may have modeled his performance at least partly on the Executive Under Secretary which Herter recommended but Rusk did not establish. Testifying before the Jackson Subcommittee in November 1963, he spoke rather frankly about the leadership challenge. Though he assured the group that "the Department is now on top of the job thrust upon it 2½ years ago" by President Kennedy, he admitted that "we have not yet found satisfactory methods of delegating the Secretary's coordinating responsibilities to officials farther down the chain of command." He pointed to the resistance to the exercise of leadership within State: "There has to be an attitude on the part of people, particularly State Department people, that we are not just part of a narrow bureaucracy, that the problems are not just State Department problems. Our attitude has to be that our problems, our interests are as broad as the whole field of foreign pol-

169

icy." And he recognized also the natural resistance of other departments: ". . . leadership, carried to its logical conclusion, means interference. It certainly is not often well received by other agencies."[22]

But State had traditionally separated "substance" and "administration," and Crockett's official sphere was the latter. Also, though the Secretary gave him considerable freedom of action, Rusk remained generally uninvolved and therefore uncommitted to Crockett's initiatives. So, given his restricted mandate, these necessarily were pilot efforts which sought to infiltrate new ideas and hope they could be made to catch on. They were not general reforms initiated on top-level authority.

Crockett's most important effort was the Comprehensive Country Programming System (CCPS), later revised and renamed the Foreign Affairs Programming System (FAPS). CCPS was an inter-agency system in which an Ambassador and other U.S. officials at his post worked to develop an individual "country program" which related budget and other resources to foreign policy objectives across agency lines. This was, in turn, reviewed in Washington, with the aim of having the final decisions reflected in the budgets of the agencies concerned. This effort, staffed mainly by men brought in from outside the Department and by some younger FSO's, had been expanded to include 30 overseas missions by 1965.

Other Crockett change efforts included establishment of the Center for International Systems Research (CISR) to stimulate and support innovative research and analysis, and the Action for Organizational Development (ACORD) program, which sought to promote organizational change. The latter employed methods such as "T-Group" sessions to increase individual self-knowledge and understanding of State's "living system." The aim of a broader Foreign Service personnel system was pursued through the Hays Bill providing for incorporation of State, USIA, and AID civil service employees. Other reforms were undertaken in information management, communications, and manpower planning.

Yet almost all of Crockett's efforts were on the defensive by the time he left the Department in January 1967, and CISR, FAPS, and ACORD were abolished one by one by his successor. Given the opposition of FSO's and the noninvolvement of top officials, what was remarkable is that he got as far as he did. As Harr has pointed out, "Crockett and others attempted to devise a management strategy for something that did not exist—management." A serious programming system, for example, meant "interference" in other agency budgets and thus inevitable resistance; only with strong commitment on the part of top leadership could anyone hope to put it across. As it was, the death blow was administered when the Budget Bureau pressed forward with an agency-by-agency programming system which undercut State's fledgling effort.[23]

Just as the Crockett reforms were losing their momentum, two new steps were taken to strengthen State's cross-governmental leadership, these with somewhat stronger top-level State interest. The SIG/IRG interdepartmental committee system established in March 1966 grew out of an initiative by General Maxwell Taylor, but with the active assistance of the then Deputy Under Secretary of State (for Political Affairs) U. Alexis Johnson. At the same time, State announced the establishment of the new position of "Country Director," an official who was to "serve as the single focus of responsibility for leadership and coordination of departmental and interdepartmental activities" for a particular country or group of countries. More than two years before, Secretary Rusk had told the Jackson Subcommittee that "inside of the Department our principal problem is layering," and that "one of the ways" to do something about it would be "to upgrade the desk officer." This

171

goal was sought by enhancing his title and eliminating the position of "Office Director," which had served as a "layer" between the country man and his regional Assistant Secretary.[24]

Both of these reforms provided an opening for those in State who wished to go after a broader interdepartmental role. But neither had very great overall impact. The AFSA report reflected a widespread view of the SIG/IRG reform in saying: "It was a wise decision. It has not been made truly effective." Few could avoid a similar judgment of country directors. Said Joseph Yager in the IDA report, "Unfortunately, this promising concept has not been fully realized, and few country directors have performed the role envisioned for them. Most are desk officers with a new title."[25]

The reasons for disappointment were several. In many cases neither the country nor the regional Assistant Secretary level was a logical one for considering major interdepartmental problems. The "Country Director" had no natural counterpart in some agencies, and Assistant Secretaries could resolve little regarding European affairs or Vietnam given the extent of White House and State Seventh Floor involvement. Another obvious problem was that FSO's had traditionally construed their roles much more narrowly than this, and formal changes alone could hardly alter a pattern which the system had nurtured for years. But as Yager remarks about the country director system, "Some blame" must "be attributed to the failure of those higher in the chain of command to adjust their own ways of doing business." And the point applies to the SIG/IRG system as well. Just as, in Yager's words, "A country director whose superiors treat him like a junior desk officer cannot easily deal with relatively senior officials in other agencies," so also an Under Secretary cannot make others take a SIG seriously unless it is evident that his boss does and treats it as possessing delegated authority for him. Rusk

172

did not, nor did President Johnson. One critic likened it to the Indian rope trick—you climb up and up with your problem and finally both you and the problem disappear.[26]

So though the SIG/IRG-Country Director package had different origins than the Crockett reforms, it suffered a strikingly similar malady—a combination of non-enthusiasm and/or tacit opposition in the career ranks and a lack of a serious push by the policy leadership. Given this situation, those in the middle who sought to make the reforms effective could accomplish something on an *ad hoc* basis, but no comprehensive or enduring changes in the system resulted.

But in 1967 the new reform movement received another boost from a hitherto unlikely source—the American Foreign Service Association. Considerable discontent had grown over career prospects among junior and mid-career officers, ranging from salaries and promotion rates to the unchallenging jobs many officers occupied and the unimpressive leadership State was exercising in interdepartmental matters. Led by 31-year-old Lannon Walker, and campaigning under the slogan, *"Un Peu de Zèle,"* the discontented organized themselves into a sort of political party and won what had previously been a *pro forma* election for the key AFSA offices. The same general group repeated their triumph in early 1970.

In several respects the "Young Turks," as they were inevitably named, represent a marked departure from the subculture we have earlier described. They are attracted rather than repelled by the "new diplomacy," and have placed heavy blame on the Department and its officer corps for failing to adapt to a changing world. They are certainly still "careerist" in the sense of pursuing what they see as the interests of the Foreign Service. But they construe these interests not as the preservation of the purity of a narrow, elite "calling," but as a much enhanced responsiveness and "openness" to the broad

173

issues and changes which affect the conduct of foreign affairs.

In 1968, AFSA released a report by its "Committee on Career Principles" headed by Ambassador Graham Martin, entitled *Toward A Modern Diplomacy*. As the title of the first chapter—"The Foreign Service of the United States: Whatever Became of It?"—implied, the report was centered on strengthening the broad foreign policy role of the career service, and only secondarily on the management of foreign policy from the vantage point of the Administration.[d] It supported such traditional objectives as "restoration of the statutory independence of the Board of the Foreign Service." Its major organizational recommendations—a Permanent Under Secretary of State, strengthening of SIG/IRG system, upgrading of the principal Under Secretary, better staff support for top officials, broadening of the Foreign Service to include AID and other agency personnel— were generally replications of those in earlier reports by other groups. And the level of analysis in the report was quite uneven. After a perceptive discussion, for example, of "the nature of American bureaucracy" as encouraging other agency officials to be responsive mainly to their own line superiors, it reached the remarkable conclusion that "only one major action would be necessary" to alleviate this problem, the bringing of USIA within the formal structure of the Department of State "as an autonomous unit." AID was already in a similar position,

[d] This is true despite such assertions as: "We believed it necessary to start with the role of the new President." (*Modern Diplomacy*, p. 19.) Lannon Walker's *Foreign Affairs* article, "Our Foreign Affairs Machinery," places greater emphasis on the Secretary of State's management problem. In fact, the Walker article is in some respects a better representation of AFSA views than the report, which reflected in considerable measure the personal predilections of Ambassador Martin. But if the lines of argument differed somewhat, the basic recommendations of the two were the same.

174

yet had proved markedly less amenable to State policy guidance than USIA had from the "outside."[27]

But the report's defects were outshone by its virtues. It was, for one thing, a lively document which despite its production "in committee" did not hesitate to make outspoken judgments and interpretations. But more important, it was evidence for the first time of strong Foreign Service support for significant reforms. Its endorsement of the leadership role, of the idea of a broad service with broad perspectives and responsibilities, and of the SIG/IRG system—all these were encouraging. And while the main report said little about the Crockett-type management innovations, its tone was at least tolerant and open-minded toward them. It recommended that "the new Administration investigate thoroughly the applicability of new technology to the problems of foreign affairs," and its Subcommittee on Organization and Leadership showed strong interest in the possibilities of PPBS.[28]

Earlier reforms had died from disinterest among both career officials and top departmental leadership. Seeking to turn this situation around, AFSA's leaders talked to many potential "Secretaries of State" just after the 1968 election. But William P. Rogers was not on their list. And Nixon's clear decision to build a White House-centered foreign policy system was a major blow, as was the contrast between the immediate flow of initiatives from the quickly assembled Kissinger staff and the slow start of State's new leaders. The major ambition of the Young Turks, to bring State and the Foreign Service into the center of foreign policy-making and management, had to be indefinitely postponed.

But there did develop, in the early Nixon Administration, a significant reform commitment on the part of certain high State officials. If Secretary Rogers followed the example of his predecessors in being relatively in-

175

different to organizational matters, his first deputy, Elliot Richardson, took an interest, and Richardson's central position in both departmental and interdepartmental matters suggested that this interest could be
quite productive. In May 1969 he assumed the chairmanship of a revamped Board of the Foreign Service,
the first man of his rank to hold this position. On July
3rd of the same year he announced the formation of the
Planning and Coordination Staff (S/PC) to improve
staff support of the principal Seventh Floor officials and
strengthen State's contributions to the NSC system.[e] And
on January 14, 1970, Deputy Under Secretary Macomber
announced the appointment of thirteen task forces composed of departmental employees to study and make
recommendations on a wide range of personnel and
management problems.[f]

Macomber's strategy was to capitalize on reform interest in the career ranks, and to avoid Crockett's problem of having his innovations identified with externally
recruited "management types" rather than professional
diplomats. 250 career officials were recruited to serve on
the task forces, submitting their draft reports in June
1970. They were published after modest, non-substan-
tive editing the following December under the title,
Diplomacy for the Seventies, together with a thirty-page
summary. At the same time, Macomber's office released
a list of 505 separate recommendations contained in the

[e] The experience of the Planning and Coordination Staff is discussed
at some length in Chapter Eight.

[f] The subjects covered by the 13 task forces were: (1) Career Management and Assignment Policies under Functional Specialization; (2)
Performance Evaluation and Promotion Policies; (3) Personnel Requirements and Resources; (4) Personnel Training; (5) Personnel Requisites:
Non-Salary Compensations and Allowances; (6) Recruitment and Em-
ployment; (7) Stimulation of Creativity; (8) Role of the Country Director; (9) Openness in the Foreign Affairs Community; (10) Reorganization of the Foreign Service Institute; (11) Roles and Functions of Diplomatic Missions; (12) Management Evaluation Systems; (13) Management Tools.

reports, and the Department's tentative action plans on each. Somewhat over half were approved for implementation. Most of the rest were tabbed for further study and decision within 90 or 180 days.[29]

In general, the reports showed refreshing candor in admitting past departmental and Foreign Service inadequacies. Macomber's speech announcing the reform program had already recognized State's post-war difficulties: "Our problems started in the years immediately following World War II, years of enormous creativity on the American foreign policy scene, with the development of new instrumentalities such as USIA, Foreign Aid, and CIA. Unfortunately, when faced with these developments, the instinct of the traditional foreign policy establishment was to protect its exclusiveness and high standards."[30]

And if some of the summary report's language suggested that the arts of diplomatic understatement and bureaucratic positive thinking were far from dead,[g] some of the task forces were quite blunt in their self-analysis. One found that, "With the exception of an active period at the end of the forties, the Department and Foreign Service have languished as creative organs, busily and even happily chewing the cud of daily routine while other departments, Defense, CIA, the White House staff, made more important innovative contributions to foreign policy." Another reported, "The Department of State moves into the 1970's with attitudes toward personnel training that ring of the 19th century." A third observed that "Psychologically, the Foreign Service officer is a permanent transient; his home is his profession. . . . These conditions of the profession en-

[g] The report conceded that "in spite of outstanding achievements by individual officers at all levels, the Department as an organization has sometimes been disappointing in its performance" of the coordinating role (p. 4), but assured readers that, "by any standards, the Department is very good indeed." (State, *Diplomacy for the Seventies*, p. 2.)

gender a clan mentality, a sense of detachment from the physical environment of the moment and from the community of ordinary Americans as a whole. Clannishness can result in a 'don't rock the boat' attitude as well as a career protectiveness against outsiders and new ideas."[31]

The reports make strong recommendations to increase the "openness" of the Department and Service to outside influences, to encourage increased creativity and policy debate within the Department, and to strengthen State's ability to exercise cross-governmental foreign affairs leadership. Their overriding theme, however, is the characterization of State's basic problem as "management." Macomber had signaled this emphasis by attributing past weaknesses to the fact that "management has not been our bag." The summary report found that the "principal cause" of the Department's failings in inter-agency coordination was "its weakness in the area of management capability."

> Because of the diversity and complexity of our overseas activities, effective coordination calls for a wide range of management skills and management tools. The traditional reliance of Foreign Service officers on experience and intuition is no longer good enough. The diplomacy of the seventies requires a new breed of diplomat-manager, just as able as the best of the old school, but equipped with up-to-date techniques and backed by a Department organized on modern management principles.[32]

Seven of the task forces focused on how to recruit, train, develop, and promote career officials so as to develop more of this "new breed," and encourage their rise to the top.[h] Two more investigated, respectively, the

[h] One major concern of the personnel task forces was the implementation of Macomber's earlier proposal to restructure the career recruitment, assignment, and promotion system around four functional "cones"—political, economic/commercial, administrative, and consular

general problems of "creativity" and "openness," while one concerned itself with the role of diplomatic missions. The remaining three addressed questions of Washington organization and management of current policy issues. But two of these in turn were relatively specialized, one concentrating on the role of country directors and another on development of a "management evaluation system." It was left to Task Force XIII to deal with the Department's overall role in United States government foreign policy-making, and to consider what "management tools" could be applied to make it more effective.

Task Force XIII's report divides the Department's role into four basic functions: decision-making, managing of its own resources, cross-governmental foreign policy leadership, and communication with Congress and the public. Its general theme, however, is the need to "interlock" the Department's processes for dealing with the first two, and thereby strengthen its effectiveness across the board. The "principal recommendation" is that "the Department devise and base its activities on a system which identifies U.S. interests, estimates foreign interests and environmental trends, matches U.S. strategies to the identified threats to the preservation of U.S. interests and opportunities for their advancement, and selects and costs preferred and alternative objectives and courses of action."[33]

This "Policy Analysis and Resource Allocation" (PARA) system is to be coordinated by a "seventh floor staff capability" developed specifically for this purpose, and by "a similar staff capability with the equivalent mission" at the regional level. Both are to be linked to the State-chaired NSC committees—the regional Inter-

---

—and to create a new career corps of Foreign Affairs Specialists. The Macomber program has also sought to balance the somewhat conflicting goals of maintaining intra-service competition yet providing greater career security for FSO's. This problem is discussed further in Chapter Nine.

departmental Groups (IG's) and the Under Secretaries Committee (USC)—so that the overall system can be "integrated into the various planning and program budgeting cycles of the other agencies." Finally, the "principal officers of the Department (Under Secretaries and Deputy Under Secretaries) . . . together with necessary staffs should be incorporated into a Strategic Management Center immediately available to the Secretary of State." Similar "Bureau Management Centers" would be established at the regional level. Both would "bring responsibility for policy analysis and decisionmaking, on the one hand, and resource allocation, on the other, under unified control, thus ending the present separation between policy formulation and resource management." The target here, of course, is the old "substance-administration dichotomy," under which the best FSO's ignored management problems, the "administrators" defined them narrowly so as to keep them within their limited mandate, and the Department continued as an "anti-organization."[34]

In basing so much on the PARA system, the report seems to have overreacted to the "intuitive" Foreign Service approach of the past and placed too much faith in man's ability to "rationalize" the foreign policy process. The notion of a top-level "Strategic Management Center," however, has considerable appeal, particularly to those who feel that improved responsiveness to Presidents is a prerequisite to an enhanced State role. The task forces say little directly about State-White House relations, though Task Force XIII recognizes that "the effectiveness of the Department's role in foreign affairs must ultimately be judged in terms of its responsiveness to the needs of the political leadership, principally those of the President."[35] But a strengthened State Department Seventh Floor, working systematically to play a comprehensive foreign policy role, would almost inevitably serve the President better than State has served him in the past.

Yet the report's description of the proposed Center does not go beyond broad generalities. It is notably unspecific on what creating such a Center might mean in terms of modifying, merging, maintaining, or eliminating the various existing Seventh Floor staff units. Particularly remarkable is the lack of reference to the Executive Secretariat (S/S), which now serves as the Department's major operational coordination arm and provides daily staff support to the Secretary. Any effort to restructure the Seventh Floor requires careful attention to the Secretariat's present and potential role. Yet S/S is mentioned but twice, and rather peripherally, in the report of Task Force XIII; and only three times— also peripheral—in the 160 recommendations dealing specifically with departmental management.[36/i]

It might have been counter-productive, of course, for the Task Force to make detailed recommendations on Seventh Floor restructuring without the close collaboration of those top officials who would have to both approve and use the new arrangements. But this points up a broader problem with the entire "reform from within" approach. In order to maximize creativity and minimize

[i] On July 6, 1971, Macomber issued a Management Reform Bulletin (No. 24) dealing explicitly with the Seventh Floor. It announced the establishment of a "Senior Management Team," described as "in concept the equivalent of the 'Strategic Management Center' recommended by Task Force XIII." "The integration of the principal management functions of the Department (personnel and budget) into the management team" is to be accomplished by strengthening the role of the principal Under Secretary and making him "responsible for the overall management of the Department's processes of planning, evaluation, and resource allocation." Little is said about the Secretariat except that it (like the Planning and Coordination Staff) will henceforth serve all five of the department's top officials. Previously it served mainly the top three.

How and whether these changes will affect actual Seventh Floor (and Departmental) operations only time will tell.

vested interests, task forces were not generally composed of people with direct, present responsibility for the specific problems they investigated.[j] But while this tactic seems to have been successful in getting task force members to think in terms of the Department as a whole, it meant that the completed reports faced the same obstacle as do studies by outside groups or consultants—the need to win the commitment of those in the Department with specific responsibility for the operations to be affected. It is hardly surprising that implementation has proceeded much faster on the personnel management side—which is within Macomber's recognized general sphere of responsibility—than on the questions of departmental organization and procedures which intimately involve his superiors.[k]

The lack of specifics on Seventh Floor procedures and staff roles meant that Task Force XIII's recommendations could be only a conceptual beginning for creating anything like a top-level Strategic Management Center. And the sporadic involvement of the four departmental

[j] An exception to this rule was the task force on country directors, a number of whose members held that position. Not surprisingly, it concluded that "the country director must more and more serve as a focal point, providing leadership and insuring coordination of bilateral relationships throughout the U.S. Government." (State, *Diplomacy for the Seventies*, p. 342.)

[k] Over 70 per cent of the 345 "Recommendations on Personnel" were listed by the Department in December 1970 as "approved for implementation," compared to under 25 per cent of the 160 "Recommendations on Management." (*Department of State Newsletter*, January 1971, pp. 20-43.) And none of the first ten "management reform bulletins" issued by Macomber's office to report implementation steps dealt with organizational structure or procedures affecting policymaking. The subjects they covered were: (1) general; (2) recruitment; (3) entrance examinations; (4) lateral entry; (5) centralization of personnel programs; (6) allowances; (7) security practices and dissent; (8) a new personnel system for specialists; (9) encouragement of dissent at field missions; and (10) information management. The eleventh bulletin reported implementation of certain organizational recommendations by the Bureau of African Affairs, which stressed that in its case "the proposed reforms could be implemented with relatively minor organizational realignment."

officials senior to Macomber meant not only that task force proposals affecting the Seventh Floor had a long road to travel before they could bring about effective change. It also signaled to regional Assistant Secretaries that they need not go beyond token implementation of policy-related staffing and procedural recommendations affecting them, and as of mid-1971 they had not. For despite the considerable effort and creativity which officials in the ranks have devoted to the process, the Macomber program in no way reflects a commitment of top-level executive energy remotely approaching the McNamara reform effort in Defense. Secretary Rogers has enthusiastically backed the effort but stayed out of its substance, and the departure of Under Secretary Richardson has taken away most of the effective interest in such questions above the Macomber level.

Because of both the sensitivity of the issues involved and the constraints imposed by prior White House decisions, the reports could deal only indirectly with the critical determining question of State's relationship to the President. Similarly, White House interest in the reform program seems limited to the belief that it won't change very much. Fulbright's skeptical 1970 comment remains apt: "I have been convinced for some time, and am still convinced, that the problems of the Department of State and the Foreign Service cannot be solved exclusively from within, in part because many of the problems stem not from within the Department but from other departments and agencies over which State has no control."[37]

For all the efforts of the "new reform movement"—with its encouraging emphasis on foreign policy leadership, on innovation, on "management"—have remained some distance from the center of the bureaucratic political system in which foreign policy is made. They have drawn support from groups and places that have often been resistant to change, and this is a major gain. But

183

they seem likely to have more impact on the way State handles those matters clearly within its departmental purview than on its role in the broader system, though the two are by no means unrelated.

One problem, ironically, may be that the very stress on "management," such a forward step in so many ways, tends to obscure the dependence of anything initiated "from within" State on how the broader political system for making foreign policy is operating. There are many advantages, of course, to treating organizational problems as "management" questions. By no means the least is that "management" is uncontroversial, favored by most forward-looking people, whereas "effectiveness in bureaucratic politics" still has serious invidious connotations or is threatening to competitors. And by comparison with both the traditional values of the Foreign Service subculture and the overemphasis on formal structure which has plagued reorganizers, seeing problems in terms of management is a major advance.

It is a sharp break from the policy-operations dichotomy, and from the old "passive" diplomatic role of observing and reporting. Instead, it sees State's central role, and that of its key officers, as "running things." With this emphasis it also parts company with the substance-administration dichotomy within the Department, since the range of resources and "administrative" devices become tools which the "manager" must use to "run" his Embassy or his area of policy and program responsibility. The focus on mobilizing people and resources to achieve particular objectives, in fact, makes "management" a close relative of the political art of "leadership."

In the State context, "management" also means a broadening of concerns, in terms of the range of substantive activities State officials feel responsible for, in terms of the new technology and "tools" which a management orientation naturally leads men to seek. It also means attention to long-neglected problems—like for-

184

eign affairs personnel planning and career development
—to reshape a system which has led to gross overpopulation of the senior ranks, and to demoralization of both
senior officers who find rank does not bring responsibility
and juniors who despair of attaining either.
Finally, a "management" approach sees organizational
devices and formal procedures not as ends in themselves
but as "management tools." This comes quite close to a
bureaucratic political strategy which seeks to use formal
structures and processes as devices to strengthen the
bargaining advantages of major officials and their en-
tourages.

Yet if the "management" framework for considering
the problems of foreign policy-making and action can
get us a long way, it cannot get us far enough. There is
logic to Harr's argument, for example, that "a comprehensive managerial strategy will be required . . . to
change the Foreign Service system so that it will fulfill
the requirements of the new diplomacy and to change
the Department of State so that it will fulfill its management role in foreign affairs." Certainly it is wrong,
as he points out, either to dissipate change efforts "on
details or piecemeal reforms," or to believe that "the
challenge can be met by a single stroke."[38] But the strategy he advocates ends up looking not all that different
from the sort of "scientific," "businesslike" administration that Woodrow Wilson thought possible if only it
could be freed from "politics."

There is, for example, the movement from the conviction that more systematic management is urgent to
the notably apolitical concept that what is needed is a
"sustaining manager,"[l] an "Executive" or "Permanent"
Under Secretary of State, an individual whose main task

---

[l] The phrase, "sustaining manager," is from Harr, who suggests that
he could be either the present Under Secretary or a new Number Three
man. (*Professional Diplomat*, pp. 334-6.) Similarly, Smith Simpson
urges a "general manager." (*Anatomy of the State Department*, pp.
246 ff.)

185

will be to perform this job. The concept owes much to the "Permanent Secretary" who is the top career official in British Cabinet Ministries.

The recommendation derives from three undeniable conditions—a "management" function that is not now being performed, the need for it to be performed, and the evidence of the past that, in the Herter Committee's words, neither the Secretary nor his principal deputy "can give continuous attention to the management of programs and activities of the Department of State and to their coordination with the programs of other Government agencies engaged in foreign affairs."[39] In fact, the Macomber experience adds further fuel to this argument, since the lack of effective interest above the Department's fifth-ranking man is probably its major weakness. But the conclusion drawn—that the problem can be resolved by creating a new "No. 3" official and giving him the responsibility—follows logically only if one buys the assumption that formal structure is *the* major influence on how things get done. If one assumes instead a bureaucratic political system of decision-making, one must ask further questions—what will this man's relationship be to the Secretary? How will he develop the "bargaining advantages" sufficient to allow him to prevail in bureaucratic combat with those inside and outside State that he seeks to "coordinate"?

These questions are either evaded entirely or discussed only tangentially by the advocates of this proposal. Yet they are absolutely critical. Other officials seeking for their own good reasons to erode or undercut this Number Three man's authority would appeal or go directly to the Secretary. They would do this not just on unambiguous "management" issues, but on questions with strong policy implications, on which they themselves had strong claims to Secretarial support. Far from having this man lighten his load as the proposal implies, the Secretary would feel a lot more heat, and would frequently be called on to support the man and argue before the President in his behalf. This would be especially true if his role went beyond the "State family" (State, AID, and USIA) to include the activities of Defense and CIA, as it would have to to have really broad impact. Unless the Secretary were intimately attuned to such a "manager's" work, moreover, he might well seek to cut him down to size rather than build him up, seeing him as a threat to his own authority, since the "manager" would have a sharply different perspective yet a mandate to "run the Department."

An unusually apt illustration of the fallacy underlying the proposal appears in the Mosher-Harr case study of the State country programming enterprise. Newly appointed Under Secretary Katzenbach sought to recruit Thomas Schelling of Harvard in 1967 to develop an effective foreign affairs programming system and make the SIG/IRG machinery work. Schelling at first agreed, but later reconsidered, apparently seeing the obstacles to success as greater than could be overcome in the time he could commit to the job. Also, write Mosher and Harr, ". . . as the spring weeks passed, it appeared that Katzenbach and Schelling came to view the job in different ways. For Katzenbach, it would make possible the delegation to an able and reliable person of responsibilities in which he (Katzenbach) had less than primary interest, so that he could deal with more important things. For Schelling, success in his prospective role would require a very close relationship with the Under Secretary and progressively greater involvement of Katzenbach in interagency decisionmaking, using SIG and the products of systems analysis."[40]

Schelling recognized that if "management" were to be serious, it had to help shape major substantive policy decisions, that a serious inter-agency coordination and programming system could not be separated from Katzenbach's personal job but had to be an integral part of it.

187

He may well have gone further and concluded that the Under Secretary needed the strong support of the President and the support, interest, and involvement of the Secretary of State if his office was to become a center of strength of the kind sought. And the evidence, in fact, is that Katzenbach did not have such support. President Johnson reputedly told the Under Secretary when the latter sought his backing on a matter critical to making a go of the SIG—"That is the kind of problem I pay *you* to handle."

For ultimately "management" can be more important than "administration"—in the traditional, narrow State sense of that word—only to the extent that it shapes "substance." A "management system" can have comprehensive impact only if it shapes the way the most important issues are decided, in other words the way top officials deal with them and the considerations they make paramount. For this to happen, given the inevitable tendency of bosses to want and need to handle particular issues in their own ways, "management" cannot be a function or activity delegated or set apart from the President and the Secretary of State—management must *be* the President and the Secretary. This hardly means that they have to do everything themselves. And there can be—in fact there urgently needs to be—a team of top officials working intimately with the Secretary, one of whom might specialize in "management systems." But the top man and his team have to set the management priorities just as they do the policy priorities, just as McNamara and his band did at Defense. Otherwise they will have no involvement in them, no stake in them, no reason not to overrule and thereby undercut the "manager" on issues that rise to their level. In this case, a "sustaining manager" might carry out a number of useful programs and activities insulated from the pressure of day-to-day decision-making, but his role would be no broader than that of the present Deputy Under Secretary for Administration.[m]

The Macomber reports do not propose a sustaining manager. Task Force XIII, in fact, put the problem perfectly in urging "that the principal management functions of the Deputy Under Secretary of State for Administration be an integral part of the Department's top decisionmaking center," and recommended four alternative "organizational arrangements which could accomplish this."[41] But if taken as the basis for an organizational strategy to enhance State's overall foreign policy role, Task Force XIII's "principal recommendation" may be even more politically unrealistic. For as discussed further in Chapter Seven, it is most unlikely that a formal "Policy Analysis and Resource Allocation" system can be of more than modest aid to top State officials in their efforts to influence specific decisions, no matter how careful its conception or how high-level its sponsorship. All of the limitations on the application of general decisions to daily cases apply here, as do the limits on the role of analysis in the bureaucratic political process of foreign policy-making.

The implications are somewhat sobering. Only top officials can "manage" foreign policy-making and a foreign policy-making organization. But do they want to? Secretaries of State have not. They will probably continue to see "management" as relatively low priority until they recognize that it can pay them dividends in strengthening the roles they do consider important, such

---

[m] Harr recognizes certain "political" problems related to the proposal, suggesting that "the *cost* of the absence of this role [of sustaining manager] is *not* fully seen by the White House" and "by the political leadership of the State Department." He also recognizes that such a manager would need the "full understanding and unflinching support" of the Secretary. But he still seems to see "management" as an activity relatively distinct from the Secretary's personal role. (*Professional Diplomat*, pp. 334-6.)

as advising the President. That it can pay such dividends seems a reasonable supposition. But to focus it in this direction will require rather a different emphasis from that which "management" advocates have thus far provided: away from separating the job from the Secretary but still somehow partaking of his authority, and toward involving him; away from the problems that seem urgent to them but secondary to the Secretary where he sits; away from the implicit aim—present, it appears, in the work of Harr and Scott—of building a rational organization and a rational foreign-policy-making system, and toward supporting the Secretary in the kitchen where he feels the heat. There are costs to this approach, in terms of the ideals of good management which men do well to keep well toward the front of their minds. But the cost of separation from the political leadership is irrelevance in the things that count. Such management as is sought may simply not be possible in the rather untidy political world of foreign policy decision-making. But it certainly cannot be achieved by the "short-cut" of a new separation of administration from politics, however pressing the need for better management may seem.

The need to relate management tools to the politics of decision-making does not, however, mean that they might not be highly useful under the right circumstances. The problem, rather, becomes one of determining just what these circumstances may be. To that end, Chapter Seven investigates four different formal management approaches which have been tried in State and elsewhere in the foreign affairs government. Chapter Eight then considers the problem of building effective staff support for the Secretary of State and other key foreign policy officials.

CHAPTER SEVEN

Formal Approaches to Coherent Foreign Policy

ONE of the lessons of Chapter Five was the limited effectiveness of a system where only one official can speak for the President. One of the lessons of Chapter Six was the limited utility of a State Department reform effort attuned neither to Presidential nor Secretarial priorities. Together they reinforce the conclusion that bureaucratic actions—whether on policy or internal reform—will promote Presidentially-based policy coherence only to the extent that men possessing his confidence, attuned to his perspective, can influence them.

Yet at best only a modest number of men will be able to speak or act for the President. And the foreign affairs government will be taking far too many daily actions for this small group personally to affect. Rusk told the Jackson Subcommittee in 1963 that he saw "20 or 30" of the 1,300 incoming State cables each day, and "perhaps 6" of the 1,000 outgoing ones. Rogers apparently sees no more. Assistant Secretaries are responsible for reading and approving a larger number of messages. Yet even were they in close communication with the President—and those in the present Administration generally are not—they could hardly hope even to *know* the details of all important U.S. actions in their regions, much less influence specific decisions on them.[1]

Ways are required, then, to stretch the influence of the President and his men. One need is for organizational devices to make lower-level decisions more likely to reflect higher-level purposes. Another is for means to force important issues up for consideration by the men at the top. And when such issues are brought to them, top officials also need information and analysis designed

191

to help them clarify their choices and make decisions that can have practical effect.

One useful device for meeting part of this problem is Nixon's national security studies system, described in Chapter Five. Another thing top officials can do is to build substantive staffs to supply them information and analysis, and fight bureaucratic battles for them on particular issues. This will be the subject of Chapter Eight. There are also, however, at least four other relatively formal steps government leaders can take to affect the broad system in which lower-level decisions are taken. One is *organizational integration,* bringing different foreign affairs programs and functions into the same line organization, with the hope that subordinate officials in the new, "integrated" organization will have to be responsive to a range of problems and pressures approximating that of top-level officials. A second is to provide *comprehensive formal policy guidance* in writing. A third is to sponsor the development of *programming systems* which seek to relate resource uses to specific policy objectives on a government-wide basis. And the fourth is to establish *general, fixed-membership coordinating committees* to provide focal points for decision on interdepartmental issues.

1. *Organizational Integration*

With the post-war proliferation of overseas programs, one recurrent proposal to improve overall coherence has been to place more activities under the formal authority of the Department of State. McCamy has proposed that all non-military foreign affairs government units be brought into State, including the international offices of Treasury, Agriculture, Commerce, and Labor.[2] More frequently, debate centers around the more limited question of whether aid and information/propaganda programs should be inside or outside the Department.

The McCamy proposal is both unrealistic and un-

192

desirable. Domestic departments did not establish their own "foreign offices" just because they yearned to get into the overseas action. These arose more because of the close relationship between the departments' major domestic responsibilities and constituencies and major U. S. international objectives. The food aid program, for example, requires not just negotiation of agreements with recipient countries. It also requires crop production targets which assure that our grain will be available in needed amounts; expertise in such matters as commodity markets and grain transportation and storage; and the general support and cooperation of agricultural interest groups.

AID and USIA do not have this type of justification for independent existence. But the importance of whether they are formally in or out of State is open to debate. In the sixties AID was inside and USIA outside, but the latter was considerably more responsive to State foreign policy influence.

If integration is carried further, however, it can have a serious impact. AID as a whole is included in State as a "semi-autonomous" agency. But its Latin America bureau has been merged with State's Bureau of Inter-American Affairs, so that one man holds the joint position of Assistant Secretary of State for Inter-American Affairs and head of the regional aid program, and the formerly separate State and AID country desks have been merged under common Country Directors. And there have been proposals to extend such integration to other regions where we have aid programs.

For those whose aim is increased foreign policy coherence, the arguments for this type of arrangement are considerable. State-AID integration for Latin America, for example, tends to push a broad foreign policy perspective down into State's line organization. Assistant Secretaries and Country Directors are made personally responsible for both "State" and "AID" activities in their areas and are put under pressure to relate one to the other and both to broad policy objectives. A second reason for such integration is that it recognizes the interdependence of aid and diplomatic relations. Aid can be a source of U. S. leverage on other issues; conversely, general U. S. diplomatic pressure may be necessary to convince a country to adopt those major internal policy reforms on which development often depends. Third, integration can provide a very important bargaining advantage—official line authority over aid—to Assistant Secretaries and Country Directors who have general foreign policy coordination responsibilities. Fourth, it gives Foreign Service officers an opportunity both to broaden their experience and develop executive skills, as often they cannot in standard State assignments like political reporting. Fifth, it simplifies day-to-day bureaucratic operations and focuses responsibility by eliminating State-AID lateral clearance requirements at the desk level. Sixth, it provides a promising base for development of a comprehensive programming system— like the one the Latin America bureau has adopted— since aid activities are more amenable to quantitative methods and concrete policy goals than many other U. S. overseas activities.

But there are significant counter-arguments. The central criticism of such integration is that the "integrated function"—development aid, in this case—will not be given sufficient priority in the general organization, State.[a] State has limited competence in aid, for example, though integration would presumably mean its absorption of AID development economists and other specialists. Moreover, State has tended to subordinate long-term development objectives to short-term political aims

---

[a] This is, of course, the same argument that is used against abolishing the Office of Economic Opportunity and dividing the domestic poverty program among various parts of the Department of Health, Education and Welfare and other established agencies.

—pleasing incumbent governments, "buying" diplomatic support. Kennedy argued in proposing establishment of AID in 1961: "Economic development assistance can no longer be subordinated to, or viewed simply as a convenient tool for meeting short-run political objectives. This is a situation we can ill afford when long-range, self-sustained economic growth of less developed nations is our goal. Development assistance, therefore, must—and shall—take its place as a full partner in the complex of foreign policy."[3]

A related argument is that integration would bury important issues too low in the bureaucracy. It would force some issues higher: the lowest level at which aid resource allocation choices could be made among regions would be raised from the AID Administrator (who would either cease to exist or become a staff officer) to the Secretary of State. But differençes on the relative importance of U. S. "development" and "foreign policy" objectives in a particular country could be resolved, under the integrated arrangement, at the Country Director level. AID officials who consider such choices to be very important policy issues argue that separate State and AID line organizations should be maintained to fight over them and push them upstairs.

Another argument against integrating a particular program into a general region-based organization arises when the program depends for its effectiveness on separate identity. This argument is a decisive one against, for example, integrating the Peace Corps into State, since relating it so closely to day-to-day U. S. foreign policy would probably make it unpalatable to many recipients. More dubiously, it is held that aid recipient countries will accept more easily, and take more seriously, pressure to reform their internal policies if it comes from an AID Mission Director rather than an Ambassador. But another argument against integration has considerable merit—that aid may be more able to maintain domestic political support if it has separate institutional existence, or is not identified with controversial foreign policies like Vietnam.

A final argument against integration would be that the program to be brought into State was only of peripheral foreign policy importance. It would then prove an encumbrance to the central agency, costing more in administrative effort than it provided in strengthened central foreign policy influence. This view, of course, has been held about aid by many Foreign Service officers, long after the facts seemed to indicate otherwise. But as aid continues to decline, the view takes on more and more validity.

If one's aim is to enhance policy coherence, the balance of the general argument would appear to lie in integration's favor. But development program objectives do tend to be compromised by too-close association with day-to-day foreign policy. Thus the organization Kennedy created to stress economic development ended up with half of its overseas personnel in Vietnam, and with its "Rural Development Annex" serving as a CIA front in Laos. And the problem of building domestic support for aid programs poses another strong obstacle to a merger of State and AID.

The Nixon Administration has proposed major organizational changes to meet these problems. If adopted by Congress, their total effect would be a move both toward and away from integration. Security-related economic aid programs are to be brought under direct State management, though probably not under the regional bureaus. Also, a Coordinator of Security Assistance is to be established at the Under Secretary level to coordinate these and the military assistance and sales programs run by Defense. Development assistance will not only be outside of State, but divided among three separate agencies performing capital assistance, technical assistance, and overseas private investment promotion functions.

Moreover, the Peterson Task Force which recommended these changes argued that the United States should not seek "any specific short-term foreign policy gains from our participation in international development." Nixon's two messages on aid do not go this far, but the program structure they propose is generally consistent with this view.[4]

Other good candidates for integration are hard to find. One logical possibility is the Arms Control and Disarmament Agency, which is now officially independent though housed in State. Incorporating it in State's Bureau of Politico-Military Affairs might increase, at least potentially, the contribution of ACDA experts to the broad policy issues of weapons systems development and general U. S.-Soviet relations, both critical to arms control prospects but both tending to fall outside of ACDA's effective influence. Also, ACDA's role as arms limitation advocate tends to make other agencies discount its views, though far less so at times (like the present) when it has the "bargaining advantage" of a major negotiation like the SALT talks to manage. Yet integration of ACDA would be interpreted, both at home and abroad, as a reduction in the priority given to arms limitations, so action in this direction would probably on balance be unwise at this time.

Control of the CIA is a very serious organizational problem, one which will be discussed further in Chapter Nine. But since both its intelligence gathering and its clandestine operations require a certain separation from State—the former to promote objectivity, the latter to mask responsibility—integration does not seem relevant. This leaves but one remaining candidate—USIA. Since its Washington personnel are largely within its specialized media divisions, integration on a regional basis would have only limited impact. More important, however, is the question of whether USIA's activities in defending America's overseas "image" are not a Cold

War vestige which should be de-emphasized if not eliminated. And its cultural activities—overseas information libraries, the Voice of America—would benefit from less identification with day-to-day foreign policy, not more.[5]

Thus if the logical case for integrating specific foreign affairs program activities under State seems reasonably strong, the only specific case where the principle seems applicable is security-related economic assistance. Efforts to improve foreign policy coherence will have to depend mainly on other devices.

2. *Formal Policy Guidance*

As another means of getting the government to do what they want, Presidents and lesser officials can issue written directives. The Kennedy and Johnson Administrations transmitted a series of National Security Action Memorandums (NSAM's) for Presidential orders on matters of particular importance or concern. The Nixon National Security Decision Memorandums (NSDM's) have a similar purpose. The use of both has been frequent and *ad hoc*, for whatever orders these Presidents wished to convey formally and on-the-record.

But specific top-level directives can affect only a fraction of what the foreign affairs government does, so periodically there are efforts to provide more comprehensive policy guidance. A representative argument for such guidance is provided by Hoopes: "A foreign-military establishment as large and as far-flung as ours requires that policy be something more tangible than a thesis carried in the minds of an Assistant Secretary and a few opposite numbers. Granted its fluid and perishable nature, policy must be generalized, written down, and each part coherently related to the other. There must be an agreed and stated vision of the whole. Otherwise the many parts of the establishment will function and comprehend in the manner of the blind men examining the elephant."[6] The idea is also attractive to advocates of the standard organizational doctrine of "centralized policy-making and decentralized operations." If executives can provide clear guidance as to what their central objectives and priorities are, it is logically argued, they can delegate responsibility for specific applications without loss of control.

To provide such guidance requires first that it be drafted by officials knowledgeable in the areas with which it deals. Thus the Eisenhower Administration spent countless hours working on broad policy guidelines ranging from the annual Basic National Security Policy (BNSP) to many other documents covering particular countries and geographic areas. These guidelines came before the NSC and, after Presidential approval, became the official "policy" that the various agencies were expected to follow.

The Kennedy-Johnson Administration abandoned this degree of formal policy guidance in favor of a more *ad hoc* approach to making Presidential wishes known. But an effort was made, centered in the State Policy Planning Council and spurred by Walt Rostow during his chairmanship, to develop National Policy Papers (NPP's) setting forth U. S. objectives in selected countries and areas. The Nixon Administration's restoration of a more formal system did not include revival of the BNSP, but a number of NSDM's have flowed from broad National Security Studies, and one important purpose of the general Presidential foreign policy messages of 1970 and 1971 has been to guide the bureaucracy on general Administration policy objectives.

The idea of a systematic effort to communicate thorough policy guidance to officials at all levels has considerable appeal. But in practice it becomes difficult to get beyond meaningless generalities. In "a foreign-military establishment as large and as far-flung as ours," it may be impossible for such guidance to be specific enough to affect day-to-day decisions without robbing those dealing with specific cases of needed flexibility. For as any bureaucrat can testify, the greater the number of general rules promulgated to guide his behavior, the more effort he must spend bending them or going around them to cope with the many cases that have the nasty habit of not conforming to blueprints developed at headquarters. And even if they are relevant when drafted, they are forever being rendered obsolete by new information and events.

 Bureaucratic politics also poses several severe barriers to development of meaningful policy guidance. One is the almost inevitable recourse to committee drafting. Obviously, contributions from several agencies are required if the "policy" is to reflect a realistic sense of actual government activities, and to weave these into something resembling a coherent whole. But committees encourage low-level compromises, and the men who serve on them are wary of any language that could pose a threat to their abilities to do their jobs as they see them. Thus a favorite mode of resolving inter-agency differences is to "increase the vagueness and generality" of what is said.[7]

The Rostow NPP's sought to avoid this problem. The effort consciously sought "to avoid the weaknesses of 'drafting by committee' by designating a senior officer to chair each working group and by charging him with responsibility for the product." Still, they had little impact. And one reason was another bureaucratic political problem—the lack of clear endorsement of their specific substance by top officials. Rostow had won a strong general Presidential mandate—an NSAM "stating that completed NPP's signed by the Secretary of State would be authoritative and binding on all agencies covered by the NPP." Yet because of limited high-level participation in their drafting, they "were not regarded as authentic enunciations of Presidential policy." Nor were they seen as reflecting the priorities of other high officials. So "the second and third levels of government, taking their cue from Rusk and McNamara, treated the National Policy Papers with indifference."[8]

It is hardly surprising that hard-pressed top policy officials would not become sufficiently involved to place their personal imprints on the drafting of such papers. Though there are exceptions—such as Nixon's recent messages—heavy immediate pressures encourage the view that such documents are distinctly marginal in importance. Furthermore, top officials identified too closely with such detailed policy elaboration documents risk encumbering their personal freedom of action. They need not wish to keep every option open, but they will not want to close all of them either. So when they are involved personally we sometimes get formulations like President Nixon's statement of his "doctrine": "America cannot—and will not—conceive *all* the plans, design *all* the programs, execute *all* the decisions and undertake *all* the defense of the free nations of the world."[9] It is hard to think of any policy action which we might conceivably undertake which would not be consistent with this ringing resolve. Yet one important purpose of the President's general messages apparently is to communicate new policy directions to the foreign affairs government.

There may, of course, be important gains from attempts at "policy codification" other than the increased direct control which is their primary goal. They may on occasion highlight important issues or program conflicts, which tend to be overlooked if each agency goes its separate way with only intermittent or *ad hoc* policy coordination from the top. In fact, Ponturo reports, the "foremost defenders" of the Eisenhower system state "almost to a man" that "the *process* of producing the policy documents was a more important contribution to effective policy making than the documents themselves," since a large number of officials were forced "to interact

201

and collaborate with each other." The "codification system" itself, however, was closer to a "conspicuous facade, with the important levers and controls not among the carefully processed policy papers but elsewhere in the daily pull and tug of bureaucratic politics."[10]

For even if it is relevant, formal policy guidance will often not be decisive. The middle-level officials who are its targets are not simply neutral public servants who seek the most objective interpretation of our broad "policy" and faithfully execute it. They are men who may have strong policy views themselves, as well as a range of pressures of their own to resolve in order to do their own jobs. They are likely to treat formal policy guidance not as the final word, but as one part of a broad legacy relevant to today's problems, a legacy including what has been done in the past. They will view this legacy the way a lawyer views the law, as a living body which grows and changes through decisions on particular cases. Granted it may impose certain limits on the permissible. But it is also a set of precedents useful in buttressing one's own side of a case and moving policy in directions one desires. Well-conceived guidelines on specific issues can strengthen the hand of those in the government who agree with top-level objectives on these issues. If they are explicit and emanate clearly from the top, they can also take advantage of the rather widespread bureaucratic belief that Presidential orders ought to be obeyed. But it is unreasonable to expect formal policy guidance to do very much more.

3. Foreign Affairs Programming

A more recent, and more promising approach to strengthening top-level foreign policy influence has been the effort to develop a comprehensive "programming" system. The aim is to tie allocation of budgetary and personnel resources to a sophisticated system of analysis which relates overseas programs to specific foreign policy

202

objectives. These efforts start from the premise that certain general foreign affairs decisions do need to be made well in advance of the actions they bring about. Funds must be allocated, programs geared up, personnel recruited and trained, long-term agreements negotiated with foreign governments. For these program-type activities some general planning is inevitable; the question is how well it will be done, how centrally it will be done, and who will do it.

The foreign affairs programming idea owes its general inspiration to McNamara's Planning-Programming-Budgeting System (PPBS) for defense. The primary focus of efforts to date is on U. S. activities with relation to particular countries. U. S. foreign policy objectives are established and clarified for each country. At the same time, comprehensive data and other information are sought about what our various agencies are doing in that country. Then an effort is made to analyze both how consistent our "mix" of programs in a country is with our objectives, and how successful these programs are in furthering these objectives. The ultimate aim is to change the allocation of resources among the programs— the amount of money spent, the numbers and types of personnel, etc.—to make what we do relate more effectively to what we want to achieve.

The most sustained effort to put these ideas into practice was the campaign of Deputy Under Secretary Crockett and his aide, Richard W. Barrett, to develop a Comprehensive Country Programming System under State Department leadership. Rusk and other senior State officials showed only limited interest, except for Rostow, who saw it as a way to give his NPP series operational meaning. There was also deep Foreign Service skepticism about both the broad concept of programming and the foreign affairs "management" role that it required. Still, its developers managed to keep the effort going and attract scattered support among Ambassadors and others in the foreign affairs government until the fall of 1965. Then the Budget Bureau, following up on President Johnson's directive of August 25th establishing a government-wide PPB system, pushed through an approach which circumvented the State effort by calling for individual agency programming efforts to be channeled directly to BoB.

From this blow State's programmers never recovered. In 1966 a committee under Charles Hitch (who had masterminded the Defense system) recommended a comprehensive, inter-agency system and saw "no technical obstacle" to its establishment.[11] But no implementing action was taken, and Under Secretary Katzenbach failed in his effort to recruit Thomas Schelling to head up a State programming effort. There was, however, one surviving offshoot—the Country Analysis and Strategy Paper (CASP) system adopted by the integrated State-AID Latin America bureau in 1967 under the active leadership of Assistant Secretary Lincoln Gordon and his deputy, Robert Sayre. More recently, the Nixon Administration has shown serious interest in foreign affairs programming, with the NSC staff leading a major effort in this field. There is also increased support in the State Department ranks, reflected in the task force proposal to center State leadership around a comprehensive Policy Analysis and Resource Allocation system.

Obviously the programming approach is no magic solution to the overall problem of foreign affairs coherence. Added to the inherent limitations of general decisions made in advance is the point stressed by Schelling, that in foreign affairs "the hard decisions" tend to be of the "non-budgetary sort."[12] But if looked on as a means to bring greater coherence to a large area of foreign affairs government activities of considerable importance and impact—aid, information, military assistance, perhaps some of the efforts of the primarily domestic agencies, perhaps broader overseas deployment of armed

204

forces, perhaps the Peace Corps—then programming is promising. Difficult analytic problems abound at each stage—in clarifying objectives, in developing categories in which to place particular program elements, above all in measuring "outputs" (results) caused by our "inputs" (specific program activities). Moreover, since resource allocation involves choices among values and beneficiaries which no analysis can conclusively resolve, it inevitably becomes a political process which programming can influence but not fundamentally alter. Still, the better its analysis of the effects of particular resource uses, the more one might expect the influence of programming to be.

A programming system could also be a very useful handle for a central agency seeking to exercise comprehensive foreign policy leadership. Reviewing the potential effects of PPB in domestic agencies, Charles Schultze concludes that it can change the internal political balance in two ways. It can introduce a new set of "partisans" into the policy process, programming staffs which advocate greater program efficiency and effectiveness and draw on their analysis for such advocacy. And it can strengthen the role of department heads in relations with their subordinate units, by providing new information and analysis illuminating Cabinet-level choices.[13]

This implies that a Cabinet member should support the "partisans" who are building a programming system as a means of enhancing his own influence. But Rusk did not. As a Stanford Research Institute Report put it: "In the Department of Defense there was an executive looking for a management system. In the State Department you had the case of a management system looking for an executive."[14]

There is room for debate about whether the Budget Bureau or the Foreign Service was most culpable in the murder of CCPS, but certainly its separation from the Seventh Floor policy makers and their failure to back it in 1965-66 must be rated a major reason for its demise. For similar reasons, skepticism is warranted about the proposed PARA system. Conversely, the modest success of the Latin America CASP system has been closely related to its sponsorship by the regional Assistant Secretary during its birth and the strong interest of his office since then.

The Schultze analysis also assumes another thing— that the Cabinet member will have the prerogative of making budget choices once he gets the analysis. Yet the major review of foreign affairs budgets occurs not in State but in the Budget Bureau (now OMB). This suggests that the critical question is not the means, programming, but the end, stronger influence on resource allocation by central foreign policy officials. If a State-centered programming system is to be effective, State's policy officials must develop a major role and a frequently decisive voice in executive branch budgeting for overseas programs.

A formal State review prerogative would need, of course, to be supported by staff capability to analyze the various budgets and programs in terms of effectiveness and alternative resource use choices. It would not necessarily require the imposition of a single analytical system. No matter how advanced a system could be developed, it could only be advisory to top officials.[b] For the latter must weigh not only the substantive considerations they feel the analysis has slighted but the multiple pressures of bureaucratic politics as well. Yet a programming sys-

[b] The Hitch Committee recognized this limitation. Its letter to Secretary Rusk characterized a "well-designed programming system" as "a major *tool* for carrying out your responsibility for the direction, coordination, and supervision of the foreign affairs activities of the U.S. government" (italics added). But much of the literature of programming has tended to slight both its political limitations and its implications for the bureaucratic balance of power. (See Frederick C. Mosher, *"PPBS: Two Questions,"* Letter to Editor-in-Chief, *Public Administration Review*, March 1967; reprinted in Jackson Subcommittee, *Planning-Programming-Budgeting: Selected Comment*, pp. 23-28.)

tem could also help them cope with these pressures. It could give legitimacy to their exercise of budgetary influence, since this would appear less an exercise of arbitrary whim and personal bias and more a result of a "rational," "objective" process of analysis and evaluation. Such trappings of rationality proved a tremendous bargaining advantage for McNamara, not only with the services but with Congress as well, at least in his initial years.

4. General, Fixed-Membership Coordinating Committees

Finally, top officials can seek increased influence and improved foreign policy coherence by establishing fixed, general interdepartmental committees to consider important policy questions.

Committees are the bane of the foreign affairs bureaucracy, and old ones are damned even more frequently than new ones are created. Some, like the National Advisory Council on International Monetary and Financial Policies (NAC) chaired by the Secretary of the Treasury, have survived efforts to abolish them yet played only perfunctory roles. Others have labored in anonymity, like most of the 160 interdepartmental committees that Nelson Rockefeller counted during the Eisenhower regime. Still others are like the Agriculture-based Interagency Staff Committee, which does useful coordination work on the food aid program at the cost of scores of man-hours every Thursday afternoon.

Only recently, however, have reigning administrations created networks of general interdepartmental committees, restricted neither to a specific substantive sphere nor to a particular "component" of the "policy process" like "planning" or "operational coordination." In March 1966, President Johnson established the SIG/IRG system to "assist the Secretary of State" in his responsibility for "the overall direction, coordination and supervision of interdepartmental activities of the United States Government overseas." The Nixon Administration made significant changes in the system the day it came to office, but retained the principle of general interdepartmental committees at the Assistant Secretary level and above.

The Johnson system had two tiers of committees: Interdepartmental Regional Groups (IRG's) for area problems and the Senior Interdepartmental Group (SIG) for broader and more important ones. The former were chaired by Assistant Secretaries of State, the latter by the Under Secretary. Both included representatives of the Secretary of Defense, the Joint Chiefs of Staff, CIA, AID, USIA, the NSC staff, and whatever other agencies the chairman might wish to invite for a particular meeting.

The committees were given broad mandates, including jurisdiction over agency programs "of such a nature as to affect significantly the overall U. S. overseas program in a country or region." Problems could come before them on appeal from lower-level officials, or assignment from the Secretary, or through their own initiative. The SIG, for example, was specifically mandated to conduct "periodic surveys" on "the adequacy and effectiveness of interdepartmental overseas programs and activities."[15]

Thus the system seemed to recognize that foreign policy-making was a flow of issues defying categorization into components like "planning" and "operations," and that any coordinating system would need a mandate to intervene in whatever part of this flow was important for a particular problem. And it was designed to deal with a major problem of the Johnson *ad hoc* decision-making system—the lack of focal points for coordination below the President, and the resultant tendency of the system to bring coherence, at best, on only the few issues to which the President and his immediate aides gave extended personal attention. To avoid the vices of committee decision-making, the committee heads were made "executive chairmen," "with full powers of decision on all matters within their purview" subject to appeal to higher authority by a disagreeing member.[16] Thus the system combined the placing of responsibility in one man with a recognition of the bureaucratic political fact of (and need for) "escalation" of issues upward. Moreover, the appeal procedure encouraged chairmen to resolve issues along lines consistent with higher-level policies and priorities, a central virtue for any such "control" device.

Yet despite these apparent advantages, the system did not prove very effective. It was established by Presidential order to aid the Secretary, but there is little or no evidence that either took it seriously enough to support it or use it in their handling of day-to-day issues. When Under Secretary Katzenbach, after succeeding George Ball, eventually tried to make something of the SIG, Johnson reportedly refused to back him in his efforts to gain Congressional sanction for a strong staff. Nor should such non-support be considered very surprising, since no President is likely to delegate real authority to a "mechanism" unless he participates personally in it or places primary reliance for overall foreign affairs leadership on the men who were to run it. Probably the major contribution of the SIG was to serve as an excuse for a small but talented staff, which was able to play an important and constructive role on a range of policy matters.

The IRG's were somewhat more useful. They were able to coordinate with some effectiveness in regions like Africa and Latin America, where the Assistant Secretary of State was considered a natural interagency leader and problems could be resolved at his level. By contrast, the IRG for Europe never achieved a useful role, since the heavy involvement of higher-ranking officials in State, Treasury, Defense, and the White House required the Assistant Secretary for European Affairs to fight just to be heard on important policy issues.

The Nixon Administration made four major formal changes in the fixed committee system. It removed AID and USIA from regular membership, changed the names of the committees to Interdepartmental Groups (IG's) and the Under Secretaries Committee (USC), restricted the general role of the latter to "operational matters," and, most important, created a Kissinger-chaired NSC Review Group to which both the IG's and the USC were to report. But, like their predecessors, the Nixon committees have proved effective only when they were consistent with the prevailing bureaucratic balance of power. Except for Latin America with its special CASP system, the IG's have played little role except to process studies assigned by the White House. This reflects a system where only Kissinger has an effective Presidential leadership mandate.

The Kissinger Review Group has, not surprisingly, been much more active. But it apparently proved much more useful after it was reconstituted as the Senior Review Group, with agency representation raised from the Assistant Secretary to the Under Secretary level. In the six months after the change it met 31 times, compared to only 15 in the six months before.[17] And the reason seems clear. The Assistant Secretary-level officials who represented State and Defense on the old Review Group were not men of major influence in their departments. The Under Secretaries who replaced them are.

But even when they reflect the current distribution of bureaucratic power, fixed committees have other disadvantages which limit their utility as comprehensive coordinating devices. They have, for one thing, what a former White House staff official has called a "fixed tendency to expand, and no capacity for shrinkage." Once a committee is established and regular meetings are scheduled, it is important to bureaucrats' prestige (and sometimes to their effectiveness) that they be present. This is true also for that oldest of general committees, the National Security Council. Yet serious business is seldom transacted before a crowd. Even so ardent an advocate of formal systems as Eisenhower aide Robert Cutler recognized that once "more than a certain number of persons sit around the Council table," officials "do not discuss and debate; they remain silent or talk for the record." According to one member, the Nixon NSC staff made sure that the order removing USIA and AID from regular fixed committee membership was issued on the afternoon following the inauguration. For should they once establish a "right" to attend in the new administration, it was felt they might prove impossible to dislodge.[18]

The Nixon Administration has sought to maintain the utility of the NSC by severely restricting the members allowed to attend. But it has still faced another recurrent problem with fixed committees—that the men they place around the table are often not the group most appropriate for dealing with a particular problem. Thus, in preparation for his Cambodia decision, President Nixon preferred to meet with a smaller group which included only three of the five statutory NSC members. Similarly, reports Schlesinger, President Kennedy "could not understand . . . why serious matters of foreign policy should be discussed in the presence of his first director of the Office of Emergency Planning, a garrulous southerner who had a flow of irrelevant opinions on everything."[19] During the Cuban missile crisis he brought together the men he wanted, and christened them the "Executive Committee of the National Security Council" for public relations purposes.

Yet another problem for top officials is that fixed committees tend to feature well-known meeting times

211

and agendas circulated in advance—multiplying the likelihood of leaks to the press. This provides just one more reason why it would be impossible to "rationalize" the bureaucratic politics of foreign policy-making by channeling it neatly through a limited number of fixed forums or "decision-making" bodies.

Still, if a more modest role is contemplated, fixed committee systems can have their uses. For an official given broad coordination responsibilities, chairmanship of a general interdepartmental group can both symbolize his role and provide him a mechanism for exercising his leadership where issues can be resolved and counterparts given their "right to be heard." Fixed committees also provide lower-level officials from State and other agencies with places to refer issues which they need to have resolved, and an institutionalized appeal system should encourage lower-level officials to resolve matters as they think their superiors would. And in those situations where the membership is appropriate to a wide range of problems and attendance can be kept limited—both of which could be encouraged by giving the chairman substantial authority to prescribe who can come—such committees can bring to foreign policy-making the advantages of both worlds: a clear focus of responsibility and the handling of issues by the most useful and relevant group.

In summary, none of the four general devices discussed here provides a major "short-cut" to the achievement of coherence in foreign policy. Yet when tied to, and used by, important foreign affairs officials, certain of these devices—programming in particular—can be of significant aid. They can help increase these officials' leverage, and sometimes also their understanding of important issues. Once again, examination of specific organizational mechanisms leads one away from treating them as ends in themselves, toward an approach which asks, first, who

212

should be strengthened in the bureaucratic political system, and second, what contribution can these "mechanisms" make to such strengthening. These are also important questions to ask about foreign affairs substantive staffs, the subject of the chapter that follows.

CHAPTER EIGHT

The Uses of Staffs

ON JULY 3, 1969, Under Secretary of State Elliot Richardson announced the creation of a new departmental unit, the Planning and Coordination Staff (S/PC). He characterized it as a "counterpart for the Seventh Floor" of the President's NSC staff. Its approximately twenty professionals were to be divided between a "planning" group "focused on longer-range problems" and a "coordination" group concerned with "major day-to-day policy decisions."[1]

S/PC replaced the once-renowned Policy Planning Council, whose work on the broader and longer-range aspects of policy had grown less and less relevant to top officials' immediate priorities and preoccupations. And the lack of a Secretarial staff substantively involved in current policy questions had cost State dearly during the Rusk era. Power flowed elsewhere because it was widely felt no one could speak for the Secretary. The White House staff rewrote State policy papers and took over critical issues, all the while berating the Department's lack of responsiveness. Meanwhile, across the river, good staff work assured that when Defense Department papers "came to the White House, they bore Secretary McNamara's personal imprint, and, unlike the more impersonal State Department memorandums, they almost never required supplementary analysis or information."[2]

In the early Nixon Administration, the imbalance worsened. Kissinger recruited a strong staff before State's leaders had settled into their offices, and the White House inundated State with study requests and directives. What came back had the new NSC staff members echoing the old, concluding that State was unable to produce the kind of analysis of current policy issues that was broad-gauged, terse, relevant to Presidential choices, and on time. Their dissatisfaction found a parallel in Secretary Rogers' comment early in his tenure. "I don't feel I have an action group at my command as they do at other departments," he said. "Sometimes I have a feeling things aren't going to get done."[3]

In the face of these problems the Department of State emulated its competitors, and created for the first time a Secretarial staff unit with an explicit mandate to involve itself daily, across-the-board, in the substance of current policy issues.

The Planning and Coordination Staff, said Richardson, would provide analyses on current policy issues independent of operating bureaus, and encourage "actual head-to-head debate" between "divergent views." It would also "help us manage the Department's input into the National Security Council system as well as our follow-through from it." The Under Secretary made the required assurances that the new staff would not be a "layer" or "competitor" which would "get between the operating bureaus and the Seventh Floor." But he apparently wanted a strong staff, sensitive to the Secretary's and the President's broad responsibilities, which would provide recommendations on current problems, conduct an ongoing critical review of bureau activities and proposals, and involve itself more generally in bureaucratic operations of importance to State's top officials. The "coordination" component of such a staff could not help intervening in relations between the bureaus and top Seventh Floor officials. Indeed, one of its aims would be to exert enough pressure on the bureaus—through its analysis and review role—to make them more responsive to the Secretary and his top subordinates.[4]

Another important aim was to prevent further enlargement of personal staffs to the several top Seventh

Floor officials, since infighting among such staffs had long hampered development and implementation of coherent departmental policy positions.

All of these were worthy objectives. Yet by early 1971 it was evident that the new Planning and Coordination Staff had had only a small impact on State Department practice and Washington policy-making. It had been unable to develop strong substantive influence on a broad range of issues. The regional bureaus felt only sporadic pressure from S/PC in relation to their own work. Nor was the new unit even able to bring significantly greater coherence to the scene on the Seventh Floor.

In retrospect, it is hard to see why S/PC's creators felt it could accomplish any of these objectives. For, like any large organization, the State Department is filled with offices and officials who fear losing influence if a central staff starts to gain. There are of course the regional bureaus, particularly the older ones like EUR (European Affairs) and NEA (Near Eastern and South Asian Affairs), who tend to feel that problems involving "their countries" are "their business," to be protected from ill-informed intruders. But State also features a far-flung and fragmented Seventh Floor. Housed there, clear in rank but uncertain in relationship, are the five top officials—presently named[a] the Secretary, the Under Secretary, the Under Secretary for Political Affairs, the Deputy Under Secretary for Economic Affairs, and the Deputy Under Secretary for Administration. Serving them are scores of professional staff personnel: men with venerable titles, like the Counselor or the Ambassadors-at-Large; men with unusual titles, like the Special Assistant to the Secretary for Fisheries and Wildlife; per-

[a] State's number three official can also have the title of "Under Secretary for Economic Affairs" if this is felt to be more appropriate for a particular occupant. Similarly, prior to 1969 the number four position was generally designated "Deputy Under Secretary for Political Affairs."

sonal aides, several of whom work for each official; and the Executive Secretariat, State's operational coordination center. The new Planning and Coordination Staff absorbed none of these, though it did incorporate the small group which served the Under Secretary as head of the NSC Under Secretaries Committee. Thus it must spar with these competing staffers for influence, in an arena characterized by some observers and participants as one of the few extant examples of classical free enterprise.

What bargaining advantages might S/PC bring to this fray? Foremost, one might expect, would be the known confidence and support of the Secretary and Under Secretary who created it.[b] The logical case for the Secretary supplying such confidence is strong. S/PC was established to defend his perspective against the presumably narrower viewpoints of lesser jurisdictions. Its Director, lacking a separate statutory base or specific operational responsibility, would be clearly dependent on Secretarial support for his influence. Such dependence would foster loyalty and day-to-day responsiveness, making the Secretary more willing to grant the needed support. At the same time, the Staff Director's rank—equivalent to an assistant secretary—appears sufficient to be taken seriously when joined to a Secretarial mandate.

Yet confidence is a peculiarly personal matter. High officials tend to bestow it not on formal units but on men, and to require more in exchange for this confidence than that a man be loyal and doing a job which

[b] The two major Seventh Floor staffs—S/PC and the Executive Secretariat—have the responsibility of serving all three of the top officials, and to some degree the Deputy Under Secretary for Economic Affairs as well. Thus the problem of top-level confidence involves the staff's relationship with not just one boss but several, and in fact S/PC has tended to serve the principal Under Secretary more than the men above and below him. But the following pages discuss the problem in terms of the Secretary, for simplicity of presentation and because he is the most important.

tends to reinforce their own. Bosses also want to feel that a subordinate shares their assumptions, identifies himself with them, works well with them, and is effective in getting things done. And a boss tends to deal with a staff of any size predominantly through its director. Looked at in these terms, the man appointed to head S/PC—William Cargo—entered his job with certain liabilities. As a career FSO whose last three assignments had been overseas, Cargo had neither a prior personal relationship with the Secretary, nor an identification with his Administration, nor high-level bureaucratic experience in post-Eisenhower Washington.

Such handicaps were not insurmountable. But to overcome them required that Cargo and his staff establish their usefulness to the Secretary not in terms of broad aims such as "improved policy analysis" or "better planning," but rather by proving to the Secretary that they could help him cope better with his daily bureaucratic business. To do this, they needed prerogatives for influencing the flow of current issues, bargaining advantages to substitute for the Secretarial confidence they aspired to but did not yet possess.

But in seeking such involvement the staff suffered from having an indirect relation to a critical action flow —the papers moving to the Secretary and his top subordinates for action. These are controlled by the Executive Secretariat, which organizes them for the Secretary, assures that the right people in the Department have been consulted, and alerts the Secretary and other top officials to developments meriting their attention. S/PC gets copies of all such papers, but is not generally responsible for action on them. Kissinger has no comparable problem, no separation of such "operational" matters from his bailiwick. This illustrates the costs of building the new substantive staff from the old Policy Planning Council, rather than broadening Exec Sec into an "Office of Policy Review and Coordination," as proposed in the IDA report.[5] Two important bargaining advantages were lost: the regular relationship with the Secretary across the range of his responsibilities and involvements, and the "handle" which the role of operational coordination provides for making inputs to substantive issues. Perhaps equally important, his "off to one side" position in the regular action processes is likely to make the S/PC Director less sensitive to the broad range of the Secretary's involvements and needs, and thereby less responsive to them. He then is in danger of being relegated to a partial and limited role, only occasionally able to get effectively involved in important current business.

This danger may have been exacerbated by what would seem to be a useful bargaining advantage—S/PC's role in the NSC planning process. The staff's responsibility for helping assign action within State for work on National Security Study Memoranda (NSSM's), for broadly monitoring study preparation, for reviewing studies prior to Secretarial approval and then staffing State's participation in the Senior Review Group which decides on further action—all these assure involvement in a major new Nixon policy process.

The problem is that it is not at all clear just what the Secretary's role in the whole process is. Broad policy responsibility as well as authority for "managing" the system clearly rests with the White House; detailed work on the studies is done in the regional bureaus, frequently at the desk level. Regional State people wanting authoritative guidance on the policy intent of a NSSM naturally call the White House. NSC operations staff officials who want to stay on top of developments and guide them naturally call their regional contacts directly. S/PC is caught in the middle. For unless it is clear that the boss (or bosses) have important influence in a process, a staff has little basis for developing its own influence.

Yet the NSC system involvement has taken a great amount of time, apparently over 50 percent for many Cargo staff members. This burden is hardly theirs alone, of course. But it has tended to mean that in the Seventh Floor competition they have been relegated to this specific role rather than across-the-board substantive involvement; and that this "NSC system" role can prove more form than substance, since the policy initiative and the system's driving energy come not from Cargo's boss(es) but from the White House.

This does not mean, of course, that the staff has had no influence or usefulness. It has, it appears, improved the quality of State's contributions to the NSC system, and particular individuals have reportedly made important contributions on specific issues. Its role as staff arm to the Under Secretaries Committee has given certain staff members an important influence over issues in the foreign economic policy area that transcend regional boundaries but are not considered important enough to occupy NSC (or Kissinger) time. But S/PC has not succeeded in its larger aims. It has not enhanced the broad policy role of the Secretary or provided the type of analysis capable of making him a markedly stronger adviser of the President on complex policy issues. Cargo has not developed an especially close relationship with the Secretary, nor has Rogers set out to use the staff in a consistent and determined way. Denied the leverage which would come from his clear backing and confidence, staff members have had to fall back on other bargaining advantages—such as their personal reputations and contacts within the Department, or their ability to serve the interests of officials in the line bureaucracy.

Why Staffs?

Some would argue that the mistake was in seeking such a staff at all. The traditional State view is that the whole department is "staff" to the Secretary, and that to put a strong group of analyst-coordinators on the Seventh Floor is to commit the sin of "layering." Rusk was consistent with this view when he told the Jackson Subcommittee, "I look upon these senior officers of the department [Rusk's two top deputies] as comprising my staff," and reacted to Neustadt's proposal of a staff the Secretary "can call his own" with no apparent understanding of what it meant.[6] This view is likewise reflected by critics who, seeing decisions delayed and responsibility fuzzed by multiple clearance requirements and the proliferation of staffs and functional offices, urge as a solution the trimming of the organization to focus clear authority and responsibility in the line geographic bureaus.

But this "line solution" to foreign affairs organization ends up weakening the Secretary's control over his department, and thus his ability to respond effectively to the White House. A formal organization chart suggests otherwise. A trim structure seems to provide every subordinate with a clear and separate responsibility and make each man report to the top boss through an explicit chain of command. But bureaucratic politics renders such control illusory. The boss learns about organizational activities mainly from those directly responsible for their success, men whose perspectives are narrower than his own. They tend to define the way he sees issues by the problems they pose to him and the help they seek. Not only will they report achievements and problems in ways that reflect credit on themselves, on occasion consciously deceiving the boss and blocking information from him. They will, even with the highest motivations, tend to deal with the boss as a means of strengthening their own ability to do their own jobs rather than his ability to do his. They will want support, intervention on their behalf, adequate funds. They will not want the boss to dip too deeply into their problems

221

at any particular time, since (as they see it) this can only make things harder for them.

Thus a simple "line solution" to organization tends to meet the needs of subordinates at the expense of their superiors. The former get what they want—clear mandates and the presumption of higher-level support. But the boss tends to become the captive of those over whom he ostensibly has undiluted authority. As Frankel has written: "Tidy tables of organization are instruments by which a top administrator makes his life more "efficient" by arranging to be systematically uninformed or deceived. When information and advice flow upward through ever narrowing channels, the paneling on the walls and the rugs on the floor of his office do not save the man at the top from living in an isolation cell."[7]

To prevent such capture by their subordinates, top officials need staff men responsive to them who do not have fixed program or operational responsibilities and can constitute an alternative resource for information, analysis, and action.[c] Moreover, the two broad divisions in S/PC highlight the two major general purposes that substantive staffs tend to serve. One, often labeled "planning," involves analyzing problems broadly, in terms of geography, the full range of functions and programs involved, and time. Such analysis should reflect the boss's

[c] The problem of defining what is "staff" and what "line" is not an easy one in the foreign affairs government. It is not a matter of "planning" vs. "operations," nor can it be said that line officers have sole action authority with staffers simply "advisory." The problem will be resolved here by considering those units to be "line" which have *primary* action responsibility for a certain geographic area, or range of substantive functions, or a particular overseas "program." Thus State's Bureau of European Affairs is a line unit and its Assistant Secretary a line official. CIA and USIA are likewise line organizations. Staffs do not have such responsibility, except where a boss may assign it tentatively on an *ad hoc* basis. They are created, rather, to support particular line officials in the exercise of their functions.

As this suggests, the discussion here concerns staffs working on substantive policy problems. It does not relate to those units—likewise often called "staffs"—that provide specialized services or administrative support.

total responsibilities but contrast with the line officials concentrating on narrower groups of problems in terms of today, tomorrow, and next week. The second general staff purpose is that day-to-day operational involvement often termed "coordination"—seeking to assure that line officials with differing responsibilities and perspectives act in harmony with one another and consistently with top officials' purposes.

But if such staff support is necessary, the S/PC experience underscores the difficulty of providing it. The State Department's problem remains one of how to design a staff to give it a better chance of effectively serving the Secretary of State and other top departmental officials.

The organizational literature on staffs is extensive, but not terribly helpful in answering this question. As far back as 1902, Secretary of War Elihu Root was telling Congress of the need for an army general staff. In the 1930's, Gulick and Urwick provided quite explicit descriptions of staff roles and responsibilities. But they tended to assume staff effectiveness rather than analyze its preconditions, taking on instead the impossible task of showing that properly designed staffs would not interfere with the authority of line officials.[8] The reaction of more recent students of organization has been not to develop a more realistic idea of "staff" but to turn their attention to other things.[d]

Foreign affairs organizational reports have likewise neglected the effectiveness problem. In the past five years, the Heineman, IDA, AFSA, and Macomber reports have all urged stronger staff support for key State policy officials. But none focuses on the problem of how

d Problems of staff and line are not singled out for discussion in James G. March's *Handbook of Organizations* (Rand McNally, 1965), which seeks to summarize present knowledge and research about organizations generally. Nor does the word "staff" appear in any of the 206 "variables" about organization set forth in March and Simon, *Organizations*, pp. 249-53.

staffs can get the leverage to do what they are supposed to do. It was rather a critic, the Jackson Subcommittee, which raised the issue most strongly. Reacting against a 1958 proposal to create a Presidential Staff Agency for National Security Affairs, it concluded that "Lacking the autonomy and fixed entrenchments of a departmental base, such an agency could not compete for long, on favorable terms, with State, Defense, or Treasury."[9]

For indications on how staffs might be made effective, then, one must turn to the post-war experience of the foreign affairs government.

Two Types of Staffs

There have been two general types of foreign affairs staffs, corresponding roughly to the two subdivisions within S/PC. Of these the one most written about in foreign policy literature is that whose role is termed "planning."[e]

State's early Policy Planning Staff fits Parkinson's criterion for a needed organization—it was put together on a crash basis because urgent problems demanded it. On April 29, 1947, Secretary of State Marshall called George Kennan into his office, and asked him to assemble the staff without delay and to develop a set of recommendations for dealing with the crisis in Europe within "ten days or two weeks." He gave his famous terse advice: "Avoid trivia." The staff did so, making a central contribution to what was soon dubbed the Marshall Plan.[10]

---

e The word "planning" has no precise meaning in foreign policy; an earlier draft of this work listed fifteen different uses of the term by writers and practitioners. Most persons concerned with planning staffs would probably accept George Allen Morgan's general formulation—"Planning is thinking ahead with a view to action."—but would include in the concept efforts to bring about the action. ("Planning in Foreign Affairs: The State of the Art," *Foreign Affairs*, January 1961, p. 271.) A good discussion of several types of planning is Arthur R. Day, "Planning in the Conduct of Foreign Affairs," *Polity*, Summer 1969, p. 412.

The staff was created to work directly for the Secretary. Kennan reports of his relationship with Marshall that "from May 1947 to the end of 1948, I had the only office adjoining his own, and enjoyed the privilege (which I tried never to abuse) of direct entry to him, through our common side-door." As Acheson later described Marshall's intentions:

> The General conceived the function of this group as being to look ahead, not into the distant future, but beyond the vision of the operating officers caught in the smoke and crises of current battle; far enough ahead to see the emerging form of things to come and outline what should be done to meet or anticipate them. In doing this the staff should also do something else—constantly reappraise what was being done. General Marshall was acutely aware that policies acquired their own momentum and went on after the reasons that inspired them had ceased.[11]

Over the years, the Staff could claim credit for a number of important policy innovations. Kennan's successor Paul Nitze spearheaded the drafting of "NSC-68," a general planning document which served as the basis for our arms build-up after the onset of the Korean War. Under Dulles' planning chief, Robert Bowie, the Staff was responsible for creation of the Development Loan Fund. In the next decade it pushed the idea of an Asian Development Bank. And in all of these, it worked not as a group of detached men limiting their activity to broad analyses but as an in-house lobby maneuvering its ideas through the bureaucracy.[12]

It has also accumulated a considerable body of argument in support of its role. Advocates of this type of staff start from the evident fact that line officers are heavily preoccupied with handling immediate problems and have little time or incentive to give attention to broader trends or to the interrelationship of various policy areas. As an antidote, they see a need for a small number of exceptionally able men, drawn from both government and the academic world, to carry out policy analyses in broad perspective. They should have regular access to high policy officials, it is felt, seek to make their work relevant to the problems faced by these officials, and press for policy changes consistent with their findings.

Such a staff, its advocates further argue, should be neither so distant from operations as to encourage ivory-tower thinking nor so involved in them as to negate the special contribution that only those free from overwhelming daily pressure can make. Operational involvement would overwhelm them with immediate problems and make them advocates of the policies of their bosses rather than skeptics providing needed critical analysis. Yet in Bowie's words, "the purpose of a policy planning staff is not merely to produce literature, but to produce results." And "if insights and thinking on long-term factors are to be effective they must be brought to bear on such decisions as they are made."[13]

Discussions with former members indicate some difference of emphasis on the best strategy for achieving this end. One stressed the importance of getting to the Secretary personally and affecting his own thinking. Policy changes, he argued, are most unlikely to happen unless the Secretary pushes them strongly. A colleague of his emphasized, rather, the need to work with officials at various levels in the Department, using one's advantages of *time* to investigate issues and *independence* from too close attachment to any high policy-maker to encourage these officials to see problems in broader perspective.[14]

But the problem, as Hoffmann suggests, is how to structure a planning staff so as to avoid both "the Charybdis of irrelevance" and "the Scylla of overinvolvement in the present." Observers of the State group agree that it was most effective when it dealt with policy problems top officials considered urgent, and when it worked very closely with the Secretary. But then it loses much of its "independence" and flexibility. For example, "planning" advocates criticize the "tendency to pull the Staff into operations to an undue degree," like Acheson's use of Nitze in connection with the Iranian oil crisis negotiations. But this is a natural response of a Secretary who has the confidence in the staff director that is virtually a prerequisite for consistent staff influence.[15]

In fact, one of the early Policy Planning Staff's major triumphs—NSC-68—illustrates the difficulty of making broad analysis relevant to top officials when it does not treat their immediate problems. For how was the State-Defense group under Nitze able to get its recommendations for major defense spending increases cleared by two Cabinet officers in early 1950 for presentation to the President? Only, says Hammond, "by avoiding practical considerations of two kinds: it had avoided dealing with concrete programs and it had ignored the problem of reconciling what seemed desirable with what was (or was thought to be) possible. As a consequence, until unforeseen events changed the whole frame of reference for policy, it was threatened with irrelevance. Were it not for the start of the Korean War, its value would, very probably, have been only historical."[16]

If it took a shock as unexpected as Korea to shatter old assumptions about U. S. defense spending and render NSC-68 "relevant"—despite Nitze's intimate relationship with Acheson, despite the Secretary's strong sympathy for the proposal—one must temper his expectations about the extent of the contribution such a planning staff can make to actual policy. It seems built into the planning staff's nature either that its effectiveness will be intermittent and to some degree accidental, or that it will be pulled into operations and become the type of staff that S/PC is designed to be.

It may well be, as one former member suggested, that if a planning staff can win an important policy change once every two or three years it is doing very well, and is more than worth the money. But will it continue to be worth the time and attention of top officials? Experience suggests it will not. Under Dulles the Policy Planning Director lost the office adjoining the Secretary. Under Rusk the staff was expanded and renamed the "Policy Planning Council." But according to a member of that period, "the planning process during Secretary Rusk's tenure was probably more divorced from vital decisions" than ever. The Council became a "bureau of studies," writing papers "dealing in depth but somewhat uselessly with policy issues affecting individual countries."[17]

General Substantive Staffs

As the Council's star declined in State, a second type of staff rose to prominence in the White House and the Pentagon—much more involved in current issues, much more concerned with responding to the daily needs of the policy official it served. One example of such a "general substantive staff" was the NSC staff under Kennedy-Bundy and their successors. Another is the Pentagon's "little State Department," the Office of International Security Affairs (ISA).[f]

The post of Assistant Secretary of Defense for International Security Affairs was established in 1953 to coordinate Defense participation in foreign policy problems. During the Eisenhower years his office focused heavily on military aid, then central to most political-military issues. It also supported the Secretary by co-

---

[f] ISA is not unambiguously a staff office. Much of its work—general direction of the military assistance and sales programs, handling of day-to-day problems in liaison with State and the armed services—is closer to a "line" function as we have defined it. But ISA has proved most important as a staff agency, supporting the Secretary of Defense on foreign policy issues.

ordinating Defense participation in the Eisenhower NSC system and developing Defense Department policy positions on political-military questions.

Hoopes suggests that ISA has "inherent clout" deriving from its position "at the crossroads of foreign-military affairs." But others have stressed the inherent weakness of its liaison role between two large departments. The Haviland report in 1960 remarked that "The position of the Office of International Security Affairs between the professional corps of the Armed Forces and the Department of State has been a difficult one to create and maintain." Military officers, especially those trained in international relations, often prefer to deal directly with State. State officials in turn sometimes like to go around the intermediary. How to avoid losing influence on the substance of the action is a serious problem for such an office.[18]

But the 1960's brought substantial change. Secretary McNamara took a broad and active view of his foreign affairs role. He determined at the start to look to ISA for general foreign policy staff support, and recruited a series of exceptional ISA Assistant Secretaries: Paul Nitze; William Bundy, who held the position briefly before becoming Assistant Secretary of State for East Asia; John McNaughton, a brilliant, tough law professor from Harvard; and Paul Warnke, a lawyer who served both McNamara and his successor Clark Clifford with exceptional effectiveness.

ISA also had a staff of considerable talent. It had depth—approximately 200 professionals, somewhat more than half of them civilian. It was not "careerist" in the sense of having loyalties to any one career service which would conflict with loyalty to the Secretary. And though most of the Office was inevitably inundated with day-to-day business like "line" counterparts around town, the highest ranking and best officials were very much oriented toward the Secretary, in terms of both serving him and seeking his backing for foreign policy causes which they considered urgent. The result was that ISA played a considerable role from the time Nitze was designated to chair Kennedy's Cuba task force in 1961 to its 1968 fights to turn Vietnam policy around and inaugurate arms control talks with Russia. This role ended when Secretary Laird entered office determined to restrain OSD staffs in their battles with the military, and when President Nixon appointed an Assistant Secretary who was out of the mainstream both in his policy thinking and his attunement to bureaucratic life.[19]

But when ISA was "effective," it was very much so. And what it did was similar in many respects to the work of the White House national security staff. Evidence from interviews and published sources suggests that both of these "general substantive staffs" have concentrated on four broad types of activities: servicing the day-to-day business of the boss (meaning the President or Secretary); providing him a range of information and analysis; stimulating review of present policies and working for needed changes; and performing operational coordination. Under Nixon the White House staff added a fifth function—managing a general policy formulation process.

General servicing of day-to-day business includes such things as organizing and channeling the "decision papers" and other material that cross the boss's desk; preparing briefings for meetings, whether a courtesy call from a foreign diplomat or a "war summit" conference at Honolulu; and drafting speeches, letters, and official statements, important or routine. Sometimes the staff will write briefings or speeches itself. Sometimes they will be handled by others, either at the boss's or the staff's request. But at minimum the staff will assure that the work is done and, when necessary, "checked out" with the appropriate people. After the quick drafting of Kennedy's American University speech on the arms race, for example, the President gave a high NSC staff official a long list of people and told him to get reactions and proposed changes from each. *Providing a range of information and analysis* occupies a major portion of staff time. Getting a large enough flow of "facts" is no problem. Rather, the need is to select and glean from the avalanche of cables, intelligence summaries, and other reports that which is most important for the boss to see; to assure the accuracy of information and its relevance to current major issues; to fill in "holes" in the knowledge available; and to guard against biased reports, particularly from line sources.

One element of this staff task is providing bureaucratic political intelligence. Presidents often want to know what and who is behind a particular proposal, not just who signed the paper transmitting it. President Johnson, said one staff aide, wanted to know whether State Department documents came from "Rusk or Ben Read's typewriter."[9] Kennedy also felt that information about bureaucratic political interplay was vital to his ability to size up situations and issues.

Staff analytic work is aimed at illuminating issues in a way responsive to the boss's broad perspective as well as to his immediate pressures. This involves both soliciting studies by others and doing independent staff analysis. A strong staff takes a direct hand in preparing many papers the boss actually sees, and often tacks its own brief analysis onto papers provided by others. It will also seek to protect him from line subordinates who want ratification of their own policy choices rather than examination of alternatives—assuming that the boss wants such protection.

[9] Benjamin H. Read was Executive Secretary of the State Department during the Johnson Administration. Presumably, a document from his "typewriter" was one that came up from the ranks and had Rusk's formal endorsement but not his personal involvement.

Stimulating policy review and change comes closest to the "planning staff" role. This includes looking ahead and assessing the likely effects of present policies continued into the future; forcing up issues that are being ignored; and working for changes through day-to-day bureaucratic involvement. This role is not planning in the comprehensive sense. It is closer to *ad hoc* troubleshooting. ISA has had a subunit called "policy plans," described by former Deputy Assistant Secretary Adam Yarmolinsky as "a kind of free-wheeling adjunct to the regional and subject-matter specialized units" which worked "on whatever problems might be assigned to it from time to time." And as emphasized by one member of this group, the actual "planning" took only a small portion of their time. The main energy was given to bureaucratic political maneuvering to win acceptance of the "plans."[20]

Operational coordination is the best description for the fourth function, which is particularly important to the role of White House aides. Partly it is following up on Presidential (or Secretarial) policy decisions, prodding and weighing in on discussions of *how* a decision will be implemented, since such discussions may in fact determine whether it will be carried out or diverted. In such situations staff members often try to have their views regarded as authoritative interpretations of what the boss wants. Sometimes they succeed.

Coordination can also include providing service to the bureaucracy, bringing the relevant parties together on an issue, acting as "honest broker" in representing their views to the boss and sometimes to each other, serving on inter-agency task forces and linking their efforts to the boss's broader policies. If it does this job right, a staff, far from "layering" or blocking communications, actually serves as a channel for them. It often provides the only means line officials have to get a quick decision from the boss on issues defying lower-level resolution.

232

Bundy was regarded as particularly adept at this function. It is also a role for which a skillful Executive Secretary in the State Department can win the appreciation of numerous State line officials in addition to his boss and men from other departments.[h]

Managing of a general policy formulation process is important to such a staff only when important to the current administration. The State Department National Policy Paper exercise in the 1960's was given low priority by White House and ISA staffs because this was the view of their bosses. By contrast, the emphasis Nixon and Kissinger have given the national security studies program has made it a major concern for all general foreign affairs substantive staffs. Similarly, such staffs are also involved in fixed interdepartmental committees— NSC staffers sitting in for the White House, ISA men representing the Secretary of Defense.

The Problem of Staff Effectiveness

All five of these general activities require that staffs get deep into the substance of foreign policy if they are to do their job usefully. And if this picture of staff activities is at all accurate, it confirms in practice what the bureaucratic politics view of foreign policy-making logically implies—that there can be no neat division of labor between general substantive staff members and

[h] An insightful description of this liaison role in the military is provided by Urwick. Official "channels of communication," he says, are "supplemented by a network of personal contacts of all kinds between the staff officer and other staff officers of the same branch above and below him, the heads of specialist services above and below him, and the commanders of fighting troops whom he serves. The minute such personal contacts degenerate into personalities, anyone concerned can get back into 'official channels.' But everyone concerned also knows that the official channels are slow and the necessities of war urgent. The importance of these personal contacts as supplementing and expediting official procedure is a feature which is emphasized in all staff work. If there are no officials whose specific function it is to secure such liaison, misunderstanding and friction are almost inevitable in any large organization." (*Papers on Administration*, p. 67.)

line officials. There are certainly differences in emphasis. Line officers, for example, tend to be much more concerned with the "nuts and bolts" of particular operations, and much less inclined toward seeking broad policy review or even welcoming it. But overlapping is unavoidable. For if policy is largely made not by general proclamations from on high but through day-to-day decisions at all bureaucratic levels, then a staff which follows the traditional prescription to "stay out of operations" will also "stay out of influence."

But if staff "interference" in operations is unavoidable, so too is line resistance. The problem is not one of staffs messing up clear lines of authority. Line officials do not have clear "authority" in the first place, but only strong mandates to fight for greater actual influence within their areas of "responsibility." But a strong staff can complicate their fight considerably. It is at minimum one more center of power to be coped with, one more constraint on decisions and actions. Sometimes, as in the circuit-connecting function, a staff can serve line officials' interests. But what strong Assistant Secretary of State for Inter-American Affairs would not believe that *he* should have primary responsibility for a Presidential Latin America policy speech, rather than have it result, like Nixon's in 1969, from a broad NSC staff effort involving each of the five types of activities described here? What officials who are themselves deep in policy battles want *their* facts or analyses challenged by "people with no responsibility?"[21]

So all staffs face the problem of State's new Planning and Coordination Staff, that of building sufficient bargaining advantages to give them a policy impact. And unlike planning staffs which can settle for intermittent victories, the general substantive staffs discussed here have the day-to-day job of speaking for the perspective of the boss and making it prevail in bureaucratic combat. They will not, of course, be hard put to keep busy.

There are plenty of routine duties to be performed, much paper to be moved from in-box to out-box. But it is harder to make a substantive impact, to move, in Neustadt's phrase, from clerkship to leadership.

How can such staffs develop the leverage to perform their roles effectively? In certain respects, they build their influence through the same sorts of devices as other officials. They develop networks of relationships with officials who can be helpful to them; they try to build up personal reputations for skill in analysis and argument, for dependability as an ally and troublesomeness as an opponent, for ability to get the relevant information and interpret it intelligently. But two bargaining advantages seem critical to the effectiveness of general substantive staffs. One is *a close relationship to the boss and the boss's interests.* The second is *a regular role in important policy-making processes.*

The confidence of the boss is critical to the staff's effectiveness. Important also are his strong interest and involvement in the staff's substantive area and his determination to use the staff as a means of expanding his own influence. Since the boss will usually deal with the staff mainly through its director, and since most executives think more in terms of personalities than organizational units, the key to confidence will usually be the boss-staff director relationship. The director must be a man whom the boss trusts and who can "deliver" what the boss wants, a man whom he finds it congenial to work closely with and rely heavily on. The Kennedy-Bundy and Nixon-Kissinger relationships provide ample illustration, as do the close ties between Secretaries McNamara and Clifford and their ISA Assistant Secretaries. Negative illustrations are also available, like the present State Planning and Coordination staff, and the Policy Planning Council under Rusk.

But the confidence of the boss in the director may not flow down to the staff; it may stop with the director's person. This has tended to be the case with the Kissinger staff. Secretary Dulles relied substantially on planning staff director Bowie, but Bowie reportedly relied less on his subordinates, and the staff began its decline during that period. By contrast, a man who served on the Nitze staff cited in an interview the flow of confidence not just from President Truman through Secretary Acheson to Chairman Nitze, but the extension of this line of confidence from Nitze to individual staff members. If any link in this chain had been weak, he said, their influence would have been far less.

Intimately related to the benefits of such confidence is how the boss sees his own role. The more interested he is in foreign policy, the more he construes his role broadly and plays it aggressively, the greater the potential for staff influence. ISA's Vietnam influence would probably have been close to nil had Secretaries McNamara and Clifford seen their jobs as Neil McElroy saw his, limited to efficient management rather narrowly defined. And even a much more aggressive State political-military affairs staff than that of the early and mid-sixties would have been sharply constrained by Secretary Rusk's reluctance to do battle with the Pentagon.

If a staff seeks broad effectiveness, however, it needs not only a close relationship with a strong boss but a "handle" for learning about and getting involved in the important foreign policy issues. Knowledge of "what's happening," both overseas and within the bureaucracy, can be supplied in considerable measure by access to cables and intelligence reports. Thus Bundy insisted that the White House get "raw" cables and intelligence data directly, not pre-screened by the departments. Thus the State Planning and Coordination Staff is supposed to get copies of all cables and papers coming through the Department's Executive Secretariat.

But knowing about things is not enough. Bureaucrats everywhere tend to resist the interference of "plannerkibitzers" wherever located. So unless his boss has a clear personal interest in a particular issue at a particular time, a staff man may find it difficult to tie into day-to-day decision-making on the issue even if the general line of confidence down to him is strong.

Hence staffs need a prerogative, or an occasion for asserting their influence. For White House staff men this comes primarily from their regular review of analyses and decision papers which go before the President. For ISA, at least as important has been the "handle" provided by its daily "working level" operational liaison role on political-military issues. Membership in interdepartmental committees and task forces is a major bargaining advantage to both staffs. So also is an understood right to clear certain cables. And once a staff has both the confidence of a strong boss and a specific handle for influence on issues, it can use these to get other handles. A White House staff known to review decision papers coming from the departments to the President is better able to insist on clearing cables on particular issues, and bureaucrats will then begin to send documents over in draft form.

Ultimately, though, what is most important is that the two types of bargaining advantages tend to reinforce each other. The right of "clearance," for example, is of only limited use to ISA if others regard its role as merely "liaison," representing no one with a right to an independent substantive input. Conversely, the general confidence of the boss is inadequate if the staff cannot get a handle on important issues. Nor could it retain such confidence for long without such a handle, because the boss would not find the staff sufficiently useful to him.

Yet the staffs analyzed here show an interesting lack of dependence on certain processes often considered crucial for central control. Stephen K. Bailey writes, for example, that "the *essential* controls of an agency head over constituent units are three, and only three: (1)

control of legislative proposals; (2) control of budgetary totals; and (3) control of major personnel appointments and assignments." The staffs we have discussed are not uninvolved in these, an example of the last being Carl Kaysen's role in Averell Harriman's selection as our chief test ban treaty negotiator. But they are not heavily involved in any one, or dependent on it for influence the way the Budget Bureau has relied on the annual budget cycle. The "handles" for influence discussed earlier may fit Neustadt's emphasis on staffs' need for action-forcing processes. But with occasional exceptions—like the Nixon national security studies program and the Latin America CASP exercise—they are not so much general processes (like the budget) intended to establish the broad framework within which more specific agency actions must fit, as flows of day-to-day activities giving staffers a shot at issues one "piece" at a time.[22]

Will Staffs Serve the Purposes of the Boss?

If an organizational reformer must seek to make staffs effective, he must also recognize that effectiveness is not an end in itself. The problem is more than one of giving staffs adequate power, though that is difficult enough. It is also one of insuring that a staff uses that power to further the purposes of its boss rather than to embark on crusades of its own. It may, of course, make important contributions to shaping that boss's purposes. But it must remain responsive to him and subordinate to him. Otherwise staffs become a force for incoherence in a government already plagued with more than enough.

Staff men, by definition, tend to be more dependent on their bosses than line officials with operating programs to run. Such dependence breeds responsiveness, based on a need to make oneself useful in the boss's eyes. Yet staff members are individuals whose perspectives cannot be identical with that of the official they serve. How large are such differences likely to become? Will they grow sufficiently great to call into question the utility of general substantive staffs as instruments for coherent policymaking?

Logic and experience suggest that staff-boss divergence will be the greater to the extent that staff members:

1. are loyal to (and/or dependent on) a larger organization, career system, or professional discipline;
2. possess a special staff tradition or sense of identity and *esprit de corps* which predates their present boss;
3. have only limited personal contact with their boss;
4. hold strong personal views on policy differing from those of the boss;
5. have strong bargaining advantages independent of the immediate involvement and confidence of the boss; and
6. are large in number.

Loyalty to a larger institution or career system can be strong enough to create a fundamental divergence of interest between staff and boss. Thus the Joint Chiefs and the Joint Staff, whose only official role is to advise the Secretary of Defense and the President, are correctly regarded by them as spokesman for service interests. Both the White House staff and ISA have a mixture of individually recruited (so-called "political") and career officials. But "careerists" have been drawn from several systems—foreign, military, and civil services—and therefore no single career group is likely to achieve dominance or "set the tone" for the staff. In fact, in both cases it has been in-and-out, "political" officials who have filled most of the top positions and played most of the leading roles. By contrast, 63 percent of S/PC members are career State officials, and the Director and his two deputies are FSO's.[i]

[i] The 19 Planning and Coordination Staff members listed in the

239

Similarly, a staff identified with a particular professional discipline or methodology is likely to diverge from its boss, even if its *raison d'être* is to promote analysis in his broad perspective. The Defense Department Systems Analysis office developed a vested interest in its own mode of analysis, and thus only partially reflected the range of factors (including bureaucratic and partisan politics) the Secretary had to take into account.

A staff can also develop *a loyalty to itself,* its own identity or tradition or *esprit de corps* which goes beyond its immediate boss. Few close to the old Bureau of the Budget would deny that it had its own special pride and institutional existence as a servant of the *Presidency,* distinct from (and sometimes not entirely consistent with) service to a particular President. Such a tendency exists for smaller staffs as well. But it is often mitigated by rapid turnover. For example, few men in ISA's regional offices, military or civilian, had held their jobs longer than three years as of the fall of 1969. And sometimes a boss encourages or forces such turnover. Nixon and Kissinger retained only two of the Rostow staff members they inherited, though partisan allegiances

February 1971 Department of State telephone directory included 8 FSO's; 4 departmental civil service employees or Foreign Service Reserve officers on the rolls over five years; 2 military officers; and only 5 "outsiders," including one present and one former White House fellow. All three top officials were FSO's, though Miriam Camps, an "outsider," was Deputy Director for Planning for the first year of the staff's existence.

The 63 per cent of S/PC staffers who were FSO's or regular departmental employees, can be compared to 29 per cent for the Kissinger staff as of April 1971. Fifty-two per cent of the NSC staff was recruited from outside State and the military services, compared to 26 per cent for S/PC.

In all these cases, people outside the foreign or military services are counted in terms of what they did prior to joining the staffs, since many outsiders come in under civil service or foreign service reserve appointments.

seem not to have been at issue, and in fact the new men came from backgrounds similar to the old.

Staff members' perspectives can grow to differ from those of the boss through *lack of personal contact with him*. And of this both the NSC and ISA staffs have had but limited doses. Their directors have been in close, usually daily touch. But others have seen the boss far less. Secretaries McNamara and Clifford dealt predominantly with the ISA Assistant Secretary, and seldom with Deputy Assistant Secretaries. Presidents Kennedy and Johnson had personal relationships with several of their NSC staff members but dealt mainly with their Special Assistants. Nixon deals just about exclusively with and through his. Thus if the White House and ISA staffs have not in general been afflicted with careerist allegiances or institutional identity, the lack of regular personal communication between the boss and most staff members has been a factor creating separate interests and perspectives.

Members of both staffs have also tended to develop and press *strong policy views of their own*. If Bundy was careful not to become identified with particular positions, Rostow's hawkish Vietnam line was concealed from no one. Kissinger also entered office with a strong and widely disseminated set of opinions, though he has been more successful than Rostow in avoiding the image as an advocate of particular policy courses within the bureaucracy. And there are other examples of policy "advocates" within the White House, such as Kaysen and Wiesner as proponents of arms control under Kennedy, and James C. Thomson, Jr., who won from his superior the accolade, "My favorite dove."[23]

ISA has if anything featured even stronger advocacy. McNaughton has been characterized as "deeply disenchanted with the Administration's Vietnam policy" before his untimely death in 1967, and his successor Warnke has been described as "perhaps the most anti-

Vietnam high official in the building."[24] In the later Johnson years, ISA men also grew increasingly skeptical about our existing scale of military involvement and foreign base arrangements, pressing a policy reassessment which eventually led to the return of Okinawa to Japan, and pushing the rewriting of a general U. S. government policy document on "counterinsurgency" to incline it toward keeping us out of local conflicts rather than getting us in. Ironically, in the Nixon Administration, ISA's policy stance has moved 180 degrees to a "hard-line," pro-military position.[j]

Thus foreign policy staffers are anything but anonyms who easily and automatically would make the views of the boss their own. Yet there are striking parallels between the views of staff men and their bosses. Rostow was characterized as a hawk, but he was also accused of telling the President what he wanted to hear. Similarly, Kaysen and Wiesner on arms control, and McNaughton and Warnke on Vietnam, were pressing a policy direction which their bosses found increasingly attractive. Thomson may have been counter to the trend on Vietnam, but he held a junior position and was shortly to leave the government. For in each case cited the staff man would have been (or, in Thomson's case, was) helpless in promoting his views without the sympathetic ear of the boss. ISA's differences with the military under McNamara reflected the attitudes of an aggressive boss determined to secure his own control. Its changed nature under Laird was consistent with his inclination to be far more conciliatory toward the services.

But staff members might be able to press divergent views more effectively if they had *bargaining advantages* which gave them leverage *independent of their imme-*

---

[j] Joseph Kraft has characterized the new men brought in by Secretary Laird and Assistant Secretary G. Warren Nutter as "a corps of right-wing clowns," a view widely shared in Washington. (*Washington Post*, May 5, 1970, p. A17.)

diate relationship to the chief. Inevitably they will have some. Indeed, they will need some to complement this relationship and provide a "handle" for involvement in issues. But in fact, the type of influence on broad policy sought by aggressive NSC and ISA staff men has been available to them almost solely through their ability to maintain the confidence and support of the boss. Success for each in his most important causes has required that the boss make them his own. Moreover, the staff man's broader credibility in battles he personally fights is heavily dependent on others' belief that he had topside support. Had these staffs a comprehensive role comparable to BoB, however—a prerogative to "decide" on budget amounts subject to reversal by the President— their independence from the boss could have been considerably greater.

There is, finally, the question of staff _size_. Obviously an ISA of 200 professionals lacked close attunement to the priorities of the Secretary of Defense except near the top levels. Staff-boss divergence must have been increased by the Secretary's practice of dealing largely with the Assistant Secretary alone, and by the preference of at least one Assistant Secretary for conducting serious business primarily with the Deputy Assistant Secretaries. A similar situation has developed in the Nixon NSC staff. The lack of a fine attunement even to Kissinger's perspective is reflected in his creation of a small personal staff within the staff, one of whose roles is to assure that the work of his regular staff members meets his personal needs.

In general, then, one can conclude that while White House and ISA staff views and perspectives have hardly been identical with those of their bosses, forces have operated to keep the differences from getting too wide. Most important has been the heavy dependence of staffers seeking effective influence on the confidence of the boss. And the tendency of staffs to, in fact, seek such

243

influence has been strengthened by the prevalence and dominance of short-term in-and-outers.

A related and more serious possibility is that staff-boss divergence might be solved on the staff's terms—by its "capture" of the boss and effective control of him. Rostow has been characterized as "a total ideologue with a captive President, a Rasputin with a Czar coming under siege."[25] But this view is surely exaggerated. Johnson met regularly on Vietnam with his Secretaries of State and Defense, and frequently consulted other personal advisers like Acheson, Clifford, and Abe Fortas. The Nixon-Kissinger relationship poses greater danger of such "capture" since the President likes to conduct serious foreign policy business so overwhelmingly through one man. Yet though it is impossible to know the balance of influence in such an intimate relationship, Kissinger seems—in Acheson's phrase—not to have forgotten "which is the President." And though dependence in such relationships runs two ways, the balance tends to be decidedly uneven, especially if the staff man likes his job as much as Kissinger seems to. The boss can often get another comparable assistant. The staff man can seldom find a remotely comparable boss.

Yet there can be a more subtle form of capture. If a staff man knows what the boss wants and responds instinctively and immediately, the boss may find it more productive—and more comfortable—to deal through him. If this becomes the predominant pattern, the boss may find himself less capable of effectively using other sources of aid and counsel when he wishes to, because he has gotten out of touch with them. This has probably occurred with Nixon and Kissinger.

But even if a boss can avoid such capture and keep his principal staff men well-attuned to his priorities, he must recognize that, at the lower levels of general substantive staffs, business is likely to be transacted in which he is neither involved nor much interested. On these matters staff influence is inevitably much reduced. But it is also less likely to be exercised in close harmony with the boss's priorities and purposes. Junior staff men have little communication with the boss, and often little more with the staff director. Their effectiveness—measured on a much reduced scale—will depend relatively more on their lateral contacts and relationships, and relatively less on lines of confidence upward. This suggests that efforts to promote policy coherence by increasing staff size become quickly subject to the law of diminishing returns.[k]

Other Problems With Staffs

Staffs are often compared to kings' courts, with members forever intriguing to win the sovereign's favor. Reedy so pictures the White House staff, though he seems to exempt its NSC component.[26] And though foreign affairs staffs seem to have been free of the more invidious forms of this malady, infighting inevitably occurs when jurisdictions are cloudy. Thus the early Kissinger staff saw considerable jockeying over who was responsible for what. And the ISA "policy plans" office maneuvered systematically and successfully to achieve the lead role within the shop on a number of critical issues. There is often a sense of power lying around waiting to be grabbed, especially in the early days of an administration. But if the effectiveness of an individual

[k] It suggests also that the NSC and ISA staffs are a *hybrid*, bridging the useful distinction between *personal* and *institutional* staffs which Neustadt likes to make. ("Staffing the Presidency," in Altshuler, *Politics of the Bureaucracy*, pp. 109-13; Jackson Subcommittee, *Administration*, Hearings, pp. 81ff.) They are institutional in the sense that they have relatively fixed substantive policy areas and sets of bureaucratic relationships, that most staff members do not deal personally with the boss, and that relationships within the staff are strongly influenced by hierarchy. They are personal in the sense that their bargaining advantages rest heavily on the confidence of the boss and that the men who play the most important roles on them are usually individually recruited. Above all, they are very personal at the top and quite institutional at the bottom.

staff man will depend in considerable degree on his skill at political maneuver, internal infighting may have the effect of "selecting" for key roles those most able to play them strongly. And as the game has been played to date, the capacity to analyze issues and size up policy and bureaucratic situations has been quite important in winning the boss's approval. So competition should also favor those with analytical skills.

A more serious problem is whether staffs seeking effectiveness will tend to become too bureaucratic politics-oriented. Put another way, since such staffs will spend a great deal of effort fighting bureaucratic battles but have very little direct experience in dealing with actual foreign policy problems where they happen (i.e., overseas), will they not tend to define problems in terms of the need to win at bureaucratic politics and selectively interpret overseas events in directions which strengthen their hand in immediate arguments? If, for example, a staff man's main job in a particular month was to secure inter-agency agreement to a proposal for a treaty "regularizing" the status of West Berlin, would he give full credence to reports that East Germany planned to sabotage such an agreement, since such reports would be ammunition in the hands of those within our government who thought such a treaty an unwise objective?

A variant of this problem is that posed by Hughes—whether substantive staffs spawn and reward individuals without strong policy convictions of their own but capable of presenting all sides of a question and arguing any one of them. Similarly, Thomson writes of the "effectiveness trap," which causes men to avoid fighting today in order, they think, to conserve their effectiveness for the fights of tomorrow. Thus, he concludes, the decision to make Vietnam "our war" was not challenged by enough dedicated dissenters. This tendency is to some degree built into staffs. Though they often contain members with strong policy convictions, their job is both to give their boss all sides of a question and to work to promote his policy views. The incentives will certainly be weighted against strong challenges to these views once the boss has "opted." Yet countering this is the fact that it is often those who have strong policy convictions who will commit the energy required to press effectively for policy changes. Thus Henry Owen, who "cared passionately" about the Development Loan Fund, worked tirelessly and successfully to bring about its creation.[27]

The conflict between the roles of "objective" analyst and policy advocate is likewise built in, as it is for all persons who are "part of the action" in foreign policymaking. The "reasoned analysis" side of the staff man's contribution to government may however be strengthened by the fact that he will often not go into battle with explicit orders from his boss and assurance of his backing. Often Presidents (or Secretaries of State) don't want their staffers phoning around town saying, "The President (Secretary) wants it just this way." They may fear that a staff man with such a strong mandate will go into business on his own. Or they may recognize what all chastened staff men eventually learn: that even though they may reflect the chief's perspective better than anybody else, though they may be in daily contact with him, though there may be the maximum of loyalty in both directions, there is still an inevitable—and substantial—gap between the way the staff man sees things and the chief's personal assessment of the substance and politics of an issue.

So substantive staff men will often find themselves armed with their boss's general confidence and a "hunting license" to see how far they can get on an issue, but without a clear advance guarantee of support. When this is the case, they gain to the degree they can put issues on an analytic basis, bringing them out on the table for a full airing, hoping to gain from an ability to analyze and persuade what they lack in power to compel. Thus the capacity to reason can assume special importance for the staff man. His bargaining advantages give him a hearing and may even make others want to go along with him, if they can do so in a way consistent with how they see their own responsibilities. But they must be persuaded, and persuasion requires reason, directed both at the substance of the issue and its relation to others' perspectives and interests. It may range from low-key nudgings to sharp challenges that cut through bureaucratic logic and narrow objectives. But in a strategy seeking greater overall coherence and rationality in foreign policy, it clearly has a useful place.

Staffing the Secretary of State

How does this broader analysis of staffs relate to the problems of the Secretary of State? What lessons does it offer about how to build an effective central staff responsive to him?

Certainly the most effective foreign affairs staffs of the sixties were deeply involved in the day-to-day flow of foreign policy business. And the transformation of the Policy Planning Council into the Planning and Coordination Staff was a clear step in this direction. But if the NSC/ISA experience suggests that this was the right way to move, it also highlights the limits of State's recent effort in terms of staff effectiveness. For S/PC has developed neither the strong confidence of the boss nor a handle on current business. Moreover, the recruitment of the staff primarily from within the career service not only lessened the likelihood that it would be attuned to the interests of the Secretary. It also had the effect of linking the staff to a subculture which, as discussed in Chapter Six, has not placed high priority on Washington bureaucratic effectiveness.

Manning the staff predominantly with insiders must have reassured those in State long biased against direct

Secretarial staff support. But the conclusion drawn by many on the outside was that State's top officials were just not that serious about getting a handle on their shop, or providing the type of shake-up of the way the Department does its business which seemed necessary to staff the Secretary and the President in a more responsive way. To them the lesson of the sixties was that you don't bring more aggressiveness and Presidentially-oriented analysis to a Department by depending mainly on a Foreign Service which had failed to provide it in the past. The appointment of Cargo was, therefore, not regarded as an indication that State sought to "take charge" even within the limits imposed by the Nixon system. And the frequent comments heard about the staff in late 1969 and early 1970—"Of course they've just gotten organized," "It'll take time to see how the new organization works out," etc.—could hardly have been more different than the talk about the Bundy or Kissinger staffs or McNamara's men during their early months.

If State's top officials really wish to strengthen their Department's role, one thing they must do is to break through the pattern of nonresponsiveness to Presidents which has caused power to drift to the White House. In particular, they must seek a cure for State's chronic inability (or unwillingness) to: develop and analyze the widest range of policy options; challenge and evaluate the expertise of others; take the broadest view of issues and its mandate; write good, concise prose for high-level readership, and in general respond quickly and appropriately to Presidential needs.

Since these are precisely the sorts of things which general substantive staffs can do well, there is every reason for a Secretary of State to create a group of people who are outside of the old pattern—recruited predominantly from outside the career service, placed in staff positions where they can do the tough work of developing and evaluating options, challenging others' exper-

249

tise, and riding herd on key policy issues. They must be *the Secretary's men*, and so viewed by him and the bureaucracy at large. They would, of course, draw heavily on the rest of the Department for support, just as the NSC staff does. They would also fight with the rest of the Department. They would be distinct; and much of the work they would do for the Secretary—and for the President in his behalf—should be free from the elaborate clearance requirements that have cost departmental staff work so much in time, content, and lucidity.

They would need to be in daily touch with officials in State's bureaus and in other departments. Indeed they could not afford not to be. But the Secretary and his men are going to have to think of themselves as a group quite distinct from the Department at large. They will need to be:

far more present-oriented in terms of tying their ambitions to performance on their present jobs (but not in tying their sights to their in-baskets);

far more "Presidential"—oriented to the President's broad view of policy, his need for illumination of choices, his need for tough questioning and analysis of pet bureaucratic doctrines; and

far more inclined toward maximizing their influence in Washington decision-making.

None of this is meant to imply that the ISA or White House examples are perfect models that a Secretary of State need only copy. ISA, for example, was not a comprehensive staff for the Secretary of Defense. Its mandate covered only a portion of that Secretary's total responsibilities, with other staffs like Systems Analysis working in different (though overlapping) spheres. But the Secretary of State needs a staff concerned with the totality of his foreign affairs responsibilities, both to strengthen his influence over his Department and other agencies and to achieve that responsiveness to the President which is a prerequisite if State is to play the central policy role.

Yet he cannot concentrate so much on building a strong staff that he destroys the effectiveness of his key line officials—the regional Assistant Secretaries. For what is needed is neither the trim line organization favored by some nor the top-heavy staff model presently in vogue at the White House. For if the line-dominant solution keeps issues buried, to be resolved by those with narrow perspectives, the staff-dominant solution undercuts the development of organizational strength anywhere below the top. The line solution places undue faith in organizational tidiness and trim lines of authority. The staff solution ducks the problem of reforming the general organization at all, by the device of creating another above it to do the really important work. But it can never do this without growing to such a size that it develops "line-type" interests and biases which make it far from "Presidential."

It is easier, of course, to talk about the need to strengthen both staff and line than to argue convincingly that it can be done. For staffs tend to bring problems up to the level of their bosses and weaken those who seek to resolve them below that level. At minimum they need the ability to do this in order to influence lower-level decisions. Yet the foreign affairs bureaucracy is simply too large and complex to be run from one level of authority. If one tries, the result is likely to resemble the Nixon Administration, where the mandate to bring coherence to the whole enterprise rests predominantly on the shoulders of one harassed White House aide.

What is required, instead, is an organizational strategy which recognizes the indispensability of general substantive staffs, yet does not expect them to carry more of the burden for bringing coherence to foreign policy than they are able to bear. This suggests that such staffs should be strong but relatively small, so as to promote responsiveness to their bosses and to discourage any illusions that they can handle the whole foreign policy job. It suggests further that, if staffs are required both to enhance the control of key officials and to analyze ongoing policies in broad perspective, they should be created to serve line officials at several points in the hierarchy.

The aim should be to produce a creative tension between adjoining bureaucratic levels. A foreign affairs organizational strategy must begin at the top, because the President's influence is necessary for any approach to coherence, and because pressure from above is necessary to force line officials to broaden their perspectives. The fact that State has taken any action toward strengthening its Seventh Floor staff is due considerably to the challenge posed by an enhanced White House role. Similarly, Kennan told the Jackson Subcommittee of a recurrent phenomenon during his Policy Planning Staff days:

> As we took a problem under discussion in the staff and as we began to discuss various ideas of what could be done about it, we would invite representatives of the various divisions of the Department of State to come down and talk with us and hear what we were saying. They would sit there and hear all of this, and run back to the divisions saying, "You know what the planning staff is thinking of doing? We had better do something ourselves, quickly, before they go ahead and write a paper about it." . . . they didn't want the recommendations to come from any other source.[28]

One would hope, then, that a strong State Seventh Floor staff would challenge regional Assistant Secretaries to provide improved policy analyses themselves in order to preserve their own influence, and that the need to do this would cause them to create the bureau-wide substantive staffs which several of the Macomber task forces

252

have recommended to so little avail. But if a Seventh Floor staff becomes too strong, or if Assistant Secretaries respond by refusing to communicate rather than by joining in a policy dialogue and seeking to win it, the result of staff pressure can be a defensive reaction among the very line officials who are needed to exercise broad leadership. State as a whole has repeatedly responded to White House pressure by clinging to a relatively narrow role. Similarly, regional Assistant Secretaries and their subordinates can take refuge in the bargaining advantages that accrue from sitting astride communications with embassies and foreign governments. They can become—as they sometimes now are—the spokesmen for traditional Foreign Service priorities and for overseas constituencies both American and foreign, rather than the indispensable agents for turning Presidential objectives into actual government policies.

Is it possible to devise an organizational strategy which stands a reasonable chance of preventing this outcome? Can one dare hope to organize for foreign policy in a way that strengthens both general substantive staffs and key line officials? It is certainly important to try. The rest of this book seeks to describe how one might go about making the attempt.

CHAPTER NINE

Building Lines of Confidence:
A State-Centered Organizational Strategy

To COMBINE the realist's caution and the reformer's zeal has not been an easy task. This study has sought to stress the urgent need to bring greater coherence to foreign policy through organizational change. But it has found no shining solutions that others in their blindness have failed to perceive. Rather its pages tell a tale of proposals and approaches that have worked only partly when at all; of pervasive and persistent patterns of bureaucratic behavior which have prevailed over man's efforts to rationalize the foreign policy process.

Perhaps when more scholars have studied the foreign affairs bureaucracy and its many particular parts, we will learn more ways to bend it to central objectives. It would certainly be useful to have more on the written record about the contexts in which programming systems have been most influential; about the reasons why men do sometimes find coordinating committees useful; about the relations of staffs to their bosses; about the origins and development of the major foreign affairs staffs and the purposes their bosses intended them to serve. Perhaps also technological breakthroughs—like the ongoing revolution in information management—can enhance our means to control the large organizations we must create to serve our large purposes.

But the foreign affairs organizational problem exists today, to be dealt with by responsible men today. So the purpose of this final chapter is to suggest what might be done about it. It is written under a certain handicap. The author has never worked at the center of the foreign affairs government, though he has dealt with it from positions in four different places on its periphery.[a] He is therefore susceptible to what Anthony Downs has called the "superman syndrome," which affects "planners" with broad mandates and no operational responsibilities. "Unfettered by reality," Downs writes, such planners "can develop far more original, daring, sweeping, and internally consistent visions of what should be done than if they actually have to deal with the disenchanting welter of conflicting interests in the real world."[1] And though his complimentary adjectives may seem misplaced, there is the clear possibility that the foreign affairs organizational strategy put forward here will seem to the experienced eye no more practical than the product of the average metropolitan planning commission, and far less aesthetically pleasing.

Hopefully, however, the approach taken here has provided some insurance against this malady. The objective around which the book is written would no doubt please the most utopian seeker after rationality. But, while insisting on the importance of our government making coherent and purposive foreign policy, we have emphasized at least equally the futility of trying to make the foreign policy process conform to a rational design, and the consequent need to base organizational reforms on our best understanding of the nature of that process and what moves it. This has led to concern about leverage, about effectiveness, about the various means by which individuals can achieve influence over government actions. For once it is decided to treat policy-making as a bureaucratic political process, any approach to coherence must try to assure that the men and institu-

[a] As Assistant to Senator Walter F. Mondale; as Staff Associate to the President's Task Force on Government Organization; as Regional Coordinator for Asia of the International Agricultural Development Service; and as Consultant for Special Programs to the American Foreign Service Association.

tions on which it is based can be influential in that process. Nor do there exist any attractive formal short-cuts like coordinating committees or central staffs. For our investigation indicated that these tend to prove in-effective unless tied to officials who already have power and who see such devices as means to protect or augment that power.

If building toward coherence thus requires enhancing the leverage of individuals motivated to seek it, there is only one place for an organizational strategy to begin. But a President works largely through other men, so a decision to start with him raises as many questions as it answers. The first of these is the question that opened this book: On whom should the President *primarily* rely for directing foreign policy? Assuming that the President spends much of his time on other things, the amount of coherence attainable will be very limited unless he gives an individual short of himself a mandate to exercise government-wide foreign policy leadership. But the need goes beyond this. For our overseas involve-ments are necessarily so large and complex, and the con-tribution of lower-level decisions to policy so critical, that there must be *lines of Presidential confidence* ex-tending beyond this individual—at least down to the Assistant Secretary level—if the President is to harness very much of the foreign affairs government to his pur-poses. Put otherwise, the quest for coherence requires an effort to build central organizational strength span-ning several hierarchical levels and to provide key men at each level with the leverage, the motivation, and the mandate to fight for the President's priorities in the bureaucratic political arena.

This need to develop strength in depth suggests that it is unwise to build a strategy around the President's national security adviser. As noted in Chapter Five, his job as staff aide requires him to concentrate heavily on meeting the President's immediate needs and protect-

256

ing his operational flexibility. This makes it very difficult for the Assistant to delegate authority and confidence to foreign affairs government officials below him. The Secretary of State feels a similar conflict between the needs of the President and the needs of his subordinates, but he is in a much better position to reconcile the two. His job is less that of providing personal staff service to the President. And, more than the Assistant, the Secretary derives leverage from his formal position: as head of the senior Cabinet department. He has important officials who report to him—Under Secretaries, Assistant Secretaries. All of these distinctions suggest that he can at least partially avoid the Kissinger bind, that his relationship with the President can be somewhat different, that he will not be so dominated by pressure to serve the man above that he is unable to support those below. Yet the influence of any Secretary seeking primacy in the foreign affairs government still depends strongly on known Presidential confidence. So the President ought to be able to keep the Secretary faithful to his policy priorities.

But the Secretary of State presides over a department which is markedly un-Presidential. Should one then not consider establishing an entirely new official and institution to direct foreign policy? One possibility would be to limit the Assistant's job to that of personal aide, and to create a new agency in the Executive Office of the President with more comprehensive responsibility for foreign affairs coordination. There is a parallel in the primarily domestic Office of Management and Budget (OMB). And such an Office of National Security Affairs has been frequently proposed. But it does not seem a good solution. Lacking the personal Assistant's intimate ties with the President, the Office Director and his staff would find bargaining advantages hard to come by unless able to impose a clearance system over departmental cables and other action documents which would constitute "layering" in its worst form and demoralize State beyond belief. In addition, comprehensive operational coordination from the Executive Office would require a unit far larger than the present NSC staff. Three or four European operating officers, for example, may well be able to keep on top of matters of reasonably immediate Presidential importance. They cannot hope to manage the general flow of foreign policy business.

By contrast, a State-centered strategy has no such depth problem. And building "Presidential" strength around the senior Cabinet official has the further marked advantage of reversing the recent Presidential tendency to give up on the regular departments and try to run the government from above them. The results of this approach tend to be a White House several steps removed from the bulk of day-to-day policy and program activities, and a permanent government demoralized and defensively confirmed in its parochialism. And if, as discussed in Chapter Three, one key problem of foreign affairs organization is to counter the bureaucratic political pressures that force officials' attention from international to intra-governmental developments, there are clear gains in basing one's strategy on men in a department which is particularly sensitive to the countries with which we deal.

For these and other reasons, the strategy proposed here will center around the Secretary of State. It will do so out of a judgment that the deficiencies of State as a Presidential instrument can be significantly reduced, whereas the weaknesses of White House-centered approaches seem close to insoluble. But others consider coordination from the White House inevitable because they have given up on State. The excellent *New York Times* series on the Nixon Administration's foreign policy-making opens with the conclusion that State "is no longer in charge of the United States' foreign affairs and that it cannot reasonably expect to be so again."

258

Similarly, Joseph Kraft has argued that "the United States is too deeply engaged around the globe for any mere Cabinet officer to be predominant in shaping this country's role in the world." "In fact," he continues, "the only official who can harmonize the vast range of this country's foreign policy interests is the President himself."[2]

Yet the issue is not whether the Secretary or the President has primacy. Rather it is who—the Secretary or the National Security Affairs Assistant—should be the central foreign affairs official short of the President and acting, to use the Bundy phrase, as his "agent of coordination." If the President is known to rely primarily on the Secretary of State for leadership in foreign policy-making across the board, he should prove far more formidable than a "mere Cabinet officer."

The more difficult problem is whether the Secretary will really seek to "take charge," and whether his Department can give him the type of support that will permit him to play this role. If not, power will assuredly pass to the White House. For no President will stick to a general organizational design if it doesn't work for him in daily practice. Kennedy leaned almost exclusively on McNamara for defense policy because McNamara met these needs. He operated increasingly around Rusk because Rusk did not. Cabinet departments are not normally at their best when asked to act in a Presidential perspective. Reliance on the White House, then, reflects the view Neustadt has cited but fallen short of endorsing: "that the State Department cannot be at once a department and then something more."[3]

One reason for hope that this conclusion can be proved false is that its Secretary has been traditionally regarded as "something more" than a Cabinet officer. Strong Secretaries like Acheson and Dulles have been dominant figures in their Administrations. Similarly, Assistant Secretaries of State play a recognized and important coordinating role, though it is not usually the type of strong leadership advocated here. There is, therefore, some tradition of primacy on which to build.

But to center on State is not to restore some mythical bygone era but to create a leadership across a broad range of issues which has never really existed before. Much ink has been spent describing State's post-war decline, yet it was in 1946 that a prominent journalist labeled it "the most criticized, mistrusted, and ineffectual Department of government." And even in days of relative glory Secretaries and their Department have often defined their job narrowly and missed important leadership opportunities. It was in the Marshall-Acheson era that the Central Intelligence Agency was created and established a pattern of operating independent of effective State Department guidance. Nor did Acheson feel it proper to go to Truman prior to General Douglas MacArthur's Korea debacle and "urge on the President a military course that his military advisers would not propose," even though he and other top officials, civilian and military, "knew something was badly wrong." Instead he followed the common State pattern of reluctance to challenge military expertise. Similarly, Dulles was wary about moving very actively into the sphere of his strongest Cabinet competitor, Secretary of the Treasury George Humphrey. Thus, both Acheson and Dulles saw the substantive range of their jobs as much more limited than Kissinger sees his. Yet a Secretary of State aspiring to true foreign affairs leadership in the 1970's must view his responsibilities as far wider than foreign relations traditionally defined.[4]

It is hard to see any logical reason why the top of the State Department could not develop just as broad a view of foreign policy as Kissinger has, and a capability for Presidential staff work equal to that of the present White House staff. But to build this kind of Department will require a broad strategy linking appointments,

structural reforms, and close daily communications between the President and State's key officials—a strategy,
in short, much more serious, much more comprehensive,
and much more centered on Presidential needs than any
State Department reform effort that has yet been attempted.

The Basic Strategy

Our strategy centers on the Secretary of State. The
President must want him to be his pre-eminent foreign
policy official. Furthermore, he must let it be known
that the Secretary's substantive mandate is as broad as he
can effectively stretch it, not carefully demarcated to
include certain categories of issues and exclude others.
But no new statutes should be enacted proclaiming this
authority: it should come personally from the President.
The personal relationship must be exceptionally close,
with the Secretary approaching (though no man can
actually attain it) the status of a Presidential *alter ego*
for foreign affairs.

This Secretary must place top priority on making the
State Department his own, and through it the overall
foreign affairs government. He must subordinate or
delegate his role as chief diplomat and see himself above
all as the top foreign policy adviser and manager. This
emphasis is essential if the Secretary is:

1. to be responsive to the President's need for options, for tough-minded advice that challenges pet
   bureaucratic doctrines, and thereby to make it in
   the President's interest to maintain Secretarial
   primacy;
2. to achieve maximum influence on the day-to-day
   actions of the foreign affairs government, aiming
   not only at prompt and faithful implementation
   of explicit Presidential decisions but also at a more
   general line of action consistent with top-level
   objectives and priorities.

261

As the first of these implies, we assume that the President will not delegate his foreign affairs involvement or his control over the major decisions. And, if it is largely the White House that handles the work supporting him and defines the issues for Presidential consideration, the Secretary will be too much removed from dealing with the major Presidential concerns to be able to keep his primary role. Thus, if the Secretary of State is to regain the status of primary Presidential foreign policy adviser, much of the work presently done by the NSC staff must be handled by men working *for* the Secretary, *in* the State Department.

This would not necessarily mean eliminating the position of Assistant for National Security Affairs. The President will still need a small staff in the White House to help handle his personal business, to supplement the Secretary's analyses of issues and choices, to work in areas where State's policy effectiveness is weakest and leadership mandate most marginal, and last but not least to prod State to do its job and provide insurance to the President by coming to the rescue when it doesn't. For the President is unlikely to want to rely exclusively on one adviser, even though he grants the Secretary clear primacy. Yet the very existence of a general foreign affairs aide in the White House will inevitably pose a threat to the Secretary and the role he seeks to play.

This strategy assumes that that threat can be minimized. This will require, however, that both the President and the Assistant recognize that the latter's job is to be overwhelmingly that of personal aide rather than broad national security policy coordinator in the Kissinger—or the Bundy—manner. Even more important, it will require that the Secretary and his Department demonstrate daily that they can provide staff support to the President's satisfaction. Not only would State have to handle all staff work that aspired to comprehensiveness of coverage—such as the managing of regular

262

policy review and formulation procedures—but it would also have to do much *ad hoc* staff work for the President, usually through the Secretary in his role of pre-eminent Presidential adviser.[b]

Effective staff work for the chief would be accompanied by a conscious effort to build downward into the bureaucracy those *lines of confidence* from the President which Rusk described as "the real organization of government at higher echelons." Particular emphasis would be placed on building strong relationships between the President and the Secretary, on the one hand, and the regional Assistant Secretaries of State on the other. For as Robert Tufts has noted, "it is through such men that the President and his Cabinet members must work if the bureaucracy is to serve them, not the other way around."[5]

Good up-down relations would not, however, be sufficient. A central purpose of the strategy is to enable State's major officials to exercise strong leadership *laterally*, not only on aid and information activities but above all on political-military issues, including intelligence. Assistant Secretaries, for example, will require both the stature and the perception to resolve issues in a way resembling how the President would; otherwise the President cannot long afford to support them come the inevitable appeals. This in turn requires far greater attunement than State presently possesses toward the nature and depth of the interests of other governmental

[b] One further possible means of strengthening the Secretary vis-à-vis the Assistant would be to move the offices of the former and his chief aides to the Executive Office Building next to the White House. This would, however, have the serious drawback of tending to disassociate the Secretary from his Department, when the principal reason for building on him rather than the Assistant is that his Department offers the prospect of leadership at several hierarchical levels. One would hardly gain from a Secretary-based strategy if one had to convert his job to that of the Assistant in order to put it across.

Thus, such a move would probably be unwise unless it could include a considerable proportion of the Secretary's supporting cast: other Seventh Floor principals and staffs, Assistant Secretaries, and considerable numbers of *their* aides.

and non-governmental foreign affairs "players." It implies inter-agency relationships in which State officials are at once more understanding, more aggressive, and more politically calculating (meaning primarily *bureaucratic* politics) than is presently the rule.

For the aim at each level would be to build strength across the board: across a wide range of substantive issues; in "policy planning," "coordination of operations," "resource allocation," and whatever other components of the foreign policy process might be usefully separated out and defined. It would also aim to reduce or eliminate the present tendency for "crisis management" to be handled by small, "closed" groups around or above the people responsible for more routine, day-to-day actions on the same policy problems.[c] State's influence would, of course, vary somewhat with the substance of the issue; it might well not always prevail, for example, on textiles. But no State Department that stressed "political" (at the expense of military or economic) matters or otherwise guarded a narrow piece of bureaucratic turf, no Secretary who saw his Department's mandate as primarily "policy" divorced from "operations," could adequately play the central role for the President. For despite the apparent belief of many Foggy Bottom residents, State cannot have it both ways. It cannot be the President's chosen agent while remaining responsive primarily to its traditional values and priorities.

But if the Department must eschew parochialism to play on center stage, the President must also pay a certain price if he hopes to make the foreign affairs government more his own. Presidents can't have it both ways either: they cannot keep all their flexibility, all their

[c] In one provocative characterization of this phenomenon, John W. Bowling argues that at present, "Crisis management bypasses the standard policy formulation mechanism and is a separate process, with only marginal overlap." ("How We Do Our Thing: Crisis Management," *Foreign Service Journal*, May 1970, p. 19.)

options, all their prerogatives to avoid decisions or to play subordinates off against each other or to withhold their general intentions from key advisers, and yet have a bureaucracy which moves reliably in the directions they desire. The President must support his underlings if he wishes to strengthen them, avoid undercutting them while still not becoming their captive. And if he wants government actions to reflect his policy objectives, he must make clear what these objectives are. Responsiveness, confidence, communications are the key words, and all must flow both up and down. The cost to the State Department of "doing its own thing" is the "little State Department" in the White House basement. The cost to the President of playing too close a hand is the sort of gap between the inner policy circle and the broader government which has marred both the Johnson and Nixon Administrations.

The Team at the Top

Critical to our strategy is the appointment of a Presidential team of exceptional men to the key "line" positions in State—the Secretary, the Under Secretary, the major Assistant Secretaries. They would in turn be the center of a larger foreign policy team, including in particular the President's National Security Adviser and the Secretary of Defense. The President should make it clear that he regards State's Assistant Secretaries as being of Cabinet-level importance. And if the strategy works as suggested, a President giving priority to foreign policy would be likely to have more personal contact with his Assistant Secretary for European Affairs (whose bailiwick, after all, includes U. S.-Soviet relations) than with some of his domestic Secretaries. A sincere Presidential statement stressing their importance may not, initially, be believed, just as Kennedy was not (with good reason) when he announced that the post of Assistant Secretary for African Affairs was "a job second to none" in his Administration.[d] But if the President appoints men of exceptional caliber and treats them as important to him, the word will get around.

Yet these Assistant Secretaries must work primarily with and through the Secretary, not around him as was the frequent Kennedy pattern. To further the prospects that they will do so, the Secretary should be the prime source of recommendations for all State Presidential appointments but his own. A new President should most definitely not appoint around him or choose other State officials before him, as did Kennedy. But once he has this mandate to put together his own team, a wise Secretary or Secretary-designate will be responsive to Presidential suggestions and view it as an advantage, not a threat, for the President to have prior personal confidence in several departmental political appointees.

Qualifications for such positions are elusive. Obviously bureaucratic political skill is critical, as is interest, knowledge, and broad experience in a range of foreign affairs issues. As many as possible of the team should be of Secretarial caliber. Men who have strong national constituencies of their own should be avoided, since this would give them bargaining advantages usable against the President and compete with loyalty to him. This would exclude an Adlai Stevenson, but not a Chester Bowles or an Averell Harriman. Nor should appointees come from the career service. To assure prime loyalty to the President, outstanding FSO's should be expected, like their civil service counterparts, to resign from career status when accepting an appointment at the Assistant Secretary level and above. In no case should an Assistant

---

[d] Kennedy also declared in 1961 "that the regional Assistant Secretaries of State were more important officers of the government than most of the Cabinet." (Lincoln Gordon, "The Growth of American Representation Overseas," in Vincent M. Barnett, Jr. [ed.], *The Representation of the United States Abroad*, Praeger [for the American Assembly], 1965, pp. 25-6).

Secretaryship be regarded as a normal rotation post for a good career officer to fill some time in the second half of his active service.

Once the team is assembled, the Secretary should encourage the President to get to know the Assistant Secretaries, to deal directly with them from time to time, to include them in the important meetings and the crisis decisions within their jurisdictions. Sorensen writes somewhat disparagingly that under Kennedy "State Department aides grumbled privately that their prestige suffered if they were not present for key decisions."[6] But the aides were doubtless right, and if they were men the President wanted to play important leadership roles in foreign policy, he suffered also.

Finally, if we want these positions filled with strong men enjoying Presidential and Secretarial confidence, there must be a willingness to dismiss or transfer those persons who do not measure up to these exacting standards. It is hard to make lines of formal authority and lines of confidence converge if one follows the common practice of keeping on, and going around, a man who holds a key position but is weak or out of favor. Removing men who don't work out is a tough business, one that can only be partially eased by making them Ambassadors-at-Large or Counselors to the President. But building strength cannot be achieved by tolerating weakness in the most important places.

The Secretary's Deputy

A Secretary seeking to play the lead role cannot do it alone. He needs, above all, a strong Under Secretary. His aim should be to make this man a full deputy and *alter ego*, commissioned to act in his name on all issues with all people. To build the type of relationship that will permit such blanket confidence, the Secretary must invest considerable time and effort. But the returns to him—the stretching of his own influence—will make this investment more than worthwhile. And the President above him and Assistant Secretaries below will also find their effectiveness enhanced because there are two men at his level with whom they can fruitfully deal.

But in view of the great advantages of an *alter ego* relationship, it is surprising how rarely it is found in high government. McNamara and Clifford considered their deputies *alter egos*, but (at least in later years) their Assistant Secretaries for International Security Affairs did not. Probably State has not had such a team at the top since Secretary Marshall, despite a stream of able Under Secretaries. In the bureaus the phenomenon seems equally rare. So it is also in domestic government departments.

The reasons seem to be at least three. One is personal —men of the type who reach high-level office may have done so by husbanding their personal power and/or relying primarily on their own independent judgment. (Lawyers and professors may be particularly prone to this do-everything-yourself tendency.) It may seem threatening to them to reverse a lifetime of habit and share authority and responsibility so intimately. The second is that the man may play only a small role—or none at all—in his deputy's selection. The third is that officials above and below them tend to want to deal with the top man, and the distinction that *they* make tends to stick barring a determined effort by the would-be *alter egos* to combat it.

The first problem is the hardest—it can be lessened only by appointing men who are relatively receptive to this kind of relationship. The answer to the second is much simpler—to allow a chief the major role in his deputy's selection. The best answer for the third is for the President to show that he is willing to deal with either man. As a general rule, of course, it would still be the Secretary who went to the White House when both were in town.

The division of labor between the Secretary and his deputy should be their decision, and communication between them their responsibility. In general all formal authority should rest with the top man. The Under Secretary might tend to become the "executive officer" who "ran the ship," but this would be something for him and his boss to decide for themselves. To strengthen his position, however, a better title would help,[e] such as "Deputy Secretary"—like the number two official in Defense—or perhaps even "Foreign Secretary" as suggested by AFSA.[7]

Other Seventh Floor Principals

But if the number two man has a clear and needed role, others among State's ranking officials do not. Such men as the Under Secretary for Political (sometimes Economic) Affairs, the Deputy Under Secretary for Economic (formerly Political) Affairs, and the Counselor have few clearly established responsibilities. They must therefore devote much of their energy to carving out policy territory for themselves. Not only does the infighting among them and their staffs tend to reduce Seventh Floor coherence. If an Under Secretary for Political Affairs is hunting for issues to ride he is likely to pull rank on an embattled Assistant Secretary and grab his most urgent problem. This phenomenon, particularly frequent in European and Middle Eastern matters, tends to frustrate any effort to build organizational strength below the Seventh Floor.

This is not, of course, to imply that an Assistant Secretary should have equal influence over all matters within his formal bailiwick, whatever their urgency. Any system must allow issues to move up and down the hierarchy as the need arises. Any system must assume that the Secretary and the President, for example, will spend more of

[e] It would also help if the regional Assistant Secretaries could be elevated in rank to Under Secretaries.

their personal time on the most critical issues, and on these the Assistant Secretary will be more a supporter than a policy leader in his own right. But on precisely these types of issues it is particularly important to protect and build up the Assistant Secretary as a credible transmitter of Presidential wishes to the foreign affairs bureaucracy, as a central "crisis manager" if crisis it be, as the faithful executor of decisions he understands from direct participation in their making.

The best answer to these problems is *not*, as often proposed, to create a new No. 3 man, an "Executive" or "Permanent" Under Secretary, and assume that he can pull it all together. For he can't. But some restructuring is essential. Specifically, certain positions should be abolished in their present form—the Under Secretary for Political (or Economic) Affairs, the Deputy Under Secretary for Economic (or Political) Affairs, the Counselor, and as many of the special-purpose Special Assistants and roving Ambassadors as possible. The meaningless phrase, "political affairs," should be barred from all titles since it is useful mainly as a hunting license and reflects no definable substantive category.

The number three and number four positions, however, might be useful if somewhat recast. Since the increasingly important area of international economic policy involves a special group of bureaucratic actors—including the Secretary of the Treasury and others of Cabinet or near-Cabinet rank—State can benefit from having an official at the Under Secretary level devoting full time to these problems. Also, there would be good use for a Deputy Under Secretary in the political-military sphere, to take charge of State's new responsibilities for security-related assistance, and otherwise spur a strengthened State involvement in defense, arms control, and related questions. But these officials should not be floating senior staff aides, but rather have direct authority over the bureaus dealing with these matters

270

and strong, specific mandates to strengthen State's performance on economic and political-military questions. The post of Deputy Under Secretary for Administration does have a logical set of functions, but its occupant has tended to suffer from top-level indifference both to him and his mission. Hopefully, a Secretary strongly interested in remaking his Department would find "administration" more relevant to his own work. It might be useful, however, to signal a closer relationship between administration and substance by renaming the position "Deputy Under Secretary for Management."*

The Seventh Floor Staff

If a State-centered organizational strategy is to have any hope of success, the Department must produce "good staff work" for both President and Secretary. This can be accomplished only by creating a staff unit which shares their perspective, and which has both the necessary "handles" for involvement in current issues and the

*Just before this book went to press, the State Department announced several changes in Seventh Floor organization as part of the Macomber reform program. Congress is to be asked to elevate the number two official to "Deputy Secretary," and he is to head a "Senior Management Team" comprised of the principal Seventh Floor policy officials. The major purpose of this "Team" is apparently to relate departmental resource allocation more closely to substantive decision-making. Also, the Deputy Under Secretary for Economic Affairs is to be raised (Congress willing) to Under Secretary for Economic Affairs, and the number five official will be renamed Deputy Under Secretary for Management as suggested here. ("Management Reform Bulletin: The Seventh Floor," No. 24, July 6, 1971.)

It is difficult to tell whether the net result of all this will be more Seventh Floor coherence or less. The above changes are promising, but the fuzziest of the Seventh Floor jobs—the Under Secretary for Political Affairs and the Counselor—are to be retained unchanged. And further confusion may be added by the creation of "a new position of Coordinator for Security Assistance at the Under Secretary level," without a clear relationship to either the Bureau of Politico-Military Affairs and its Director or the "Political" Under Secretary. Also, the Secretariat and the Planning and Coordination Staff are apparently to be kept as separate units rather than combined as proposed below.

271

aggressiveness to exploit them. These "Secretary's men" should be identified with him rather than the career Foreign Service or departmental staff. Their director will need to have an intimate relationship to the Secretary.

They should be predominantly a "generalist" group. This is not to say that they would not require, individually and collectively, considerable foreign affairs background and specific expertise. But specialized staffs would be housed elsewhere, in places like the Bureaus of Politico-Military and Economic Affairs. The role of the Secretary's men would be rather, in Ambassador Berger's words, "to relate one field to another"[8] and to the Secretary's broader responsibilities. The work they did would be similar to that of other "general substantive staffs" discussed in Chapter Eight. While some staff members would be FSO's, the majority at least initially should not be. They, together with a non-FSO director personally chosen by the Secretary, would "set the tone" of the group, making it "Secretarial" rather than departmental or careerist. As to numbers, perhaps the present size of the Planning and Coordination Staff, 20-plus, would be reasonable for a start, though only a few at most would have direct contact with the Secretary.

But to establish such a staff as a separate entity would be to condemn it to the fate of S/PC—separation from the regular flow of business to the Secretary. The Executive Secretary's role in managing this flow tends to make him the Secretary's prime personal aide. This role would be important for the substantive staff director to play if he is to understand the Secretary's needs and priorities, and be taken seriously in the Department and elsewhere in town. Moreover, the general responsibility of Exec Sec for Secretarial business is the best "handle" for staff involvement in issues, paralleling the flow of paper through Kissinger to the President.

Thus the staff needs to be joined with the Executive

Secretariat. This new entity could be called the Office of Policy Review and Coordination as recommended in the IDA study,[9] or perhaps simply the Seventh Floor Staff. This merger would also eliminate the present unreal distinction between "policy coordination" and "operational coordination." For clearly much of what Exec Sec now does is of central policy significance—shaping and policing understandings about who has a right to be consulted on which issue, making sure, in Macomber's recent words, that the Secretary and the Under Secretary are "responsive . . . to the areas [of policy] which on a priority basis most need their attention."[10] Such matters are at the heart of a general substantive staff's functions.

Exactly how the twenty-odd "general substantive" staff members would be blended with the sixty Exec Sec professionals is a matter too detailed for treatment here. The present NSC staff provides the President both substantive analysis and operational support, and its experience could well provide relevant lessons. Doubtless there would be on the combined Seventh Floor Staff some men who mainly policed the paper flow and others who were in close touch with it but spent their time looking into, and weighing in on, substantive issues.

The staff would support the work of State-chaired interdepartmental committees at its level, and house the central analytic group for a foreign affairs programming system. Any "policy planning" group on the old State model would also be included within it. Since such a group would need to have both greater separation from immediate operations than others on the Seventh Floor and at the same time sufficient proximity to operations to do useful work, the best solution would probably be to keep the S/PC-type arrangement and provide the planning group with its own deputy staff director. This *could* mean greater relevance for this activity than it has usually achieved, since the "planning" group would be in proximity to more operationally oriented staffers with an interest in and handle for promoting change.

Assistant Secretaries and Regional Staffs

This and previous chapters have stressed the indispensable role of regional Assistant Secretaries of State as agents of Presidential influence. Yet the proposed Seventh Floor Staff, necessary to build the Secretary's ascendancy and assure responsiveness to Presidential needs, cannot help but prove something of a rival to Assistant Secretaries. What can be done to build them up in turn? Is it possible to strengthen both staff and line?

Critical, of course, are strong appointees, strong deputies to each, and Presidential and Secretarial confidence. But if "the real organization of government" is "how confidence flows down from the President," Rusk has also stressed the importance of "the performance which earns that confidence from bottom to top."[11] How can Assistant Secretaries come through with "the performance that earns confidence" if the Seventh Floor Staff is formulating issues in ways more relevant to Secretarial needs? And how can they assure that they will be more than the spokesmen of Ambassadors and Country Directors inevitably biased toward foreign clients?

To avoid such fates, they will need strong substantive staffs also. These should perform functions similar to their Seventh Floor counterpart, and be peopled with the same types. However, they would be far smaller, and most staff members at the regional level could have the advantage of regular personal contact with their boss. The best idea would probably be to begin small, with four or five professionals for each general regional staff. These staffs might be enlarged if useful, but since the bureaus are much smaller and more intimate institutions than the Department as a whole, care should be taken to avoid making them top-heavy.

274

In practice, relationships between Seventh Floor and regional staffs would likely be both competitive and cooperative. They would be raising the same sorts of questions—challenging line operators with a longer time focus and a broader geographic and substantive range. They should therefore prove kindred spirits. At the same time, they will be supporting the inevitably differing needs of different levels of authority, and perhaps different viewpoints on issues and problems as well. Hopefully, one result would be more explicit exposing of the rationales behind particular actions and programs.

Even small general staffs in the regions, however, would be a marked departure from the State tradition. The bureaus have traditionally resisted not only the development of Seventh Floor staff resources but also the creation of regional policy staffs for themselves. Latin America is to some degree an exception, but only a limited one. Nor are the reasons for such resistance hard to find. Just as a Seventh Floor Staff threatens regional Assistant Secretaries, a regional staff does the same to the next level of authority—the Country Director.

Again, there are ways that Country Directors can be strengthened, particularly removing the frequent "layer" between them and the Assistant Secretary—the Deputy Assistant Secretary with an area responsibility—and limiting Deputy Assistant Secretary positions to the one *alter ego* and others as needed with functional responsibilities. But it remains debatable whether the recent official effort to build Country Directors into senior, cross-governmental policy leaders is either realistic or wise. The basic problem is that an official seeking to play a broad coordinating role in foreign affairs can develop little effective power that is not based on a line of Presidential confidence. A Country Director's leadership becomes a sham if he lacks the strong backing of

275

superiors who themselves have bureaucratic clout. But three layers is a long way for either the President's confidence or his perspective to travel, even assuming direct President-Secretary-Assistant Secretary-Country Director relations. Thus the Country Director is likely, as one Macomber task force dissenter argued, to be "too far removed from the source of political power to evaluate, reconcile, and arbitrate the U. S. interests involved in any important issue."[12] And if the Country Director is not very likely to be sensitive to Presidential needs, he will be overly sensitive to the needs of "his" country, tending to measure success in U. S. foreign policy in terms of whether we can maintain "good relations" with it.

Thus the strategy proposed here would not place great faith in building Presidentially-related strength at the country level. Much would depend, however, on the leadership of a particular Assistant Secretary. It is probably unwise for a President—or even a Secretary—to prescribe a single organizational pattern for all regional bureaus, other than the creation of small substantive staffs. But the existence of strong Assistant Secretaries would provide a link to power which an aggressive Country Director might exploit if he could develop the confidence of his boss.

Formal Control Devices

Relatively formal mechanisms would be supplemental devices in our strategy, to be exploited as useful to strengthen central officials. There would be a general fixed coordinating committee system with the key officials as chairmen, both to legitimize their inter-agency leadership and provide them a useful tool. It would be patterned largely after the Johnson SIG/IRG system, except that the senior body would be at the Cabinet level and chaired by the Secretary. The Secretary might in turn choose to delegate much of its operation to the

Under Secretary as his *alter ego*, who would then head a formal or *ad hoc* subcommittee comprised of his counterparts around town. The National Security Council would diminish in importance but continue to exist. It would house the personal Presidential staff and be the formal focal point for discussing issues requiring Presidential decision. It might also be useful to have a staff committee headed by the Seventh Floor Staff Director to work on studies that come through the system. This would be somewhat comparable to the original concept of Nixon's NSC Review Group.

A programming system could be highly useful in establishing a central State role in shaping general foreign affairs budgets and personnel deployment. This might be developed in two stages. The first might combine a strengthening of State competence in budget analysis and an alliance with the Office of Management and Budget to assure timely State involvement in the budget cycle. This first stage would also include further and more extended experimentation with programming systems such as the Latin America CASP system. If State demonstrated its capability at this job and the utility of the process as a means for affecting important agency decisions, the Secretary could then seek to establish a formal State-centered foreign affairs budget and personnel review procedure, similar to that managed by OSD for the military and tied to a comprehensive programming system. OMB would keep its role of final review, comparable to what it has traditionally had vis-à-vis defense.

Neither the programming system nor the coordinating committees should be supported by special staffs but rather by the Seventh Floor and regional general staffs. Since programming would primarily be country-based, it should be managed as much as possible from the regions. If it became generally adopted, the need for special programming capability at the regional level

277

would probably mean expansion of regional substantive staffs beyond the size indicated earlier. State's review of the military budget, however, would be centered in the Bureau of Politico-Military Affairs.

There would be no effort at a comprehensive policy codification system. Our strategy would include, however, a modified Nixon-type policy review system for selected issues. The White House, State's Seventh Floor, and regional bureaus would all be involved in selecting the issues, and review processes would be arranged so that some were targeted for Presidential decision, some for the Secretary of State, and some for Assistant Secretaries. White House and Seventh Floor staffs would have the option of participating in all reviews, however, and could urge their bosses to pull issues up to their level if they felt important problems or possibilities were being neglected.

Political-Military Affairs— *The Crucial Bureaucratic Arena*

Essential to the success of this strategy would be effective leadership by the Secretary of State in that most urgent of foreign policy fields, that which is often termed "political-military" or "national security" policy. Military and para-military organizations, instruments and programs need to be subordinated to the broader foreign policy they are meant to serve.

But to state this aim raises the obvious problem. For the State Department can hardly hope to "run" or "control" our vast political-military apparatus in any simple sense. There is not only the problem of separate Congressional committees and strong domestic constituencies for these activities. There is also the fact that the Defense Department has a budget close to 200 times that of State and 50 times as many civilian employees.[13] For State to maximize its influence over their activities, a careful bureaucratic political strategy is required.

An indispensable prerequisite is a strong alliance with the Secretary of Defense and his office. State cannot control the military budget nor direct military operations, though hopefully it can influence both more than it has. But the Secretary of Defense and his staffs, with the support of the President and a strong central foreign affairs agency, have a fighting chance to do so. This means, of course, not only that the Secretary of Defense is inevitably a major foreign policy official in his own right, but that the Secretary of State should encourage his involvement in foreign policy issues so that his leadership of the Pentagon will reflect these concerns. To form such an alliance may involve some risk that the Defense chief will become the senior partner. But a strong Secretary of State should be able to keep this problem within bounds.

The alliance of the Secretaries should extend to their staffs and major officials. Specifically, State *needs* a strong ISA so that they can work together to subordinate overseas military activities to foreign policy objectives, since ISA will inevitably have greater depth, be closer to military issues, and be tied more directly to the Secretary of Defense. Once again, there is the risk of ISA becoming the main center for foreign policy initiative, as it was for some issues in the sixties. But this, too, ought to be manageable for a strong State Department. Much of ISA's impact in the later sixties was due to State's refusal to play the role of skeptic about overseas military activities. Furthermore, the cost to State of a weak ISA is far greater. State's ability to influence political-military matters cannot but be damaged if, as stressed by one State official interviewed, no one in OSD seems to have an effective handle on them short of Deputy Secretary David Packard. Just as a President and his top foreign policy official need centers of strength down in the bureaucracy to increase their reach and ability to influence issues, so also State needs centers of strength laterally, responsive to its leadership and able to work effectively toward common objectives. State leadership in political-military matters would require considerable personal effort by the Secretary and his *alter ego* deputy. They would need to be supported, however, not just by the general Seventh Floor Staff but by specialized staffs housed in the bureau headed by the proposed Deputy Under Secretary for Political-Military Affairs. Such staffs would need to be both capable of holding their own in technical military discussions and willing to challenge the military on its own ground. The two qualities—expertise and skepticism—do not always come together. Often an expert tends to internalize the basic assumptions of the practitioners of a field while he absorbs their specialized knowledge. But State's defense experts would not only have to be well versed, for example, about the expansion of the Soviet Mediterranean fleet. They would have to reject simplistic assertions of its "threat" to a "vital strategic crossroads" and insist on hard analysis of what types of problems it did pose for our interests. Fortunately, both the ranks of the defense intellectuals and the recent Pentagon critics contain men who combine such expertise and skepticism in ample measure.

Control of the CIA is another difficult problem, one which an outsider has special weaknesses in analyzing. Clandestine operations are particularly troublesome. In some cases, for better or for worse, they have basically *been* our foreign policy whether intended by State or not, as at the Bay of Pigs, in the overthrow of the Arbenz regime in Guatemala, and from time to time in Laos. On many other occasions they apparently have been a central element in it. There is a serious question as to how often such operations are really in our interest. But in any case they should be under the effective control of top policy-makers to avoid their being shaped primarily by intelligence operatives with an action-for-action's-sake mentality. It is quite possible, as Allen Dulles has argued, that "the CIA has never carried out any action of a political nature, given any support of any nature to any persons, potentates, or movements, political or otherwise, without appropriate approval at a high political level in our government *outside the CIA*."[14] But if central policy influence is achieved not mainly by one-shot approvals from hard-pressed high policy-makers who may or may not know all the relevant facts, but by regular involvement of central officials in details and day-to-day decisions, high-level approval is hardly enough. On the other hand, if too many people are in on a secret, it is a secret no longer.

There is surely no easy answer to this problem. But a State Department which was in fact our central foreign policy institution would provide a far stronger base on which to build effective control of the CIA than the committees of overworked men, responsible mainly for other things, upon which present control efforts apparently rest. Similarly, a strong State Department could be far more assertive in influencing intelligence-gathering priorities and in evaluating what comes in. What is needed, above all, is central foreign policy officials who have a strong stake in controlling the CIA and who have —responsive to them—the organizational strength and depth which gives them a chance to do the job.

Personnel

The strategy proposed here would be a marked departure from the practice of filling most important State Department positions with Foreign Service officers. There would be a considerable influx of new blood, particularly in-and-out types who were more analytically oriented, more inclined toward aggressive involvement in issues and risk-taking, recruited especially by the current administration's major policy officials and therefore loyal to them. Such a staffing emphasis is based on the assumption that no President of any strength is likely to entrust the success or failure of his foreign policy strategy to a career service, particularly one that has tended toward a restrictive definition of foreign policy and an aversion toward Washington bureaucratic politics. The "outsiders" brought in would include virtually all Presidential appointees, most of the substantive officers on the Seventh Floor Staff, and a considerable portion of regional staffs. The hope would be that they would think of themselves as "Secretary's men," and therefore "President's men."

There is a related assumption—that sufficient people of this type would be available with foreign affairs background and bureaucratic experience. The Bundy, Kissinger, and ISA staffs have shown that such persons can be found, though in somewhat smaller numbers. Presumably the base grows broader as time passes, and a considerable number of them would be receptive to a call by a President and a Secretary who evidenced both a determination and a strategy for really taking hold of the foreign policy process.

Quite possibly there would develop a deep gulf between the Secretary's men and the Foreign Service. This could reinforce the worst traits of the latter—resentment toward "outsiders," a sense of their business being spoiled by eager know-nothing meddlers—and create a struggle between the two groups from which neither could benefit. The parallel, of course, is the impact of McNamara's "whiz kids" on another type of career service—the military. But though it is unlikely that most Foreign Service officers would endorse the staffing recommendations of this strategy, surely more than a few of the "Young Turks" (and middle-aged and older Turks as well) would find considerable attraction in a State Department which was *really* determined to lead. They might well be quite willing to compete and show that they possessed the capabilities that many have felt lacking. If such a restructuring might seem to pose a threat to their long-term prospects, it could also mean more challenging short-term opportunities to demonstrate exceptional abilities, particularly for junior and middle-level officers. Moreover, the level of general ability in the Foreign Service is high, its general foreign affairs expertise substantial. Good outside men are usually hard to find, and, if motivated to work aggressively in such a system, it is hard to believe that many FSO's could not more than hold their own. But the strategy proposed here would be a major shock to the system, and for FSO's to adapt effectively to it would require a major modification in many elements of the "living system" or "subculture" described by Argyris and Scott. And if there is a widespread intellectual recognition within the Service that the old ways no longer suffice, this does not necessarily mean they would welcome a new regime of "outsiders" when it came.

FSO's might be more inclined to "give their all" for the current administration if the career appointment and promotion system could be radically restructured to increase upward mobility and enlarge the flow both into and out of the service. If it were clearly possible for an exceptional (but not unique) candidate to make it from FSO-7 (the usual entry level) to FSO-1 in ten years or less; if the movement in and out of the Service could be well over 10 per cent of the officer corps a year, with perhaps one third of the "new blood" coming from lateral entry;[g] if something like a 20-year retirement "norm" could be established, with only a small portion of FSO's serving beyond this period—then the incentives

[g] In no recent year has either new officer intake or "attrition" reached 10 per cent. Since 1965 the annual percentage of FSO's leaving the Service has averaged about 8 per cent, with new officer recruitment under 5 per cent. There has been a consequent decline in the corps from 3,620 to 3,089 members. ("AFSA Bulletin on Management Reform," No. 3, February 9, 1971; *Department of State Newsletter,* February 1971, p. 8.)

to make one's mark at his present job might not be out-weighed by the risks of excessive zeal to a lifetime diplomatic career. And a Washington policy position (with attendant political hazards) might become the target for more FSO's, the Ambassadorship for fewer.

It does not appear likely that the net result of the Macomber reform effort will be a move in these directions. Working under Macomber's direction, and drawing on both the task force reports and extensive further analyses and consultations, the office of the Director General of the Foreign Service has developed a tentative personnel strategy that is probably the most comprehensive the Department has yet produced. Its draft proposals were circulated for FSO comment by the Department and AFSA in April 1971, and the first implementing order was issued the following July. They center on two general objectives:

1. To bring rational personnel planning to the Foreign Service, so that recruitment and promotions are closely related to present and projected manpower needs at particular levels in particular specialties; and

2. To respond to widespread FSO discontent about the workings of the promotion system—particularly "psychological insecurity" related to perceived unfairness in performance evaluations and the threats of "selection out"; and a belief that the system has created "a 'hyper-competitive' environment in which scrambling for good jobs in order to achieve early promotion has undermined Service discipline and *esprit de corps,* and has discouraged training and other types of 'broadening' assignments which are vital for the development of more effective senior executives."[15]

To eliminate "hyper-competitiveness," two Macomber task forces recommended that mid-career promo-

284

tions for most officers be "semi-automatic," based on seniority and continued satisfactory performance.[16] The proposed program stops short of any aim to "eliminate competition for promotion opportunities" on this scale but seeks to provide security for most of an officer's tenure by dividing his period of service into three parts:

1. "A more stringent junior officer review period" (grades 8-6) after which those who pass muster are granted "full career status" by being promoted to FSO-5;
2. "Assured tenure of twenty additional years in grades 5, 4, and 3" for all officers surviving the junior officer review, with promotions during this mid-career period to depend partly on seniority and partly on competition;
3. Moderately reduced security for those promoted to grade 2 after "an especially searching review which places particular stress on executive and management skills."

By explicitly recognizing the more competitive (and less secure) nature of government policy-making in the upper echelons, the proposed new procedures seem to acknowledge the particular need at this level for bureaucratic political effectiveness and responsiveness to the leadership of the current administration. But the risks to top-grade FSO's—selection out after ten consecutive years without a promotion or after falling in the lowest ten per cent of one's class for three years—are hardly comparable to those of men whose positions may stand or fall with the reigning President or Secretary. In fact, they would be no more vulnerable than before in an absolute sense; they would just not partake of the greater security the new system offers to middle-level officers.

Nor will the best FSO's get to the top more rapidly. The sins of the past have created a gross overpopulation of the top grades. Assuming that the Service will grow markedly neither in size nor in the importance of its average job, there are only two ways to correct such a condition: a rather brutal thinning of the senior ranks or a slowing of promotions for men aspiring to attain them. Not surprisingly, the latter course has been chosen. The 1971 FSO promotion list was the smallest in many years—16.5 per cent of the officer corps, compared to a peak of about 25 per cent in 1967.[17] The "hypothetical FSO career models" in the draft proposal assume an average of 25 years service before an officer entering at the bottom reaches grade 2. The truly exceptional officer—characterized as a "Water Walker"— can get to grade 2 in 13 years, and to grade 1 in 17 years.

The proposal also makes it clear that lateral entry will be "sharply limited." Despite recommendations by at least three task forces for "more extensive use of lateral entry as a means of infusing new blood"; despite a Management Reform Bulletin in January 1971 announcing a "positive lateral entry program" with "a possible maximum target of about 50 officers per year" to be brought into grades 2 through 5 by fiscal year 1973— the April draft estimates a *total* of 34 lateral entrants in the FY 1971-76 period. This would be a slight reduction in the trickle of the years before.[18]

Such de-emphasis on lateral entry once hard decisions have to be made is not surprising. For in a relatively closed service there is a direct conflict between the goals of expanded lateral entry and faster upward mobility. Each time a middle or senior-grade position is given to someone from the outside, a promotion is denied to someone within. And it is asking an awful lot to expect that already-low promotion rates would be squeezed even further for a goal as general as "infusing new blood." Perhaps when the overpopulation in the senior ranks is corrected, there may be room for a lateral entry program which does more than bring in a token number of specialists. But the only real way to get both rapid upward mobility for the able and a large inflow of talent above the bottom ranks is to have a very considerable annual exodus from the Service. And to get this would require not only a very strong effort on State's part to explore out-placement opportunities and "second careers" for FSO's, and probably changes in the retirement system so that it would not unfairly penalize those who left before serving an arbitrary number of years in the system. It would also require a fundamental modification of the very concept of the Foreign Service as a *career* service where a man can expect to spend most or all of his working life. Instead it would need to become more a changing body of men who are involved in government foreign policy-making for significant but varying portions of their lives.

There has been considerable discussion, both informally among FSO's and in task force reports, of moving away from the concept of the Service as a "lifetime commitment," and toward a "flexible Foreign Service" encouraging "a circular flow of talent"—current FSO's moving out frequently and lateral entrants coming in.[19] Developments in this direction might not only lessen the need for "political" appointees to protect Presidents and Secretaries from capture by the career service. They might also make the whole career vs. political issue less volatile because the whole system would be more loose and open. But the strong pressure to concentrate on more rational utilization of the talent already within the system has been heightened by the inevitable tendency of a program of reform "from within" to reflect the interests of those within. This has made it impossible for plans outlined to date to move significantly toward a greater "circular flow." Thus an organizational strategy built around the Secretary of State will have to depend on a substantial influx of men who will remain outside of the FSO corps. Many FSO's might play invaluable supporting roles; a few might be induced to resign from the Service to assume responsibilities at the Assistant Secretary level and above. But there will remain an inevitable tension between the interests and predispositions of Foreign Service officers and those of Presidents. So no Secretary of State who did not build a strong "political" component into the State Department could hope to satisfy a President bent on controlling the foreign affairs bureaucracy.

The Limits of Organizational Strategies

It is asking a lot of a President to expect that he will carry out a strategy like the one proposed here in anywhere near undiluted form. It assumes both a sophisticated awareness of the problem and a decision to give control of the foreign affairs bureaucracy priority over other Presidential interests and objectives. Any strategy —particularly this one—would stand or fall on the quality of key appointments. Yet the President is likely to choose the key men before he has taken the oath of office and personally experienced the problems of controlling "his" government. In this hectic pre-inaugural period, he will probably have little feel for (or acquaintance with) the type of men he will need to fight his bureaucratic battles. But he will likely be more sensitive than ever before or after to the uses of appointments to appease particular politicians or segments of his national constituency. It is easy to argue here the critical importance of Assistant Secretary-level appointments in State, even to hold that the foreign policy team he puts together will be enhancing or limiting his accomplishments as President long after journalists have stopped writing about the political balance of his Cabinet. It is harder to believe that a President will see the priorities this way before he has personally felt the problem of making the foreign affairs government his own.

If through luck or wisdom the President does choose a good team, his Secretary of State will then face the not inconsiderable task of redesigning the oldest and most tradition-encrusted job in the President's Cabinet. Americans and foreigners alike have come to expect a certain pattern of behavior from the Secretary: frequent attendance at international conferences, perpetual appearance at diplomatic functions, recurrent testimony before Congressional committees, personal concentration on a limited number of policy problems, a reluctance to intervene forcefully in the business of his Cabinet peers, and an almost total indifference to the workings of the Department beneath him. If he enters his job inclined to "feel his way" and learn about his duties from his colleagues and subordinates, he will surely be forced into this pattern also. Yet these matters are not beyond his power to change if both he and the President are determined to do so. The United States is a strong enough world power so that we don't have to have our Secretary of State doing things just because other foreign ministers are doing them, assuming we can develop tactful explanations for why diplomatic functions must usually be delegated to less exalted men. Congressional burdens are harder to lighten, but, properly exploited, these give a strong Secretary an opportunity to solidify his leadership role. And the distribution of power in the upper reaches of particular administrations is heavily influenced by the way key officials interpret their own responsibilities. Still, a conscious and sustained effort to remake the job will be needed by a Secretary clear-minded enough to know the role he wants to play and strong-willed enough to make it stick.

If these and other hurdles are overcome, we could still not expect anything like total coherence and purposiveness in United States foreign policy. Even with the fullest implementation of this strategy, many bureaucratic actions would still conflict with one another and with broader Presidential purposes. It is well within the realm of the possible that the Under Secretary and Assistant Secretaries of State could be close enough to the Secretary and in sufficient communication with the President to make them strongly aware of and responsive to Presidential priorities. But their perspectives will remain somewhat distinct from his. And it is most unlikely that many officials much below their level will either know what the President would want in a given situation or have a strong enough incentive to act on such knowledge if they do possess it. The farther down the hierarchy one moves, the more narrow and specialized become the perspectives of officials. And in Frankel's words, the way the government operates provides these officials with "excellent defenses" against their would-be coordinators, "ranging from well-concealed bureaucratic foxholes to major legislative fortifications."[20] The foreign affairs government is filled with "working level" officials who have direct control over specialized operations. They have detailed information about these operations, coupled with a strong influence over the amount and form in which this information is available to others. They have relationships with special clients whom the President's men must take into account, from Cuban exiles to foreign governments, from Congressional subcommittees to large corporations. Such bargaining advantages have blunted the lances of many a hard-charging coordinator. There is no reason to believe they will not do so again.

Nor is coordination or coherence an end in itself. The goal must remain good foreign policy. And while consistency of purpose and action will generally contribute to this goal, it will not always do so. In some cases, dispersion of power through the federal foreign affairs bureaucracy can be the most promising force for challenging and changing outworn or misguided policy courses. It was not the White House staff or State's Seventh Floor which pressed hardest for reversal of our

Vietnam escalation in 1968. Rather it was the Defense Department's "little foreign office," which in so doing not only assumed a foreign policy mandate broader than any plan aimed at coherence might assign it, but was clearly pressing a position at variance with the President's predispositions. An effort to center foreign policy-making around a closely knit team of men, a few hierarchically-joined centers of strength, poses at least the theoretical danger of discouraging precisely this type of challenge from within, and encouraging pursuit of policies that might be coherent but are wrong.

A truly monolithic foreign affairs bureaucracy would no doubt pose a formidable barrier to change. But the more familiar case of dispersion and bureaucratic competition—or organizational attachment to familiar traditions and terrain—can create at least as strong a built-in bias against new departures. And our strategy would explicitly address these problems. One of its goals is to build considerable argument about policy into the State policy process, with the Seventh Floor and regional staffs specifically commissioned to challenge present operations and assumptions in the name of a broader perspective. And it is probably fair to assume that the more that good people close to key officials are commissioned to raise hard questions, the more likely these questions are to be heard.

But there are limits to this resolution of the problem. These staffs will inevitably be less than eager to challenge a policy line to which their bosses are firmly committed. For few chiefs like to hear frequent disagreement from their subordinates. Even fewer welcome it when the "policy" under attack is not one securely established but one they are fighting desperately to put across. Bosses who properly see their staffs as *their* instruments will want their men to fight for faithful and consistent implementation of a particular "policy" once determined, not to mount guerrilla operations against it.

291

It becomes, therefore, very difficult to institutionalize dissent, to build devil's advocates into the policy process. But the conflict between coherence and change becomes less forboding when one recognizes how far short of a foreign affairs monolith the government will inevitably remain. No conceivable strategy for enhancing Presidential influence will eliminate the existence of other centers of power within the bureaucracy with voices loud enough to be quite well heard.

If our strategy will not necessarily block needed change, however, neither will it guarantee wise foreign policy. It may improve the prospects for such policy by making better information and analysis available to those who help shape it. But the strategy presented here is primarily a strategy for redistributing and centralizing power, and power is usable for bad policies as well as good ones. Today the differences among Americans over fundamental foreign policy premises are as deep as they have been since World War II. No organizational strategy can resolve these differences, or provide "objective" means of determining which premises are "correct." But it can make the permanent government somewhat more responsive to national political currents, by making it more responsive to the President, who stands at the center of these currents. It can thus increase the chances that the advocates of a policy change will live to see bureaucrats carrying out that change, *if* they can somehow win a Presidential (or, in certain cases, Congressional) decision in favor of it. But that remains up to them.

Yet it would be wrong to end this book by emphasizing what an organizational strategy cannot accomplish. For a significant enlargement of the proportion of our foreign affairs actions that reflect Presidential purposes would be a signal achievement. It is impossible to assure total control of the bureaucracy, or total coherence in its activities. But it is highly possible to make the President's influence over that bureaucracy substantially greater than it has ever been, and to provide him with the type of analytic and operational support that would encourage that influence to be exercised in wise ways. One can justifiably indict some past reform proposals for advocating the unattainable. But far more serious has been the recurrent tendency to present one particular organizational change as *the* major solution to the problem. Every foreign affairs organizational debate has its advocates of increasing the Secretary of State's formal authority to coordinate, of creating a network of interdepartmental committees, of establishing a new senior official, or of strengthening the White House staff. But if this study has established anything at all, it is that no single formal change can bring coherence to foreign policy. It was not enough for Kennedy to designate his Secretary as "agent of coordination" when his other key State appointments had little relation to this objective. It was not enough for Johnson to establish the SIG/IRG coordinating committee system. Nor has it been enough for Nixon to inaugurate a new system to illuminate his options on major policy issues, even though the system has been designed and employed in an exceedingly sophisticated way.

For the key to the foreign affairs organizational problem lies not in any one tool but in a combination of tools. And it lies not in establishing them for their own sake, but in subordinating them to a bureaucratic political strategy which seeks to build centers of strength responsive to the President at as many levels and places within the bureaucracy as possible. If the President chooses his team of key officials wisely and picks men who want to exercise comprehensive foreign policy leadership, they will depend upon his confidence for the leverage to make this leadership effective. To maintain his confidence, they will need to work loyally and responsively with him, seeing issues in a perspective

293

close to his own. If he in turn recognizes their value to him, he will reward such loyalty with the support they require. If he places most of this team in key State Department positions, they will derive from these positions handles for involvement in a wide range of the most critical issues. Their Presidential mandates should make it possible for them to extend this range still wider. And the judicious use of staffs, programming systems, and coordinating committees can offer them further bargaining advantages for the exercise of foreign affairs leadership.

Even with all of this going for them, they will not win every bureaucratic battle for the President. Nor will the President be entirely free of bureaucratic battles with them. But such an approach represents his best hope for reasonable control of the things that matter the most.

LIST OF ABBREVIATIONS

ACDA—Arms Control and Disarmament Agency

AFSA—American Foreign Service Association

AID—Agency for International Development

BNSP—Basic National Security Policy, the most general policy planning paper in the Eisenhower NSC system, devoted particularly to broad political-military strategy

BoB—Bureau of the Budget (now Office of Management and Budget)

CASP—Country Analysis and Strategy Paper, the major document in an interagency foreign affairs programming effort begun in 1966 by the State Department's Latin America bureau

CCPS—Comprehensive Country Programming System, an interagency programming effort inaugurated in 1963 by the office of the Deputy Under Secretary of State for Administration; succeeded in 1965 by the short-lived FAPS program

CIA—Central Intelligence Agency

DoD—Department of Defense

DPRC—Defense Program Review Committee, an Under Secretary-level interagency group in the Nixon NSC system created to review defense budget and strategy issues; chaired by the Assistant to the President for National Security Affairs

Exec Sec—Executive Secretariat, the Department of State's operational coordination center; also called S/S

FAPS—Foreign Affairs Programming System, successor to CCPS

FSO—Foreign Service officer; FSO's usually enter the Service at grade 8 or 7, with lower grade numbers (e.g. FSO-1, FSO-2) signifying higher rank

IDA—Institute for Defense Analyses

IG's—Interdepartmental Groups, State-chaired interagency committees at the Assistant Secretary level in the Nixon NSC system

IRG's—Interdepartmental Regional Groups, State-chaired interagency committees at the Assistant Secretary level in the Johnson Administration; replaced by the IG's in January 1969

ISA—Office of International Security Affairs, DoD

JCS—Joint Chiefs of Staff

NPP—National Policy Paper, one of a series of planning papers dealing with policy toward specific countries; prepared in the Kennedy and Johnson Administrations under the direction of State's Policy Planning Council

NSAM—National Security Action Memorandum, a document transmitting a Presidential order during the Kennedy and Johnson regimes

NSC—National Security Council

NSDM—National Security Decision Memorandum, the Nixon Administration's NSAM

NSSM—National Security Study Memorandum, a Presidential directive calling for comprehensive analysis of an important policy problem in the Nixon NSC system

ABBREVIATIONS

OCB—Operations Coordinating Board, an Eisenhower Administration interdepartmental committee charged with overseeing implementation of Administration policy decisions; abolished by Kennedy in February 1961

OMB—Office of Management and Budget, formerly BoB

OSD—Office of the Secretary of Defense

PARA—Policy Analysis and Resource Allocation system, proposed in December 1970 by a State Department (Macomber) task force

PPBS (or PPB)—Planning-Programming-Budgeting-System, introduced by McNamara to relate DoD resource allocation to specific defense policy objectives; more generally, any programming system with similar aims and characteristics

SALT—Strategic Arms Limitation Talks, inaugurated by the United States and the Soviet Union in 1969

Seventh Floor—The floor of the State Department building housing the Secretary and his principal subordinates and their supporting staffs; hence, those officials and staffs (Regional Assistant Secretaries are on the Sixth Floor)

SIG—Senior Interdepartmental Group, a State-chaired interagency committee at the Under Secretary level in the Johnson Administration; replaced by the USC in January 1969

SIG/IRG—The Johnson Administration's interdepartmental coordinating committee system, established in March 1966

S/PC—Planning and Coordination Staff, Department of State; succeeded the Policy Planning Council in July 1969

S/S—See Exec Sec

State—The Department of State

USC—Under Secretaries Committee, a State-chaired interdepartmental committee in the Nixon NSC system; successor to the SIG

USIA—United States Information Agency

WSAG—Washington Special Actions Group, an Under Secretary-level interdepartmental committee in the Nixon NSC system charged with crisis management and contingency planning; chaired by the Assistant for National Security Affairs

BIBLIOGRAPHICAL NOTES

THOUGH this book is more an extended analytical essay than an effort at exhaustive research, many sources were consulted in the course of its writing. Most important were conversations with present and former foreign affairs government officials, including about 100 formal interviews and at least that many informal conversations. Also indispensable were a wide range of written materials, from newspaper articles to academic treatises, and from major reports to minor intragovernmental memos. These did not, however, include any classified documents.

With a handful of exceptions, interviews were conducted with officials at the assistant secretary level or below. A particular effort was made to find persons whose positions exposed them to a rather broad range of foreign policy problems and activities. In many cases these were people serving on general substantive staffs in the White House, State, and Defense, or as aides to important policy officials. Anonymity was promised to all. Thus, in those relatively rare instances where persons interviewed are quoted directly in the text, the reader will find only the rather unhelpful notation, "personal interview." For each such note, however, there were numerous uncited occasions when a conversation with a foreign affairs bureaucrat either deepened the author's factual understanding or offered an insight which opened up a whole new line of analysis and inquiry. It is to be regretted that the "facts of governmental life" make it impossible to give such persons the public credit they deserve. Certainly the book could never have been written without them.

Before the notes to each major chapter, there is a brief discussion of its principal sources. This is intended both to give the reader an idea of the range and limits of the author's research and to provide him with a general guide to published materials that are relevant to foreign affairs organization as the author has approached the subject.

CHAPTER ONE: INTRODUCTION

1 Stuart Symington, "Further Concentration of Power, Executive Privilege, and the 'Kissinger Syndrome,'" *Congressional Record*, March 2, 1971, pp. S2239, S2236.

2 Presidential News Conference of March 4, 1971, reprinted in *Washington Post*, March 5, 1971, p. A14.

3 The eleven studies referred to are: (1) the Hoover Commission report ("Foreign Affairs," A Report to the Congress by the Commission on Organization of the Executive Branch of the Government, February 1949); (2) the first Brookings study (*The Administration of Foreign Affairs and Overseas Operations*, A Report Prepared for the Bureau of the Budget, Executive Office of the President, Brookings, 1951); (3) the Woodrow Wilson Foundation study (William Yandell Elliott *et al.*, *United States Foreign Policy: Its Organization and Control*, Columbia University Press, 1952); (4) the second Brookings study (H. Field Haviland, Jr. *et al.*, *The Formulation and Administration of United*

States Foreign Policy, A Report for the Committee on Foreign Relations of the United States Senate, Brookings, 1960); (5) the Rockefeller proposal (presented in U. S. Senate, Committee on Government Operations, Subcommittee on National Policy Machinery [henceforth "Jackson Subcommittee"], *Organizing for National Security*, Vol. I [Hearings], pp. 942-1001); (6) the Jackson Subcommittee staff report ("Basic Issues," reprinted in *Administration of National Security*, Staff Reports, pp. 7-26); (7) the Herter Committee report *(Personnel for the New Diplomacy*, Report of the Committee on Foreign Affairs Personnel, Carnegie Endowment for International Peace, December 1962); (8) the Sapin study (Burton M. Sapin, *The Making of United States Foreign Policy*, Praeger [for The Brookings Institution], 1966); (9) the Heineman task force report (unpublished, submitted to President Johnson by the President's Task Force on Government Organization on October 1, 1967); (10) the American Foreign Service Association (AFSA) report *(Toward a Modern Diplomacy*, A Report to the American Foreign Service Association by its Committee on Career Principles, AFSA, 1968); and (11) the Institute for Defense Analyses (IDA) study (published as Keith C. Clark and Laurence J. Legere, *The President and the Management of National Security*, Praeger, 1969). The Sapin and IDA studies made no one specific recommendation on this issue, though both discuss it in considerable detail. The Brookings study and the Rockefeller proposal advocated creation of a new "super-Cabinet" official to coordinate foreign policy.

The warning about "super-staffs" is in Jackson Subcommittee, "Super-Cabinet Officers and Superstaffs," *Organizing for National Security*, Vol. III (Staff Reports and Recommendations), pp. 9-24.

4 Letter from McGeorge Bundy to Senator Henry Jackson, September 4, 1961, reprinted in Jackson Subcommittee, *Organizing for National Security*, Vol. I, pp. 1337-38; "White House Announcement of New Procedures for Overseas Interdepartmental Matters," reprinted in Jackson Subcommittee, "The Secretary of State and the Problem of Coordination: New Duties and Procedures of March 4, 1966," p. 1; Department of State Foreign Affairs Manual Circular No. 521, February 6, 1969, reprinted in Jackson Subcommittee, "The National Security Council: New Role and Structure," 1969, p. 5.

5 Quoted in Saul Pett, "Henry A. Kissinger: Loyal Retainer or Nixon's Svengali," *Washington Post*, August 23, 1970, p. B3.

6 Elie Abel, *The Missile Crisis*, Bantam, 1966, pp. 169-71; Chester L. Cooper, *The Lost Crusade: America in Vietnam*, Dodd, Mead & Company, 1970, pp. 336 ff.; Graham T. Allison, "Conceptual Models and the Cuban Missile Crisis," *American Political Science Review*, September 1969, pp. 706-7.

7 Quoted in John Fischer, "Mr. Truman Reorganizes," *Harper's*, January 1946, p. 28.

8 See, for example, Jackson's introduction to his Subcommittee's first reports *(Organizing for National Security*, Vol. III, 1961); and George F. Kennan, "America's Administrative Response to its World Problems," *Daedalus*, Spring 1958, reprinted in *Organizing for National Security*, Vol. II (Studies and Background Materials), pp. 225-39.

9 See Allison, "Conceptual Models," pp. 690-93.
10 Hoover Commission, "Foreign Affairs," pp. 29-32; Herter Committee, *New Diplomacy*, pp. 11-13, AFSA, *Modern Diplomacy*, pp. 25-26; John Ensor Harr, *The Professional Diplomat*, Princeton University Press, 1969, pp. 334-36.
11 *Department of State Newsletter*, April 1971, p. 43; John Franklin Campbell, "What Is To Be Done?—Gigantism in Washington," *Foreign Affairs*, October 1970, p. 88; "State-AID-USIA Telephone Directory," February 1971, p. 154; *United States Foreign Policy 1969-1970*, A Report of the Secretary of State, March 1971, pp. 612-17.
12 State, *Foreign Policy 1969-1970*, p. 320.
13 *The Budget of the United States Government: Fiscal Year 1972*, pp. 96, 86.
14 In Jackson Subcommittee, *Administration of National Security*, Hearings, p. 78.

CHAPTER TWO: HOW NOT TO REORGANIZE

The basic sources for this chapter are the studies and reports which it seeks to analyze. The most important are those cited in note 3, Chapter One, and note 1 of this chapter. The careful reader will note that they have tended to come in clusters—the first centering about 1950, the second about 1960, and the third about 1968.

By far the best general reference to the foreign affairs organizational thinking of key officials and outside analysts is the publications of the Jackson Subcommittee of the Senate Committee on Government Operations. These include not only a series of exceptionally fine hearings and reports but reprints of a number of key documents and good articles and two extensive bibliographies. The Jackson Subcommittee materials through 1964 are collected in U.S. Senate, Committee on Government Operations, Subcommittee on National Policy Machinery, *Organizing for National Security*, Vols. I-III, 1961 (henceforth "Jackson Subcommittee, *Organizing*"); and U.S. Senate, Committee on Government Operations, Subcommittee on National Security Staffing and Operations, *Administration of National Security*, Staff Reports and Hearings, 1965 (henceforth "Jackson Subcommittee, *Administration*"). Since 1965 it has operated under a third title, Subcommittee on National Security and International Operations.

For summary and commentary on various reports regarding personnel, see Arthur G. Jones, *The Evolution of Personnel Systems for U. S. Foreign Affairs*, Carnegie Endowment for International Peace, 1965; and Frederick C. Mosher, "Some Observations About Foreign Service Reform: 'Famous First Words,'" *Public Administration Review*, November/December 1969, pp. 600-610. For a detailed survey of the foreign affairs government and its post-war evolution, see Sapin, *Making of Foreign Policy*. The reader seeking background on the Eisenhower Administration's formal processes may wish to read the articles and papers in Jackson Subcommittee, *Organizing*, Vol. II; IDA, *President and National Security*, pp. 60-70 and 218-28; Paul Y. Hammond, "The National Security Council: An Interpretation and Appraisal," *American*

BIBLIOGRAPHICAL NOTES

Political Science Review, December 1960 (reprinted in Alan A. Altshuler, *The Politics of the Federal Bureaucracy,* Dodd, Mead and Company, 1968, pp. 140-56); and Robert H. Johnson, "The National Security Council: The Relevance of Its Past to Its Future," *Orbis,* Fall 1969. For background on Presidential approaches since then, see the bibliographical note for Chapter Five.

1 The thirteen include the excellent series of papers edited by Don K. Price for the American Assembly, *The Secretary of State,* Prentice-Hall, 1960; the Department of State's massive internal study, *Diplomacy for the Seventies,* December 1970; and the eleven studies and proposals cited in note 3, Chapter One.

2 Hoover Commission, "Foreign Affairs," pp. 29, 32, 30. Among the critics were Brookings, *Administration of Foreign Affairs,* p. 239; and Elliott *et al., U. S. Foreign Policy,* pp. 101-2.

3 Bundy to Jackson, in Jackson Subcommittee, *Organizing,* Vol. 1, p. 1338.

4 Lannon Walker, "Our Foreign Affairs Machinery: Time for an Overhaul," *Foreign Affairs,* January 1969, p. 319.

5 Woodrow Wilson, "The Study of Administration," June 1887; reprinted in *Political Science Quarterly,* December 1941, pp. 481-506.

6 Harvey H. Bundy *et al.,* "The Organization of the Government for the Conduct of Foreign Affairs," prepared for the Hoover Commission, January 1949, pp. 71-72.

7 Joseph Ponturo in IDA, *President and National Security,* p. 220.

8 Quoted in *Washington Post,* February 22, 1970, p. A10.

9 In Jackson Subcommittee, *Organizing,* Vol. I, pp. 14, 16.

10 Hoover Commission, "Concluding Report," p. 5; "Report to the President and the Secretary of Defense on the Department of Defense," by the Blue Ribbon Defense Panel, July 1, 1970, p. 23. For elucidation of the contradiction between the Hoover Commission's preaching on authority and responsibility and some of its actual recommendations, as well as a broader discussion of this problem, see Herbert A. Simon, Donald W. Smithburg, and Victor L. Thompson, *Public Administration,* Albert A. Knopf, 1950, esp. pp. 286-91.

11 See Campbell, "What Is To Be Done?" pp. 88-89. Campbell's proposals are developed at greater length in *The Foreign Affairs Fudge Factory,* Basic Books, 1971.

12 Stanley Hoffmann, *Gulliver's Troubles, or the Setting of American Foreign Policy,* McGraw-Hill (for the Council on Foreign Relations), 1968, p. 268. The book he cites is James L. McCamy, *Conduct of the New Diplomacy,* Harper & Row, 1964. McCamy places particularly strong emphasis on making authority commensurate with responsibility. (See pp. 54 ff.)

13 Jackson Subcommittee, *Organizing,* Vol. I, pp. 944-46.

14 Haviland *et al., Formulation of U. S. Foreign Policy,* pp. 3, 64 ff. A similar proposal was advanced by Arthur W. Macmahon in *Administration in Foreign Affairs,* University of Alabama Press, 1953, pp. 92 ff.

15 Herter Committee, *New Diplomacy,* pp. 11-13, 15-18; AFSA, *Modern Diplomacy,* pp. 25-26; Harr, *Professional Diplomat,* pp. 334-36.

[16] Jackson Subcommittee, "Super-Cabinet Officers," in *Organizing*, Vol. III, p. 19.

[17] Mosher, "Observations About Foreign Service Reform," p. 604. The Wriston report is "Toward a Stronger Foreign Service," Report of the Secretary of State's Public Committee on Personnel, June 1954.

[18] Don K. Price, "The Secretary and Our Unwritten Constitution," in American Assembly, *Secretary of State*, p. 178; Herbert Kaufman, "Emerging Conflicts in the Doctrines of Public Administration," *American Political Science Review*, December 1956, reprinted in Altshuler, *Politics of the Bureaucracy*, p. 85.

[19] Arthur M. Schlesinger, Jr., *A Thousand Days: John F. Kennedy in the White House*, Houghton Mifflin, 1965, p. 414.

[20] Jackson Subcommittee, *Organizing*, Vol. III, p. 5.

[21] Jackson Subcommittee, "The Secretary of State," in *Administration*, Staff Reports, p. 37.

[22] *Ibid.*, p. 38; Kennan, "America's Administrative Response," in Jackson Subcommittee, *Organizing*, Vol. II, p. 228; John Kenneth Galbraith, *Ambassador's Journal*, Houghton Mifflin, 1969, p. 212; Campbell, "What Is To Be Done?" p. 88.

[23] Richard Holbrooke, "The Machine That Fails," *Foreign Policy*, Winter 1970-71, p. 72.

[24] Peter F. Drucker, *The Age of Discontinuity*, Harper and Row, 1968, p. 212.

[25] Richard Hofstader, *The Age of Reform*, Vintage Books, 1960, p. 248.

[26] Both quotations are from William Attwood, "The Labyrinth in Foggy Bottom," *Atlantic*, February 1967, p. 47.

[27] State, *Foreign Policy 1969-1970*, pp. 319-20.

[28] Roger Hilsman, "The Foreign-Policy Consensus: An Interim Research Report," *Journal of Conflict Resolution*, December 1959, p. 362.

[29] Hoffmann, *Gulliver's Troubles*, p. 286; Jackson Subcommittee, "The National Security Council," in *Organizing*, Vol. III, p. 33.

[30] For the classic presentation of the politics-administration dichotomy, see Woodrow Wilson, "The Study of Administration." For an example of the traditional approach to organization, see Luther Gulick and L. Urwick (eds.), *Papers on the Science of Administration*, Institute of Public Administration, Columbia, 1937. Among the critiques of traditional approaches are James G. March and Herbert A. Simon, *Organizations*, John Wiley & Sons, 1958; Herbert A. Simon, *Administrative Behavior*, Macmillan, 1957 (second edition); Simon, Smithburg, and Thompson, *Public Administration*; and Dwight Waldo, *The Administrative State*, Ronald Press, 1948. On the processes by which men with differing interests reach joint decisions, see Charles E. Lindblom, *The Intelligence of Democracy*, The Free Press, 1965; and the bureaucratic politics analysts discussed in Chapter Three.

[31] Samuel P. Huntington, *The Common Defense*, Columbia University Press, 1961, p. 146; Hilsman, "Foreign-Policy Consensus," p. 365; Allison, "Conceptual Models," pp. 690-94.

[32] Sapin, *Making of Foreign Policy*, pp. 5-7.

[33] Senator Henry M. Jackson, "Organizing for Survival," *Foreign*

Affairs, April 1960, p. 447; Haviland *et al.*, *Formulation of U. S. Foreign Policy*, p. 20; Cooper in IDA, *President and National Security*, p. 8.

[34] In Jackson Subcommittee, *Organizing*, Vol. I, p. 943.

[35] Hoover Commission, "Foreign Affairs," p. 33.

[36] Richard E. Neustadt, "Approaches to Staffing the Presidency: Notes on FDR and JFK," *American Political Science Review*, December 1963; reprinted in Altshuler, *Politics of the Bureaucracy*, p. 118.

[37] Roger Hilsman, *To Move a Nation*, Doubleday, 1967, p. 17; Harvey C. Mansfield, "Federal Executive Reorganization: Thirty Years of Experience," *Public Administration Review*, July/August 1969, pp. 334, 335.

[38] *United States Foreign Policy for the 1970's: A New Strategy for Peace*, A Report by President Richard M. Nixon to the Congress, February 18, 1970, p. 11. (All page references to the two general Nixon foreign policy messages refer to the White House press release edition.)

[39] AFSA, *Modern Diplomacy*, pp. 155, 22, 151; IDA, *President and National Security*, p. 10.

CHAPTER THREE: ORGANIZATION AND BUREAUCRATIC POLITICS

The major source for Chapter Three is the work of a limited but growing number of analysts on the bureaucratic politics of foreign policy-making. Among the pioneering efforts were those of Hilsman and Huntington already cited; a particularly fine case study by Warner R. Schilling ("The Politics of National Defense: Fiscal 1950," in Warner R. Schilling, Paul Y. Hammond, and Glenn H. Snyder, *Strategy, Politics, and Defense Budgets*, Columbia University Press, 1962); several studies by Hammond; the Jackson Subcommittee materials; and, above all, Richard E. Neustadt's *Presidential Power*, Signet, 1960.

Recent years have seen efforts to systematize, modify, and elaborate the conclusions about the policy-making process reached in these earlier works. Probably the major intellectual locus of such work is the Kennedy Institute at Harvard. Neustadt gives a brief outline of its work in *Alliance Politics*, Columbia University Press, 1970, pp. 139 ff. The most interesting and explicit analyses of bureaucratic politics to date are those of Graham T. Allison and Morton H. Halperin. Allison's broad study is scheduled for publication in the fall of 1971 (*Essence of Decision: Explaining the Cuban Missile Crisis*, Little, Brown and Company); references here are to his article in *American Political Science Review*. Halperin is now completing a comprehensive study of bureaucratic politics. Except where otherwise noted, references to his work are based on preliminary drafts made available through the courtesy of the author.

A related work which draws more on organization theory is Anthony Downs, *Inside Bureaucracy*, A Rand Corporation Research Study, Little, Brown and Company, 1967. A different kind of illumination comes from Charles Frankel's *High on Foggy Bottom*, Harper and Row, 1969. Although his position as Assistant Secretary of State for Educational and Cultural Affairs was somewhat on the periphery of the foreign affairs government as it concerns us here, Frankel's book includes a number of exceptionally cogent insights into the bureaucratic political process.

Finally, one should not neglect case studies or participants' memoirs as sources of important clues about the broader process. Among the better recent ones are Cooper, *The Lost Crusade*; Russell Edgerton, *Sub-Cabinet Politics and Policy Commitment: The Birth of the Development Loan Fund*, Inter-University Case Program, Inc., Syracuse, 1970; Phil G. Goulding, *Confirm or Deny: Informing the People on National Security*, Harper and Row, 1970; Townsend Hoopes, *The Limits of Intervention*, David McKay, 1969; and Frederick C. Mosher and John E. Harr, *Programming Systems and Foreign Affairs Leadership*, Oxford University Press, 1970.

1 Neustadt, *Presidential Power*, pp. 41, 45.

2 Frankel, *Foggy Bottom*, p. 171.

3 Max Weber, "The Ruler vs. the Expert," reprinted in Jackson Subcommittee, *Specialists and Generalists*, 1968, pp. 43-44; Dean Acheson, "The President and the Secretary of State," in American Assembly, *Secretary of State*, p. 42.

4 Allison, "Conceptual Models," p. 708. Two very different early post-war books highlighting the complexity of bureaucratic relationships within the (primarily domestic) government are Charles S. Hyneman, *Bureaucracy in a Democracy*, Harper Brothers, 1950; and Simon, Smithburg, and Thompson, *Public Administration*.

5 Simon, Smithburg, and Thompson, *Public Administration*, p. 20.

6 Hilsman, "Foreign Policy Consensus," p. 365.

7 Schilling, "Politics of Defense," pp. 10-15; Hoopes, *Limits of Intervention*, p. 225.

8 Allison, "Conceptual Models," p. 706; Hilsman, *To Move a Nation*, p. 7; Hoopes, *Limits of Intervention*, p. 163.

9 Allison, "Conceptual Models," p. 710; Hilsman, *To Move a Nation*, pp. 559-61. The term "bargaining advantage," I believe, originates with Neustadt.

10 Allison, "Conceptual Models," p. 710.

11 Jackson Subcommittee, *Organizing*, Vol. I, p. 15.

12 Morton H. Halperin, "The Decision to Deploy the ABM: Bureaucratic Politics in the Pentagon and White House in the Johnson Administration," Prepared for Delivery at the Sixty-sixth Annual Meeting of the American Political Science Association, Los Angeles, California, September 8-12, 1970, p. 8.

13 Hilsman, *To Move a Nation*, p. 561.

14 Hoopes, *Limits of Intervention*, pp. 214-20.

15 Allison, "Conceptual Models," p. 707.

16 Hilsman, *To Move a Nation*, p. 5; Lindblom, *Intelligence of Democracy*, Ch. 9.

17 Hilsman, *To Move a Nation*, pp. 541-43; Altshuler, *Politics of the Bureaucracy*, v.

18 Hilsman, *To Move a Nation*, p. 10.

19 In Jackson Subcommittee, *Administration*, Hearings, p. 403.

[20] Andrew M. Scott: "The Department of State: Formal Organization and Informal Culture," *International Studies Quarterly*, March 1969, pp. 2-5; "Environmental Change and Organizational Adaptation: The Problem of the State Department," *International Studies Quarterly*, March 1970, p. 87.

[21] Morton H. Halperin, "Why Bureaucrats Play Games," *Foreign Policy*, Spring 1971, p. 79.

[22] Jackson Subcommittee, "Basic Issues," in *Administration*, Staff Reports, p. 24; Scott, "Environmental Change: The Problem of State," p. 92.

[23] Downs, *Inside Bureaucracy*, pp. 212-16.

[24] Morton H. Halperin, "The Gaither Committee and the Policy Process," *World Politics*, April 1961, reprinted in Thomas E. Cronin and Sanford D. Greenberg, *The Presidential Advisory System*, Harper and Row, 1969, pp. 196-97; "Management Strategy: A Program for the Seventies," Remarks by the Honorable William B. Macomber, Deputy Under Secretary of State, January 14, 1970, reprinted in State, *Diplomacy for the Seventies*, p. 589.

[25] Allen Schick, "Systems Politics and Systems Budgeting," *Public Administration Review*, March/April 1969, p. 142.

[26] Huntington, *Common Defense*, p. 446; Hilsman, *To Move a Nation*, p. 549.

[27] Schilling, "Politics of Defense," pp. 25, 26, 218-22.

[28] Hoffmann, *Gulliver's Troubles*, p. 177.

[29] Roger Fisher, *International Conflict for Beginners*, Harper and Row, 1969, p. 180.

[30] Schilling, "Politics of Defense," p. 26; Henry A. Kissinger, "The Policymaker and the Intellectual," *Reporter*, March 5, 1959, reprinted in Jackson Subcommittee, *Organizing*, Vol. II, p. 259; John Kenneth Galbraith (alias Mark Epernay), *The McLandress Dimension*, Signet, 1968, p. 74.

[31] Personal interview.

[32] Gordon Tullock, *The Politics of Bureaucracy*, Public Affairs Press, 1965, pp. 167-70; Downs, *Inside Bureaucracy*, p. 262.

[33] John C. Ries, *The Management of Defense*, Johns Hopkins, 1964, pp. 49-50.

[34] John Kenneth Galbraith, *The New Industrial State*, Houghton Mifflin, 1967, Chs. 6 and 8; Warren G. Bennis, *Changing Organizations*, McGraw-Hill, 1966, pp. 11-12; Abel, *Missile Crisis*, p. 173. One wonders whether the President's invective was accurately and fully reported.

[35] Neustadt: "Staffing the Presidency," in Altshuler, *Politics of the Bureaucracy*, p. 120; *Presidential Power*, p. 17.

CHAPTER FOUR: NEED FOR A STRATEGY

[1] Kaufman, "Emerging Conflicts," in Altshuler, *Politics of the Bureaucracy*, pp. 77 ff.

[2] Harvey Bundy *et al.*, "Organization for Foreign Affairs," p. 49; AFSA, *Modern Diplomacy*, p. 19; IDA, *The President and the Management of National Security*; Herter Committee, *New Diplomacy*, p. 10.

3 Jackson Subcommittee, "Basic Issues," in *Administration, Staff Reports,* p. 9; Harvey Bundy *et al.,* "Organization for Foreign Affairs," p. 51.
4 For an amusing if rather incoherent account of the visit, see Michael E. Kinsley, "The Harvard Brain Trust: Eating Lunch at Henry's," and John Averill, "Eating Crow at Mike's," both in *Washington Monthly,* September 1970, pp. 45-50.
5 For an interesting summary of what the last generation of American students has learned about the Presidency and the need for a lowering of expectations about Presidential performance, see Thomas E. Cronin, "The Textbook Presidency and Political Science," paper prepared for delivery at the 56th Annual Meeting of the American Political Science Association, September 7-12, 1970.
6 Sam Brown, "The Politics of Peace," *Washington Monthly,* August 1970, p. 43.
7 George E. Reedy, *The Twilight of the Presidency,* World Publishing Company, 1970, pp. 1, 14. On the yellow pads, see Stewart Alsop, "The Timing of the Gamble," *Newsweek,* May 11, 1970, p. 112. On the speech, see Hedrick Smith, "Cambodian Decision: Why President Acted," *New York Times,* June 30, 1970, p. 2.
8 Thomas E. Cronin, "New Perspectives on the Presidency?" *Public Administration Review,* November/December 1969, p. 673. Bundy's book is *The Strength of Government,* Harvard, 1968.
9 Theodore C. Sorensen, *Decision-Making in the White House,* Columbia University Press, 1963, p. 44.
10 American Assembly, *Secretary of State,* p. 2; Acheson, "The President and the Secretary," p. 33; Neustadt, *Alliance Politics,* p. 103.
11 Quoted by Richard M. Nixon in his campaign address of September 19, 1968.
12 Quoted in *Life,* January 17, 1969, p. 62B.

CHAPTER FIVE: STRATEGIES OF PRESIDENTS

Aside from personal interviews, the major sources for this chapter are official documents and journalists' accounts. Of the greatest general value have been the articles throughout the decade by Joseph Kraft (including those in his *Profiles in Power,* New American Library, 1966). Also particularly useful have been Stewart Alsop's column in *Newsweek,* Elizabeth B. Drew's commentary in *Atlantic,* several of John Osborne's "Nixon Watch" pieces in *The New Republic,* and a number of articles by Hedrick Smith in the *New York Times.* David Halberstam's two *Harper's* articles ("The Very Expensive Education of McGeorge Bundy," July 1969, pp. 21-41; and "The Programming of Robert McNamara," February 1971, pp. 37-71) offer many insights into the inner workings of the Johnson Administration, though his judgments of the two individuals appear unduly harsh, Vietnam notwithstanding.

On the Kennedy and Johnson Administrations, Richard M. Moose's Chapter in IDA, *President and National Security,* is the best published description of overall White House staff operations. The Jackson

BIBLIOGRAPHICAL NOTES

Subcommittee materials are also a good source, particularly on the Kennedy Administration, as are Sorensen's *Kennedy* (Harper and Row, 1965) and *Decision-Making*, Schlesinger's *Thousand Days*, and Hilsman's *To Move a Nation*. Most "inside" accounts of Johnson Administration policy-making are Vietnam-centered, such as Hoopes's *Limits of Intervention* and Cooper's *Lost Crusade*. Also good on LBJ and the War is Tom Wicker's *JFK and LBJ: The Influence of Personality on Politics*, William Morrow & Co., 1968.

As befits its emphasis on formal procedures, the Nixon Administration has already produced considerably more official description of its policy-making system than its two predecessors combined. Nixon's first foreign policy message (February 18, 1970) includes as Part I a description of the NSC system; his message of February 25, 1971, provides useful further information in Part VI. Also important are the documents of February 7, 1969, announcing the new system, and Kissinger's letter of March 3, 1970, to Senator Jackson. Both are available in Jackson Subcommittee prints: "The National Security Council: New Role and Structure," February 7, 1969; and "The National Security Council: Comment by Henry A. Kissinger," March 3, 1970. About the only comparable documents from the Kennedy-Johnson period are McGeorge Bundy's September 1961 letter to Jackson (Jackson Subcommittee, *Organizing*, Vol. I, pp. 1335-38), and the announcement and description of the SIG/IRG system (Jackson Subcommittee, "The Secretary of State and the Problem of Coordination: New Duties and Procedures of March 4, 1966").

Seven good articles on Nixon foreign policy-making appeared in the *New York Times*, January 18-24, 1971. The sharpest public criticism of the system is Senator Symington's speech of March 2, 1971 (*Congressional Record*, S2235-40); Nixon replied at his news conference of March 4. Also useful on Nixon are Robert H. Johnson's "The NSC: Relevance of Its Past" and Edward A. Kolodziej, "The National Security Council: Innovations and Implications," *Public Administration Review*, November/December 1969, pp. 573-85.

Further especially illuminating materials published too late to be drawn on in this study include Chester Bowles, *Promises to Keep*, Harper and Row, 1971; Alexander L. George, "The Case for Multiple Advocacy in Making Foreign Policy," *American Political Science Review*, forthcoming; the "Anderson papers" on the Nixon Administration and Bangladesh; and above all the "Pentagon papers" on United States involvement in Vietnam.

[1] Jackson Subcommittee, "The National Security Council," in *Organizing*, Vol. III, p. 38.

[2] White House press release, February 19, 1961; Bundy to Jackson, in Jackson Subcommittee, *Organizing*, Vol. I, p. 1338.

[3] Bundy to Jackson, pp. 1337-38; Schlesinger, *Thousand Days*, p. 133; Sorensen, *Kennedy*, p. 269.

[4] Schlesinger, *Thousand Days*, p. 421; Mosher and Harr, *Programming Systems*, p. 30; Hoopes, *Limits of Intervention*, p. 21; personal interviews.

BIBLIOGRAPHICAL NOTES

[5] Richard Rovere, "Letter From Washington," *The New Yorker*, December 24, 1960, pp. 54, 52; Sydney Hyman, "How Mr. Kennedy Gets the Answers," *New York Times Magazine*, October 20, 1963, p. 17.

[6] Sorensen: *Decision-Making*, p. 63; *Kennedy*, p. 284.

[7] Personal interview.

[8] Moose in IDA, *President and National Security*, p. 81.

[9] Schlesinger, *Thousand Days*, pp. 422, 423.

[10] Very little seems to have been written about the task forces for public record. On their relation to crisis management, however, see John C. Ausland and Col. Hugh F. Richardson, "Crisis Management: Berlin, Cyprus, Laos," *Foreign Affairs*, January 1966.

[11] Moose in IDA, *President and National Security*, p. 71.

[12] *Ibid.*, p. 81; Schlesinger, *Thousand Days*, p. 423; Sorensen, *Kennedy*, p. 282.

[13] Kraft, *Profiles*, p. 164.

[14] "Bill Moyers Talks About LBJ, Poverty, War, and the Young," *Atlantic*, July 1968, p. 35.

[15] Moose in IDA, *President and National Security*, p. 85.

[16] For two representations of his basic views, see Walt W. Rostow: "The Great Transition: Tasks of the First and Second Postwar Generations," Sir Montague Burton Lecture at University of Leeds, England, February 23, 1967, reprinted in *Department of State Bulletin*, March 27, 1967, pp. 491-504; and "Guerilla Warfare in the Underdeveloped Areas," Address at Fort Bragg, June 28, 1961, reprinted in *Department of State Bulletin*, August 7, 1961, pp. 233-36.

[17] Moose in IDA, *President and National Security*, pp. 83, 98.

[18] Cooper, *Lost Crusade*, p. 413; James C. Thomson, Jr., "How Could Vietnam Happen?" *Atlantic*, April 1968, p. 49.

[19] Douglas Kiker, "The Education of Robert McNamara," *Atlantic*, March 1967, p. 54.

[20] Cooper, *Lost Crusade*, p. 414; personal interviews.

[21] Quoted in Sorensen, *Kennedy*, p. 285.

[22] Joseph Kraft, "Kennedy's Working Staff," *Harper's*, December 1962, p. 36.

[23] Halberstam, "Education of McGeorge Bundy," p. 29.

[24] Halberstam, "Programming of Robert McNamara," p. 62; Kraft, *Profiles*, p. 183.

[25] Quoted in *New York Times*, October 25, 1968, p. 31.

[26] Murray Marder in *Washington Post*, January 19, 1970, p. A8; personal interviews.

[27] Jackson Subcommittee, "NSC: New Structure," p. 1.

[28] *Ibid.*, pp. 1-2.

[29] Dean Acheson, "Thoughts About Thought in High Places," *New York Times Magazine*, October 11, 1959, reprinted in Jackson Subcommittee, *Organizing*, Vol. II, p. 292; Nixon, *U.S. Foreign Policy*, 1970, p. 15.

[30] Jackson Subcommittee, "NSC: Comment by Kissinger," p. 3.

[31] Nixon, *U. S. Foreign Policy*, 1970, pp. 13, 12.

[32] Jackson Subcommittee, "NSC: Comment by Kissinger," p. 2; Nixon, *U.S. Foreign Policy*, 1970, p. 15.

BIBLIOGRAPHICAL NOTES

33 Personal interview.

34 Nixon, *U.S. Foreign Policy*, 1970, p. 13.

35 John Osborne, "Nixon's Command Staff," *The New Republic*, February 15, 1969, p. 14. The original staff list is published in Jackson Subcommittee, "NSC: New Structure," pp. 2-3.

36 The number of Nixon NSC meetings is computed from information provided by the NSC staff. The Kennedy figure is from Bundy's letter to Jackson in Jackson Subcommittee, *Organizing*, Vol. I, p. 1336. Information on who attends Nixon NSC meetings is from personal interviews. On who attended Eisenhower's, see Hammond, "The NSC: An Appraisal," in Altshuler, *Politics of the Bureaucracy*, p. 146.

37 Computed from information provided by NSC staff.

38 *New York Times* editorial, February 19, 1970, p. 44.

39 *Time*, June 8, 1970, p. 18.

40 Jackson Subcommittee, "NSC: Comment by Kissinger," p. 2.

41 Nixon, *U.S. Foreign Policy*, 1970, p. 88.

42 *Ibid.*

43 Information on the date of creation of the Senior Review Group and the frequency of its meetings was provided by the NSC staff.

44 See, for example, David R. Maxey, "How Nixon Decided to Invade Cambodia," *Look*, August 11, 1970, pp. 22-25; Hedrick Smith, "Cambodian Decision: Why President Acted," *New York Times*, June 30, 1970, p. 1; and "Richard Nixon's Ten Days," *Newsweek*, May 18, 1970, pp. 36-41.

45 Nixon quoted in *New York Times*, December 3, 1968, p. 1. On Fulbright, see James Reston in *New York Times*, February 9, 1969, Sec. 4, p. 12.

46 Brooke Nihart, "National Security Council: New Staff System After One Year," *Armed Forces Journal*, April 4, 1970, p. 29.

47 News Conference of March 4, 1971, reprinted in *Washington Post*, March 5, 1971, p. A14.

48 Quoted in *New York Times*, October 14, 1968, p. 40.

49 Computed from information supplied by NSC staff.

50 *New York Times* editorial, December 4, 1968, p. 46; Nixon quoted in *New York Times*, December 3, 1968, p. 22; Chalmers M. Roberts, "Kissinger Runs a Taut Shop," *Washington Post*, May 25, 1969, p. B2.

51 Kissinger: "Policymaker and Intellectual," in Jackson Subcommittee, *Organizing*, Vol. II, p. 257; "Domestic Structure and Foreign Policy," *Daedalus*, Spring 1966, pp. 515, 507.

52 Kennan, "America's Administrative Response," in Jackson Subcommittee, *Organizing*, Vol. II, p. 233.

53 Kissinger quoted by Saul Pett, "Henry A. Kissinger: Loyal Retainer or Nixon's Svengali?" *Washington Post*, August 23, 1970, p. B3.

54 On Kennedy and Italy, see Schlesinger, *Thousand Days*, p. 878; on Nixon and Biafra, see Elizabeth B. Drew in *Atlantic*, June 1970, pp. 4-30; on biological weapons, see Seymour M. Hersh, "U.S. Still Retains Weapons It Renounced," *Washington Post*, September 20, 1970, p. B1. Beecher's article is "Foreign Policy: Pentagon Also Encounters Rebuffs," *New York Times*, January 21, 1971, pp. 1, 12.

55 Kraft in *Washington Post*, September 16, 1969, p. A21.

56 Personal interview.
57 Kissinger, "Policymaker and Intellectual," in Jackson Subcommittee, *Organizing*, Vol. II, p. 255.
58 Jackson Subcommittee, "Super-Cabinet Officers," in *Organizing*, Vol. III, p. 19.
59 This formulation of the problem is similar to Ries's criticism of Defense Department organization proposals based on a dominating "centralization" objective in *Management of Defense*, esp. Ch. XI.
60 Quoted in *Life*, January 17, 1969, p. 62B.
61 *Washington Post*, February 7, 1969, p. A7.

CHAPTER SIX: PROBLEMS WITH STATE

The major source for this chapter is the author's interviews and conversations with present and former officials in State, the White House, and other government agencies. Providing useful documentary information and general background have been the weekly *Department of State Bulletin*, the monthly *Department of State Newsletter*, and the specific materials on the Macomber reform program (above all State, *Diplomacy for the Seventies*). The author's understanding of the Department and Foreign Service was deepened by the opportunity to work as a consultant to the American Foreign Service Association while this study was undergoing final revision.

A number of informative books have been written about the State Department and Foreign Service. Among the relatively recent ones are Robert E. Elder, *The Policy Machine*, Syracuse, 1960; Harr, *Professional Diplomat*; John P. Leacacos, *Fires in the In-Basket: The ABC's of the State Department*, World Publishing Company, 1968; and Smith Simpson, *Anatomy of the State Department*, Houghton Mifflin, 1967. Also useful are Scott's articles ("State: Informal Culture," and "Environmental Change: The Problem of State"); the chapters on State by Joseph Yager in IDA, *President and National Security*; the case study on foreign affairs programming by Mosher and Harr (*Programming Systems*); the paper by Chris Argyris ("Some Causes of Organizational Ineffectiveness Within the Department of State," Center for International Systems Research Occasional Paper Number 2, Department of State, January 1967); the foreign affairs personnel studies sponsored by the Carnegie Endowment for International Peace in support of the Herter Committee's efforts; the Jackson Subcommittee materials; and the memoirs and other writings of such men as Acheson, Hilsman, Kennan, and Schlesinger.

The *Foreign Service Journal*, published by the American Foreign Service Association, provides a useful window into the Department and Foreign Service. It is also becoming less of a "house organ" and more a source for interesting articles on general foreign policy issues. AFSA's "Young Turks" produced not only *Toward a Modern Diplomacy*, but also a series of critical articles in Smith Simpson (ed.), "Resources and Needs of American Diplomacy," *The Annals*, November 1968; and Walker's article, "Our Foreign Affairs Machinery." The Association is presently issuing a series of red-edged "AFSA Bulletins on Management Reform." These parallel, and sometimes react to, the series of blue-edged bulletins released periodically by Macomber's office to report reform implementation.

1 Elliott Roosevelt (ed.), *F.D.R.: His Personal Letters 1928-1945*, Duell, Sloan, and Pearce, 1950, Vol. II, p. 914; Schlesinger, *Thousand Days*, p. 406; *New York Times*, October 14, 1968, pp. 1, 30.

2 In Hilsman, *To Move a Nation*, p. 15.

3 Sorensen, *Kennedy*, p. 287; Schlesinger, *Thousand Days*, pp. 406, 413; Jackson Subcommittee, *Administration*, Hearings, p. 81.

4 Quoted in Schlesinger, *Thousand Days*, p. 431.

5 Galbraith, *Ambassador's Journal*, p. 212. In the discussion that follows, remarks that are quoted but not cited are derived from interviews and other private conversations.

6 Schlesinger, *Thousand Days*, pp. 417-18.

7 Moose in IDA, *President and National Security*, p. 96; Paul Nitze, "Organization for National Policy Planning in the United States," in Jackson Subcommittee, *Organizing*, Vol. II, p. 287.

8 Rovere quoted in Schlesinger, *Thousand Days*, p. 384, Galbraith, *Ambassador's Journal*, p. 207.

9 Stevenson quoted in Schlesinger, *Thousand Days*, p. 408; Thomson, "How Could Vietnam Happen?" p. 50.

10 Schlesinger, *Thousand Days*, p. 878.

11 Mosher and Harr, *Programming Systems*, esp. Chs. II, III and VII.

12 Sorensen, *Kennedy*, p. 287; Harr, *Professional Diplomat*, p. 110.

13 Scott: "State: Informal Culture," pp. 2-3; "Environmental Change: The Problem of State," p. 87.

14 Quoted in Harr, *Professional Diplomat*, pp. 208-9.

15 Argyris, "Causes of Ineffectiveness Within State," p. 2; Scott, "State: Informal Culture," p. 7.

16 Stewart Alsop, *The Center*, Harper and Row, 1968, pp. 106-7.

17 Mosher and Harr, *Programming Systems*, p. 232; Daniel C. Lazorchick, "Foreign Policy and Diplomatic Initiative in Washington," *The Annals*, November 1968, p. 108.

18 Schlesinger, *Thousand Days*, p. 414; "Major Problems of Personnel Management in the Department of State," A Staff Paper Prepared for the President's Task Force on Government Organization by the White House Staff, April 11, 1967.

19 Adam Yarmolinsky, "Bureaucratic Structures and Political Outcomes," *Journal of International Affairs*, 1969—No. 2, p. 227; Yager in IDA, *President and National Security*, p. 123.

20 Herter Committee, *New Diplomacy*, pp. 4, 50, 53, 49.

21 *Ibid.*, pp. 12, 13, 19.

22 Jackson Subcommittee, *Administration*, Hearings, pp. 286, 288, 289.

23 Harr, *Professional Diplomat*, p. 44; Mosher and Harr, *Programming Systems*, Chs. II, III, VII.

24 Jackson Subcommittee: "Secretary of State and Coordination," p. 6; *Administration*, Hearings, p. 398.

25 AFSA, *Modern Diplomacy*, p. 25; Yager in IDA, *President and*

National Security, p. 121. For a more extended discussion of the "country director" reform, see Harr, *Professional Diplomat*, pp. 302-11.

26 Yager in IDA, *President and National Security*, p. 122.

27 AFSA, *Modern Diplomacy*, pp. 56, 20, 23.

28 *Ibid.*, pp. 57, 145-50.

29 Macomber's speech which inaugurated the task force effort, "Management Strategy: A Program for the Seventies," is reprinted in State, *Diplomacy for the Seventies*, pp. 587-605. The compilation of recommendations and their action status appears in *Department of State Newsletter*, January 1971, pp. 20-43.

30 State, *Diplomacy for the Seventies*, p. 589.

31 *Ibid.*, pp. 304, 111, 381.

32 *Ibid.*, pp. 588, 4.

33 *Ibid.*, p. 566.

34 *Ibid.*, pp. 567, 571, 12; *Department of State Newsletter*, January 1971, p. 35.

35 State, *Diplomacy for the Seventies*, p. 543. Task Force XIII also discusses formal White House-State relationships intermittently, especially on pp. 556, 563, and 571-72.

36 *Ibid.*, pp. 554, 567; *Department of State Newsletter*, January 1971, pp. 39, 40, 41.

37 Quoted in Patrick J. McGarvey, "State Department Answers Fulbright: 'We Can Clean Our Own House,' " *Government Executive*, May 1970, p. 47.

38 Harr, *Professional Diplomat*, p. 332.

39 Herter Committee, *New Diplomacy*, pp. 11-12.

40 Mosher and Harr, *Programming Systems*, p. 183. This conclusion is consistent with other informal accounts.

41 State, *Diplomacy for the Seventies*, pp. 568-69.

CHAPTER SEVEN: FORMAL APPROACHES

Of the four formal approaches discussed here, programming is the most extensively treated in foreign affairs organizational literature. The place to begin, once again, is the Jackson Subcommittee, which inaugurated in August 1967 a series of reports, hearings, and related publications on PPB and its possible contribution to foreign affairs. (U.S. Senate Committee on Government Operations, Subcommittee on National Security and International Operations, *Planning-Programming-Budgeting*, 1967 and after.) As one would expect, the Jackson materials emphasize the relation of programming to the real world of foreign policy-making. For an excellent discussion of the interaction of PPB and the (primarily domestic) policy process, see Charles L. Schultze, *The Politics and Economics of Public Spending*, Brookings, 1968.

The Mosher-Harr book (*Programming Systems*) describes and analyzes the Crockett-Barrett effort to build a government-wide foreign affairs programming system around State. Henry S. Rowen and Albert P. Williams treat a number of the more general issues involved in

"Policy Analysis in International Affairs," pp. 970-1002 in U.S. Congress, Joint Economic Committee, Subcommittee on Economy in Government, *The Analysis and Evaluation of Public Expenditures: The PPB System*, 1969. For the most recent account of the Defense experience, see Alain C. Enthoven and K. Wayne Smith, *How Much is Enough? Shaping the Defense Program 1961-1969*, Harper and Row, 1971.

The section on organizational integration draws heavily on an analysis done by the author for the Heineman Task Force in 1967, which in turn was based mainly on interviews. The treatment of formal policy guidance owes much to the early Jackson Subcommittee materials, and to Joseph Ponturo's treatment of the subject, "The President and Policy Guidance," Chapter X in IDA, *President and National Security*. The section on coordinating committees relies mainly on interviews and conversations with persons involved in the SIG/IRG and Nixon NSC systems, mostly in staff support roles. The basic documents of both systems were reprinted by the Jackson Subcommittee. ("Secretary of State and Coordination," and "NSC: New Structure.")

Two useful general discussions of the problem of top-level control over discretionary decisions made at various levels of large organizations are in Robert N. Anthony, *Planning and Control Systems: A Framework for Analysis*, Harvard Business School, 1965; and Ries, *Management of Defense*.

[1] Jackson Subcommittee, *Administration*, p. 388. Informal inquiries indicate that this remains a reasonably accurate picture of the cable involvement of Rusk and his successor, though there is wide day-to-day variation.

[2] McCamy, *Conduct of the New Diplomacy*, pp. 79-86.

[3] Letter to the Speaker of the House and the President of the Senate transmitting the draft bill on foreign aid, May 26, 1961; reprinted in *Congressional Quarterly Weekly Report*, June 2, 1961, p. 922.

[4] "U.S. Foreign Assistance in the 1970s: A New Approach," Report to the President of the United States from the Task Force on International Development (Peterson Task Force), March 4, 1970, p. 2; Richard Nixon: "Foreign Assistance for the Seventies," A Message to the Congress of the United States, September 15, 1970; and Message to the Congress of the United States, April 21, 1971.

[5] One recent article calling for USIA's abolition is Bruce J. Oudes, "The Great Wind Machine," *Washington Monthly*, June 1970, pp. 30-39.

[6] Hoopes, *Limits of Intervention*, p. 7.

[7] Dean Acheson, "Thought in High Places," in Jackson Subcommittee, *Organizing*, Vol. II, p. 292.

[8] Ponturo in IDA, *President and National Security*, p. 239; Mosher and Harr, *Programming Systems*, p. 57; Ponturo, p. 240; Hoopes, *Limits of Intervention*, p. 6.

[9] Nixon, *U.S. Foreign Policy*, 1970, p. 5.

[10] Ponturo in IDA, *President and National Security*, p. 227.

[11] Letter to Secretary Rusk from the Advisory Group on Foreign

Affairs Planning, Programming, and Budgeting (Hitch Committee), October 5, 1966, p. 1.

12 Thomas Schelling, "PPBS and Foreign Affairs," pamphlet in Jackson Subcommittee series, *Planning-Programming-Budgeting*, p. 2.

13 Schultze, *Politics of Public Spending*, esp. pp. 92-97.

14 Quoted in Leacacos, *Fires in the In-Basket*, pp. 363-64.

15 Department of State Foreign Affairs Manual Circular Number 385, March 4, 1966; reprinted in Jackson Subcommittee, "Secretary of State and Coordination," pp. 4, 5.

16 *Ibid.*, p. 4.

17 Computed from information supplied by the National Security Council staff.

18 Robert Cutler, "The Development of the National Security Council," *Foreign Affairs*, April 1956; reprinted in Jackson Subcommittee, *Organizing*, Vol. II, p. 175. The other information and quotations in this paragraph are derived from personal interviews and other off-the-record sources.

19 Schlesinger, *Thousand Days*, p. 420.

CHAPTER EIGHT: USES OF STAFFS

This chapter owes much to interviews with well over fifty present and former members of foreign policy staffs in the White House, State, and Defense (ISA). All took place in the 1967-1971 period, the great majority between October 1969 and June 1970.

The best published description of what a foreign affairs staff has actually done over a period of years is Moose's discussion of the NSC staff since 1947, Chapter IV in IDA, *President and National Security*. Elder's *Policy Machine* devotes a chapter to the Policy Planning Staff, and other books on the State Department (cited in Chapter Six) provide useful information. Unfortunately, much less has been written about the Pentagon's Office of International Security Affairs.

The Jackson Subcommittee materials include good general discussions of the roles and problems of staffs, particularly the 1960 report, "Super-Cabinet Officers and Superstaffs," and Neustadt's testimony of March 1963 (*Administration*, Hearings, pp. 74-104). The former includes a response to a proposal for a Presidential Staff Agency for National Security Affairs put forward by William R. Kintner in "Organizing for Conflict: A Proposal," *Orbis*, Summer 1958; reprinted in Jackson Subcommittee, *Organizing*, Vol. II, pp. 240-54.

The papers by Gulick, Urwick and Henri Fayol in Gulick and Urwick, *Papers on Administration* present traditional, relatively formal concepts of staff roles. A criticism of some of the distinctions they sought to make appears in Simon, Smithburg, and Thompson, *Public Administration*, pp. 280-91. For a practical analysis of staff-line conflict in several business firms, see Melville Dalton, *Men Who Manage: Fusions of Feeling and Theory in Administration*, Wiley, 1959.

1 Quoted in *Department of State Newsletter*, July 1969, pp. 2, 5.

2 Moose in IDA, *President and National Security*, p. 76.

3 Quoted in *Wall Street Journal*, November 12, 1969, p. 1.

4 Quoted in *Department of State Newsletter*, July 1969, pp. 2-5.

5 IDA, *President and National Security*, pp. 165-66.

6 Jackson Subcommittee, *Administration*, Hearings, pp. 400-402.

7 Frankel, *Foggy Bottom*, p. 93.

8 See Elihu Root, "The General Staff Concept," reprinted in Jackson Subcommittee, *Specialists and Generalists*, pp. 37-9; and Gulick and Urwick, *Papers on Administration*.

9 Jackson Subcommittee, "Super-Cabinet Officers," in *Organizing*, p. 21.

10 C. Northcote Parkinson, *Parkinson's Law*, Houghton Mifflin, 1957, Ch. 6; George Kennan, *Memoirs*, Little, Brown and Company, 1967, p. 326.

11 *Ibid.*, p. 345; Dean Acheson, *Present at the Creation: My Years in the State Department*, W. W. Norton & Company, 1969, p. 214.

12 For a description of how members of the Staff played this role in a particular case (the creation of the Development Loan Fund), see Edgerton, *Sub-Cabinet Politics*.

13 Robert M. Bowie, "The Secretary and the Development and Coordination of Policy," in American Assembly, *Secretary of State*, p. 70.

14 Personal interviews.

15 Hoffmann, *Gulliver's Troubles*, p. 317; Bowie, "Secretary and Development of Policy," p. 70.

16 Paul Y. Hammond, "NSC-68: Prologue to Rearmament," in Schilling, Hammond, and Snyder, *Strategy*, p. 370.

17 Zbigniew Brzezinski, "Purpose and Planning in Foreign Policy," *The Public Interest*, Winter 1969, pp. 63, 64.

18 Hoopes, *Limits of Intervention*, pp. 34, 1; Haviland *et al.*, *Formulation of U.S. Foreign Policy*, p. 89.

19 On the trend in ISA since January 1969, see Neil Sheehan, "Key Pentagon Group Dissolving," *New York Times*, April 13, 1969, p. 3; George C. Wilson, "Defense 'Statesmen' Take Turn to Right," *Washington Post*, June 1, 1969, p. B1; William Beecher, "Laird Said to Tighten Rein on the Joint Chiefs of Staff," *New York Times*, June 14, 1970, p. 1; and Beecher, "Foreign Policy: Pentagon Also Encounters Rebuffs," *New York Times*, January 21, 1971, p. 1.

20 Yarmolinsky, "Bureaucratic Structures," p. 232; personal interview.

21 The phrase is Rusk's characterization of Sorensen and Kaysen, as reported in Sorensen, *Kennedy*, p. 285.

22 Stephen K. Bailey, "Managing the Federal Government," in Kermit Gordon (ed.), *Agenda for the Nation*, Doubleday, 1968, p. 319. On Kaysen and the Harriman designation, see Schlesinger, *Thousand Days*, p. 903. For Neustadt on action-forcing processes, see Jackson Subcommittee, *Administration*, Hearings, p. 91.

23 On Kaysen's effective advocacy on the test ban treaty and other issues, see Kraft, *Profiles*, p. 66. The phrase about Thomson is taken from his "How Could Vietnam Happen?" p. 49.

24 Hoopes, *Limits of Intervention*, p. 51; Goulding, *Confirm or Deny*, p. 177.

25 By a "colleague" of McGeorge Bundy, as quoted in Halberstam, "Education of McGeorge Bundy," p. 35.

26 Reedy, *Twilight of the Presidency*, Ch. VIII.

27 Thomas L. Hughes, "Relativity in Foreign Policy," *Foreign Affairs*, July 1967, pp. 677-81; Thomson, "How Could Vietnam Happen?" p. 49; Edgerton, *Sub-Cabinet Politics*, p. 164.

28 Jackson Subcommittee, *Organizing*, Vol. I, pp. 844-45.

CHAPTER NINE: BUILDING LINES OF CONFIDENCE

1 Downs, *Inside Bureaucracy*, p. 218.

2 Terence Smith, "Foreign Policy: Decision Power Ebbing at the State Department," *New York Times*, January 18, 1971, p. 1; Kraft in *Washington Post*, February 17, 1970, p. A15.

3 In Jackson Subcommittee, *Administration*, Hearings, p. 103.

4 John Fischer, "Mr. Truman Reorganizes," *Harper's*, January 1946, p. 27; Acheson, *Creation*, pp. 468, 466.

5 Robert W. Tufts, "The Secretary of State, 'Agent of Coordination,'" in Jackson Subcommittee, *Administration*, Hearings, p. 110.

6 Sorensen, *Kennedy*, p. 285.

7 AFSA, *Modern Diplomacy*, p. 24.

8 Quoted in Jackson Subcommittee, *Administration*, Staff Reports, p. 43.

9 IDA, *President and National Security*, pp. 165-66.

10 Macomber, "Management Strategy," in State, *Diplomacy for the Seventies*, p. 600.

11 Quoted in *Life*, January 17, 1969, p. 62B; and Jackson Subcommittee, *Administration*, Hearings, p. 387.

12 Statement of Arthur Allen dissenting from the report of Task Force VIII, "Role of the Country Director," in State, *Diplomacy for the Seventies*, p. 357.

13 Computed from *Budget of U.S. Government*, FY 1972, pp. 96, 86, 532.

14 Allen Dulles, *The Craft of Intelligence*, Harper and Row, 1963, p. 189.

15 Director General of the Foreign Service, "Proposed Changes in FSO Promotion, Selection-Out and Performance Evaluation Systems," Department of State, April 19, 1971. Approval of the order for junior and middle-level officers was announced in "Management Reform Bulletin: Promotion Reform: Threshold Review and Mid-Career Tenure," No. 27, July 6, 1971. The same bulletin seems to foreshadow later approval of the proposed changes dealing with grades 2 and above.

16 State, *Diplomacy for the Seventies*, pp. 81-83, 328.

17 "The FSO and FSIO Promotion Lists," *Foreign Service Journal*, May 1971, p. 2; "AFSA Bulletin on Management Reform," No. 3, February 9, 1971.

18 State, *Diplomacy for the Seventies*, pp. 10, 286-89, 325, 394; "Man-

agement Reform Bulletin: Lateral Entry Into the Foreign Service Officer Corps," No. 4, January 8, 1971.

[19] Report of Task Force IX, "Openness in the Foreign Affairs Community," in State, *Diplomacy for the Seventies*, p. 394.

[20] Frankel, *Foggy Bottom*, p. 177.

Index